FOR JANE

DONALD LINDSAY

FRIENDS FOR LIFE

A PORTRAIT OF

LAUNCELOT FLEMING

Lindel Publishing Co.
England

II

First published in England 1981
Copyright © Donald Lindsay
Published by Lindel Publishing Company
Warwick Road, Seaford, Sussex, England.

Photoset in 10 point Times
Printed in England by
Lindel Organisation Ltd.
Warwick Road, Seaford, Sussex.

I.S.B.N. 0 9502354 3 1

FOREWORD

Raveningham Hall,
Norfolk.

Bishop and Dean, Academic and Arctic Explorer, College and Naval Chaplain, Oarsman and Rowing Coach, not many people can aspire to such versatility. Throughout his career Launcelot made countless friends in whatever sphere he then happened to be working. Some are more interested in "people" than they are in "things" and vice-versa. In the modern world to be successful one has probably to be interested in both. The odds are, however, that if you get the "people" right then the "things" are more likely to fall gently into place. As a picker of people or, if necessary, as a poacher of people from others (see Chapter 12 of the text) Launcelot was in his element. He knew so many people and so many were ready and willing to work with and for him that once he had made his choice things somehow happened. It should be added that making a choice normally took some time but he rarely made a mistake. His powers of persuasion were quite extraordinary, allied to an element of low cunning which he never hesitated to use to gain his ends. His courage, as one would expect, in overcoming his illness and in taking the unpopular course if he knew it to be right was of the highest order. To be able within a short time after his Ordination to hold a tough, critical but captive congregation in *Penola* in Graham Land was a remarkable achievement. So was the way in which despite the strongest opposition he reorganised the major part of a large rural diocese, short of clergy and low in stipends, into what is now recognised as being the only way by which the Church could be sustained. All this without any experience as a parish priest.

The care of his clergy, as one would expect from his character, is rightly highlighted throughout this narrative. One remembers when

IV

he first came to Norwich how he let it be known at once that there would be no dedications of electric light installations or consecrations of stained glass windows in churches until he had met and got to know his clergy.

The only chink in his armour was his failure to believe that others did not aspire to the high standards that he set for himself. To let him down would not merely hurt him it would also bewilder him. All Launcelot's countless friends, who hold him in great affection, must be grateful to Mr. Donald Lindsay for the admirable way in which he has portrayed his life and achievements. No better summing up of all that Launcelot has done and stood for could have been chosen than the quotation with which Mr. Lindsay concludes his appreciation and which he takes from Thomas Hardy's *The Woodlanders.* If ever the cap fitted that one does.

Edmund Bacon

CONTENTS

Chapter 1	Edinburgh 1906 – 1915	1
Chapter 2	Stubbington House and Rugby 1915 – 1925	15
Chapter 3	Trinity Hall 1925 – 1929	25
Chapter 4	Yale and Westcott House 1929 – 1933	39
Chapter 5	Exploration in the Arctic 1932 – 1933	55
Chapter 6	The British Graham Land Expedition 1934 – 1937	67
Chapter 7	Dean and Chaplain (i) 1933 – 1940	93
Chapter 8	'A Friend of All On Board' 1940 – 1946	107
Chapter 9	Dean and Chaplain (ii) 1946 – 1949	127
Chapter 10	Portsmouth 1949 – 1959 (i) Learning the Job	139
Chapter 11	Portsmouth 1949 – 1958 (ii) On the Job	157
Chapter 12	Norwich 1959 – 1971 (i) The Main Task	175
Chapter 13	Norwich 1959 – 1971 (ii) Other Concerns	201
Chapter 14	Windsor 1971 – 1976	227
Chapter 15	"Retirement"	245

ILLUSTRATIONS

Frontispiece. Launcelot, aged 7. From the painting by Paul Croeber.

Between pages 34-35
1, 2 Robert and Eleanor Fleming at the time of their marriage
3 Robert Fleming's mother

VI

4   Eleanor Fleming's father and mother
5   Robert Fleming with Bob, Archie, Jean and Launcelot
6, 7 Robert and Eleanor Fleming in later life
8   Chester Street, Edinburgh. No. 10 is the house immediately on
     the left of the archway
9   Eleanor Fleming with Launcelot and Archie in the Chester
     Street drawing-room
10   Launcelot in the school-room
11   Stubbington House School, Fareham
12   Rugby School
13   Whitelaw House, 1925. Launcelot is seated second from the
     right
14   Trinity Hall, Cambridge. The Front Court
15   Innerhadden Lodge
16   Launcelot with his first stag
17   The Cottage by the Burn, Innerhadden
Between pages 98-99
18   Commonwealth Fellows on board S.S. *Albertic*
19   Harkness Quadrangle, Yale University
20   Launcelot in Iceland, 1932
21   Members of the Spitzbergen Expedition. The leader (A. R.
     Glen) is sitting in the centre. Launcelot is sitting on the
     extreme left.
22. *Penola* in St. Katherine's Dock shortly before sailing
23. *Penola* under full sail
24   *Penola's* first anchorage at Port Lockroy
25   Building the Southern Base
26   Launcelot does his share of the cooking
27   Interior of the living room
28   The changed map of Graham Land
29   Digging a pit for geological investigations, 1935
Between pages 130-131
30   Trinity Hall Chapel
31   Trinity Hall. The Senior Combination Room
32   H.M.S. *Queen Elizabeth*

33   Launcelot emerging from the gun turret, September 1942
34   Launcelot with the Third May Boat, 1947
35   Launcelot and Charles Raven
36   Portsmouth Cathedral
37   Bishopswood
38   Running late
39   Launcelot's interest in Youth
40   Enthronement in Norwich Cathedral
41   Bishop's House at Norwich
Between pages 226-227
42   The highest point in the diocese
43   On the Broads with a group of young men from whose
      activities the Endeavour Training organisation was later
      formed.
44   Launcelot with the Brooke family in Scotland. On the left,
      Ken Mathews
45   Second thoughts on a sermon
46   Jane Agutter, 1961
47   Launcelot and Jane 1965
48   The wedding reception. On the left, Launcelot's eldest brother.
      On the right Margaret and Richard Agutter
49   Making another friend for life
50   Sunday morning in the Lower Ward, Windsor Castle, by
      Joseph Nash – 1848
51   H.M. The Queen with Launcelot after his installation as Dean
      of Windsor.
52   The entry to the Deanery, Windsor.
53   The Royal Family leaving St. George's Chapel after the
      Service of Thanksgiving for the Quincentenary, 23rd April
      1975
Endpiece. Tithe Barn, Poyntington.
Launcelot and Jane at Tithe Barn

VIII

IX

ACKNOWLEDGEMENTS

Very great gratitude for permission to reproduce photographs and other material is due to:–

English Life Publications, Ltd. No: 12
The Master and Fellows of Trinity Hall, Cambridge. Nos: 14, 31, 32
The Scott Polar Research Institute. Nos: 20–29
The Imperial War Museum. No: 32
The City Engineer's Reprographic Department, Portsmouth. No: 36
Sir Osbert Lancaster, C.B.E. No: 39
The Eastern Daily Press. Nos: 40–43
David Farrell. No: 46
Barnet Saidman. Nos: 47, 48
Derry Moore. No: 52
The Windsor, Slough and Eton Express. Nos: 51, 53
The Society of The Friends of St. George's. No: 50

Every effort has been made to trace the owners of copyright material and to ensure that permission for its use has been granted and acknowledged. Sincere apologies are offered for any omissions or errors.

The poem by C. H. Sorley on page 257 is reprinted by kind permission of the Cambridge University Press.

PREFACE

This book has no claim to be a formal, let alone a definitive biography of Launcelot Fleming. Such a book cannot be written in the lifetime of its subject. It is an attempt to tell the story of his career in the hope that something of the quality of a remarkable man may emerge. It has been written, first, for his many friends who often have only known him at one point in his career and who have said that they wished to know the whole story. A far more important purpose, and far more difficult to achieve, is to ensure that all that he has stood for, expressed both in his character and his beliefs, will not be forgotten as the years go by. I would hope that even those who have never known him personally will glimpse something of his rare spirit.

One or two of Launcelot's oldest friends have said that this book cannot and should not be written in his lifetime. This is a view which I greatly respect. At the same time a very large number of those consulted during the writing of the book have encouraged me to go ahead. Nobody is more aware than I of the difficulty of the task and of how far short I have fallen of their hopes. Ideally this book should have been an autobiography but Launcelot would never have written it. So whenever possible I have used his own words to tell the story. Inevitably it is too early for a complete account of his life, especially of the later stages of his career, to be written. This does not mean that any future official biographer is likely to discover many skeletons in the cupboard. It means that certain judgements have rightly had to be tempered while those concerned are still alive.

It cannot be easy for a very humble man to have his life story told while he is still alive and active. Yet, once convinced that so many of his friends wanted the book written he and Jane, his wife, have given me every possible assistance and encouragement for which I am deeply grateful and without which the book could never have been written. I must also thank all those whom I have consulted or who have written to me during the past three years. As they number well over two hundred I hope that they will forgive me for not naming them individually.

Two people, however, must be named. I am very grateful to Sir Edmund Bacon for agreeing to write a Foreword. As Lord-lieutenant of Norfolk during Launcelot's years there and as a Knight of the Garter who knew something of the Windsor period he was the close friend whom Launcelot hoped would undertake the task. To Mrs. Mary Horsfall my debt of gratitude is more than I can express. Not only did she decipher my handwriting and type the whole book but her critical eye has saved me from many an inaccurate remark or slipshod sentence.

'There's an awfully nice chap called Fleming, who keeps on coming into your chapters. I wish I knew him.' Such was one typical comment made by Launcelot on reading the text. Whatever judgements may be passed on the inadequacy of this 'portrait', I can only say that it has been a great privilege and often an uplifting experience to have been close to him during these years.

Seaford 1978 – 1981   Donald Lindsay

EDINBURGH

1906 – 1915

"And the Lorde was with Joseph, and he was a luckie fellowe". Thus William Tyndale's translation of Genesis XXXIX, 2. For Joseph read Launcelot. That both the Lord and the luck have been with him there is little doubt. A very happy childhood in a home where money was plentiful, the delights of Cambridge, the excitement of polar exploration, a genius for friendship with outstanding pastoral gifts and, late in life, the joy of marriage, have all combined to make his life full to overflowing and richly rewarding. However, because he knew that the Lord was with him, Launcelot has never had any doubt that what he has so greatly enjoyed was something to be held in trust, and must be repaid in a lifetime of service to others.

William Launcelot Scott Fleming was born on the 7th of August 1906, the fifth and youngest child of Robert and Eleanor Fleming. Both his parents, so different from each other, were remarkable people, and much of Launcelot's personality, far less simple than at first appears, stems from his family background.

Robert Alexander Fleming was a distinguished and deeply loved Edinburgh physician, who had been born on the 6th of September 1862 at 4, Airlie Place, Dundee. His father, a wealthy jute merchant noted for his generosity to city charities, had died at a comparatively early age. His mother, who lived to be over ninety, was a rigid Presbyterian of almost Calvinistic severity. When years later her grand-daughter announced her engagement to a man of the Jewish faith, old Mrs Fleming alone approved of the marriage, seeing it as a providential way by which a brand would be plucked from the burning. Robert's sister inherited her mother's Calvinism, and throughout her life was apprehensive that she would not prove to be one of the Elect. She was thus addicted to good works, buying up pen wipers and blotting pads at sales of work, which she then gave to the next sale and duly bought back to be given to yet a third sale. She never married but was devoted to Robert's children, who were equally devoted to her and who looked forward eagerly to holidays spent with her and their grandmother. Her austere faith had not killed her sense of humour, and Launcelot knew that he was in no danger of rebuke when he referred to her bulbous nose as 'the family disappointment'. Robert himself was less uncompromising in his religious views, but he remained a loyal and active member of the Presbyterian Church of Scotland all his life. He became an Elder at St. George's, the copper-domed parish church in Charlotte Square, a building now put to more secular uses.

Robert first graduated with an Arts degree at Edinburgh University and then turned to medicine, being awarded a distinguished "First" in 1888. Not content with this success he continued his studies on throat, ear and eye troubles in Vienna. Before returning home he visited hospitals and medical schools in Rome, Dresden and Stockholm. In the course of his European travels he became increasingly interested in neurology, in which field he became an early and noted specialist. At the same time he always set his face against the dangers of too narrow specialisation, and when back in Edinburgh he combined his University work as one of the three Clinical Tutors to the University Chair of Clinical Medicine with private practice. The coveted honour of becoming a professor at the University eluded him despite many years as the professor's right hand man. It was typical of him to conceal his disappointment and never to bear a grudge against the man elected to the post which he had for so long hoped to fill. Nevertheless his medical colleagues in the city showed their high regard and affection for him by electing him in 1928 to serve a two year term as President of the Royal College of Physicians in Edinburgh. In the same year his University work was officially recognised by the conferring on him of the highest honour which the University could bestow, an Honorary Doctorate of Laws.

Some of Robert's most valuable work, characteristic of the man, lay among the poor and outcasts of society. For thirty years he was an honorary physician to the Edinburgh Royal Infirmary. His time here coincided with the earlier entries of women students, many of whom applied to come to his wards. This was partly because of his reputation as a teacher and partly because he held the still strange belief that women could make good doctors. This belief he put into practice when in the 1930s he advised his wife to choose as her doctor Dorothea Walpole, sister of Hugh Walpole the novelist.

In days when psychiatry was a comparatively new branch of medicine Robert became famous for his work on behalf of the Scottish Prison Service. He wrote several important papers on the mentality of criminals and lectured frequently on the subject, illustrating his work from his experiences at the Criminal Lunatic Asylum at Peterhead. Both when talking to students or to friends he enjoyed beginning a story with the words, 'Such a good friend of mine – he murdered his grandmother . . .' On one occasion he was interviewing an inmate who was being considered for release. This man had killed another man with a cricket bat by smacking it down on his victim's bald pate as it glistened in the sunlight. Robert, putting his hand on the man's shoulder, asked him earnestly, 'Now, tell me, *why* did you do it?' The man replied, 'Doctor, I just couldna reseest it'. Regretfully Robert felt unable to recommend release. When he retired from the Prison Service in 1947 Robert received a personal letter from the Secretary of State for Scotland, thanking him for his years of devoted service and for his "great contribution towards our reformative training".

Robert was of middle height, spare in build, with eyes twinkling with quiet and kindly amusement behind his spectacles. He was very much a doctor of the old school, always trim and neatly dressed – a trait not inherited by Launcelot – and addressing all alike with an old-world courtesy and charm. Outside his work his interests were those of a countryman, shooting and fishing. He was a first class shot with the amiable weakness of always having a ready excuse if he missed his bird. 'That big stone took my eye off', or 'the sun got on my glasses'. 'I'll move the stone for ye, doctor, but I canna' move the sun', retorted the gillie. In 1916 he was appointed Surgeon on the staff of Officers of the King's Bodyguard for Scotland, better known as the Royal Company of Archers. Two years previously he had won the King's Prize for Archery. The gold medal carried with it an annual gift of £20, which had to be included in the Estimates laid before Parliament. As an Officer Robert proudly wore the two eagle's feathers in his bonnet and it was doubtless a comfort to his Sovereign to know that a leading member of his Bodyguard could be relied upon to make his arrows hit the "gold" or the "clout".

On 24 May 1896 Robert went to the home of his friend Henry Holland at Cornhill-on-Tweed for a day's salmon fishing. The day was a public holiday in celebration of Queen Victoria's birthday. No record survives of the day's catch, but when a little later Robert's engagement to Henry Holland's sister Eleanor was announced, the gillie commented, 'Aye, Doctor Fleming hookit a grand big one'. They married on 20 April 1897, and fifty years later celebrated their Golden Wedding eight months before Robert died.

Eleanor Mary Holland was born on 23 August 1876. She was brought up to be as staunch an Anglican as her future husband was a Presbyterian. When she was six months old her father, the Reverend William Lyall Holland, took her with his wife and their three sons to Riga, where he had been appointed Chaplain to the wealthy English jute merchants, who had a trading station there. The extreme cold of the Baltic winters may well have bred in Eleanor a belief that a Spartan upbringing was best for children. In 1881 the family came home to Cornhill-on-Tweed where for the next forty-eight years William Holland was Rector. He was a delicate man, but this did not prevent him from transforming the life of a parish noted on his arrival for drunkenness and immorality. In recognition of his devotion to the needs of his parish he became an Honorary Canon of Durham Cathedral, where his father-in-law Canon Henry Baker Tristram was a famous and colourful figure.

Durham played a big part in Eleanor's early life. Not only were her father and grandfather Canons of the Cathedral in which she was christened but a somewhat earlier ancestor, Shute Barrington, had

been Bishop of Durham. He it was whom his punning friends liked
to refer to as the only licensed poacher, when on occasion he had to
proclaim, 'I, by Divine Permission, Shute'. Eleanor had regularly
attended the Cathedral services and had there first learned to love
music. She had gone to school in the city and many of her happiest
memories were of days spent in her grandfather's home.

Canon Tristram was a splendid character. He had been born in
1822 in Northumberland and most of his life was spent in the north
of England. He had all the north countryman's sturdy independence, tenacity and prejudiced determination to uphold what he
loved best. In his case this was the Evangelical tradition of the
Church of England, the Conservative party and Freemasonry. At a
time when the effects of the Oxford Movement were being widely
felt he remained an uncompromising Evangelical. He was an
imposing figure with his flowing beard and long surplice, insisting
on celebrating Holy Communion from the north side of the altar, or
Table as he would call it, bare of candles. The new Revised Version
of the Bible was summarily dismissed by him as the Reversed
Vision. When twitted about the extremity of his views, and the
equal extremity of those of another Canon of markedly High
Church leanings, he would unhesitatingly reply, 'I am extremely
right and he is extremely wrong'. Yet despite the strength of his
opinions his great sense of humour prevented him from making
personal enemies of those with whom he was in total disagreement.

Moreover there was another side to his life which made him
known far beyond the confines of the diocese of Durham. For this
rigidly Protestant Canon was also a famous naturalist and
ornithologist, the friend of Charles Darwin and a Fellow of the
Royal Society. Ill health in 1856 had forced him to winter abroad,
and his travels began when he penetrated deep into the Sahara to
make an important study of larks and chats. For nearly forty years
he continued to travel and to write learnedly about his observations
of fauna and flora. He gained an unrivalled knowledge of the natural
history of Palestine; he travelled through much of the Middle East
and went as far as China and Japan, in which latter country one of
his seven daughters was a missionary. From this lovable and

powerful character Eleanor inherited her tenacity of purpose and her interest and skill in gardening.

Many of Eleanor's forbears had been parsons and two of her three brothers were ordained. Canon Tristram's lifelong zeal for the work of the Church Missionary Society was carried on by these grandsons. Prebendary William Holland, Launcelot's godfather, worked for thirty years as a missionary in India before becoming Rector of the City Church of St. Mary Woolnoth and a Prebendary of St. Paul's Cathedral. The second brother, Sir Henry Holland, spent his life as a medical missionary, winning great fame as an eye surgeon at the Quetta Mission Hospital in Baluchistan. Here he narrowly escaped death in 1955 when his hospital was destroyed in an earthquake. Thanks largely to his efforts the money was raised to rebuild the hospital. The youngest brother, Herbert, was also for a time a missionary, later becoming Bishop of Wellington, New Zealand, and finally Dean of Norwich.

Marriage made no difference to Robert and Eleanor's loyalty to their own form of worship. Nor did their loyalties cause any rift between them. Sunday by Sunday Robert went to Charlotte Square while Eleanor went to the nearby Episcopal Cathedral or to St. John's Church, West End. However, whenever there was an important occasion in either church both would go to the Service together. Beyond this Eleanor could not compromise, and she made sure that her children were brought up as what the Scots knew as "good 'Piscies". Sometimes on Sunday evenings Harry Millar, a wellknown and much loved Presbyterian minister, would come to supper. On one occasion the talk must have been very much concerned with the Church of England, for as Millar left the house he turned to his host and said, 'Well, Robert, I think you'd better give up religion altogether and became an Episcopalian'.

Eleanor could be intimidating and Edinburgh friends found her formidable at times. In their opinion she was the dominant member of the marriage partnership. She believed passionately in the importance of the family as the main unit in society, and she took great pride in her own family tree. She held that it was a married woman's duty to run an efficient and happy household and that a happy home was to a great extent the product of good management. The family today recall with amusement the terrible rows which she used to have with her servants. Her heated exchanges with Helen, the flat-footed housemaid from a pit village, blocked the staircase at times for half an hour or more. Yet in spite of the rows and Eleanor's exacting demands the servants remained loyal to the family and stayed for years. At moments of serious domestic crisis Eleanor would appeal to Robert for support. While never directly interfering in what he regarded as her own sphere, he would defuse a potentially explosive situation with a quiet remark. He had a gift of affectionate ridicule combined with a delicious sense of humour which relaxed the tension. Although Eleanor was a woman of powerful determination and strength of character, her deep love for her husband meant that in the last resort Robert, when he wished, was always master in his own house.

The family home in Edinburgh was at No. 10, Chester Street. Plans for this part of the New Town had been drawn by Gillespie Graham in 1826, but the building of Chester Street only began in 1862. The gracious houses in this street and in the surrounding area were then largely occupied by the well-to-do professional classes; today most have been converted into flats or office buildings. No. 10 had its main door, with Robert's fine brass plate affixed to it, on the right hand side of the street front. As with so many Scottish houses of the period, the dining-room was on the left as you entered the house, with Robert's consulting room behind it. In those days patients saw their doctor in his own home. Across the first floor was the large drawing-room with a charmingly decorated plaster-work ceiling, and behind it was Robert and Eleanor's bedroom. The stone staircase with its iron banisters led up to two more floors of bedrooms. Servants and tradesmen entered the house by a flight of steps leading down from the street into what was then unimaginatively known as "the area". Most of the houses had small gardens at the back, familiarly known at that time as the Back Green, often nicknamed the Black Green from the effect of the soot-laden Edinburgh air. Many of these plots were just put down to

grass, and on Mondays were used for long lines of washing hung out
to dry. By contrast the Back Green of No. 10 was transformed by
Eleanor into a small but colourful garden. Robert had bought the
house for £1000 and as his family increased he decided in 1902 to
build two additional bedrooms at the top of the house.

Robert and Eleanor had five children, four boys and a girl. The
eldest child was born in 1898 and christened Robert Stevenson
Tristram. Bob Fleming, who inherited much of his father's charm,
was destined to cause his parents lasting anxiety and unhappiness
with his matrimonial and financial problems. Throughout her life
Eleanor was haunted by the fear that a scandal would sully the good
name of the family, but Robert knew that, whatever the
provocation, he could never escape from ultimate responsibility for
his son. Two years later Jean was born. She inherited her mother's
strength of character, and as she grew up there were frequent clashes
of personality between her and a mother with pronounced Victorian
views on the proper relationship which should obtain between
them. Judged by modern practice, both children were strictly, if not
harshly, brought up. Jean has suggested that much of Bob's
chequered career has been due to what appeared to him to be a lack
of affection in his early days. The Spartan disregard of warm
clothing in the cold of an Edinburgh winter, the belief in corporal
punishment, the grim Sunday routine with one, or perhaps two,
formal Services and the insistence, despite Bob's bitter unhappiness,
on early boarding school, might well help to account for a life lived
in reaction against his parents and for the tragic misunderstandings
between mother and son.

In Jean's case, although she was largely subjected to the same firm
handling, her stronger character better enabled her to hold her own,
not least when it came to her marriage. Her parents found it hard to
countenance her love for a young naval officer, Daniel de Pass, who
had been brought up as a practising Jew. However, before the
marriage took place Dan was baptised and confirmed, and thereafter
both Robert and Eleanor became very attached to him. That Dan's
conversion to Christianity is sincere is proved by the part which
later in life he played in Church affairs. It was a marriage of great

happiness, for Dan was a man of charm and considerable ability, who eventually rose to the rank of Commodore.

On All Saints Day, the first of November, 1902, a second son, Henry, was born. Five months later the child contracted a virus infection and with no antibiotics available to save him he died within twenty-four hours. It was a shattering blow which only the strong faith of Robert and Eleanor enabled them to withstand. Eleanor always remembered Henry as one of the family, and years later Launcelot sent his mother a cable from the Antarctic on All Saints Day to assure her that the brother whom he had never known was remembered in his prayers. Two years later, in May 1904, Archie was born – a boy for whom as he grew up the Royal Navy was the only possible career, and one in which he was to serve with distinction. Eleanor used to say that up to this point 'we were a normal family, and then, at the end, I got a Launcelot'.

With Launcelot's arrival in August 1906 the family was complete.

Whether it was the loss of her second son or for some other reason, neither Archie nor Launcelot was subjected to as stern an upbringing as Bob and Jean. This was fortunate for Launcelot was a delicate child and a Princess Christian nurse, Miss Gibson, was engaged to look after him. During the First World War Edinburgh was shelled, and this frightening experience for a small boy upset him for six months. His early education was entrusted to a daily governess until he was nine years old. A snapshot has survived of him in the schoolroom, dressed in a sailor suit, looking virtuous and very studious. 'You must have looked quite attractive in those days,' said his wife when given the photograph.

Launcelot has always felt that he could never be sufficiently grateful for having enjoyed the security of a good home. Several times he says this in letters from the Antarctic. Life followed a clearly prescribed pattern, which is a help and not a hardship for a young child. On Sunday mornings the under-nanny, Nellie Gittins, dressed Archie and Launcelot in their sailor suits in order to go with their father to the Royal Infirmary to talk to the patients in his wards. Nurses and patients made a fuss of the boys, who enjoyed the

weekly visits until the moment came to go into the ward for
"incurables", where lay patients with every kind of deformity. This
Launcelot dreaded. In the afternoon Nellie Gittins took both boys to
the children's service at St. John's Church, West End. The vicar,
Canon Tremlett, must have made a great impression on Launcelot
for he kept the vicar's photograph on the mantelpiece of the night
nursery. Before bedtime the family gathered around the
harmonium, which Eleanor played, and sang hymns. A favourite
hymn was "For all the Saints", which she liked to have sung to mark
the continuing place of the lost child in the family.

On weekdays when lessons were over, there were walks to the
Botanical Gardens, accompanied by Jim the bulldog. Occasionally
there would be a visit to the Zoo, and on one memorable day Nellie
Gittins took Launcelot to Rothesay Mews where her father was in
charge of Lord Salverin's stables and he was put astride a horse. On
rare Saturdays when his father was not shooting he would take
Launcelot to see the ships in Leith docks – a great treat. At home in
the evenings there were fierce games of racing demon, and there was
always the No. 0 gauge model railway with its clockwork engine and
carriages from Bassett Lowke to be set in motion. At a relatively
early age Launcelot collected stamps and "founded" what he
impressively named "The Ideal Philatelic Club". From time to time
in an age before radio and television the family enjoyed a magic
lantern show. A modern child would denounce the simple and
ordered life as boring in the extreme, but to a large extent Launcelot
and his contemporaries expected to make their own amusements,
and with larger families than are common today there was no lack of
companionship.

In 1913 Launcelot clearly remembers being taken by Mrs
Anderson, the family cook, to hear a lecture by Captain Evans on
Scott's last expedition. He was greatly moved by the story, and
perhaps the occasion played some slight part in arousing his interest
in Antarctic adventure. Of greater importance was Eleanor's wish
that her children should share her own love of music. There were
excellent concerts throughout the winter in the Usher Hall to which
she took them, sometimes wisely remaining only for part of the

concert lest they became sated with more than they could appreciate. "Messiah" on New Year's Day was a particularly enjoyable experience.

Eleanor was also anxious that her children should learn to love and appreciate the countryside. She was a countrywoman, who never really liked having to live in a city. The Easter holidays were spent with her parents at the Cornhill-on-Tweed rectory. The summer holidays were usually spent in a house rented for the purpose by Robert's mother and sister, first at Gargunnock, a small castle near Stirling, and later at Mossfennan, a house on the upper reaches of the Tweed. Long carefree days in the open air bred in Launcelot a lasting love of the Scottish countryside. Archie's passion for fishing was not shared by his younger brother, though one of Archie's trout proved useful as a method of stirring Nellie Gittin's tea on a picnic. It was at Mossfennan that Eleanor organised a performance of the tea-party scene from "Alice in Wonderland". Jean was Alice, Bob the Mad Hatter, Archie the March Hare, while Launcelot was relieved to have few lines to learn as the Dormouse.

On one holiday in 1917 Eleanor and her father took Jean, Archie and Launcelot for a bicycle tour to Gatehouse-of-Fleet, some hundred miles from Edinburgh. Launcelot had been given a bicycle just in time to join the tour, though to his disgust the only model available in wartime was one for a girl. However, it had the advantage of being easy to dismount; he merely jumped into the road, throwing the bicycle into a ditch. Robert had bought his first car – a dark blue, secondhand, 14 horse power Clément for which he paid £300 – as early as 1908, and motor drives to favourite picnic places added to the joy of the holidays. It was on one of these picnics that a cousin, commenting on Launcelot's childhood habit of speaking very slowly and rather pompously, said that obviously he would have to become either a butler or a bishop when he grew up.

Despite the tensions which arise in any family in which there are strong personalities, life in the early days at Chester Street or on holiday were very happy. Discipline was strict but the rules which had to be obeyed were clearly understood. Nanny presided over the nursery life, ensuring regularity in the daily behaviour of her charges and of their bowels. 'Eat up' came the command if a particular dish was disliked. Much more vivid in Launcelot's memory was the firm administration of Gregory Powder and, worse still, of castor oil when this was considered necessary. Virtue was acquired and recognised if the medicine was 'swallowed bravely'. If Nanny's control was challenged then Eleanor's aid was invoked and this was usually sufficient to bring the culprit to penitent obedience. In the last resort Robert was expected to inflict a little corporal punishment, though he hated hurting his children and avoided taking any action if possible.

Every morning Robert conducted family prayers when the whole household had to attend. Each evening Eleanor heard the children's prayers as she came to their rooms to say goodnight. On Christmas evening the whole household, upstairs and downstairs, would meet around the Christmas tree in the large drawing-room. By the light of candles, all holding hands would sing "While Shepherds Watched Their Flocks by Night", and then the children would show their presents set out on small tables around the tree. It was a life of great joy to Launcelot and important in his development. Happiness came from security, and security, which matters more than all else to a child, was the gift of parents devoted to their children and themselves stayed on the rock of their faith.

During these years Launcelot unconsciously learned from his father the need to care for people, and throughout his whole life it has been people who matter first, last and all the time to him. Although it is about his mother that he most frequently speaks and who was the dominating influence upon him, it is his father whom he more closely resembles. 'Launcelot is not clever,' said Robert once, 'but he is very determined.' It was this determination that his mother gave him and which could, in the opinion of those who disagreed with him in manhood, verge on obstinacy. Some have even noted a streak of something akin to ruthlessness when finally convinced that the course which he had decided to take was right. His mother's religious upbringing and her strong personality played a big part in decisions which had to be made at turning points in his life. To her he instinctively turned for advice but, as with his father, in the last resort the decisions were his. Determination and compassion do not always go together, but thanks to his parents they are both found in Launcelot. It has been said that the two qualities which make a fine doctor are great skill in diagnosis allied to infinite compassion. On this definition Robert was certainly a fine doctor, from whom his youngest son inherited his remarkable sensitivity in understanding people's troubles and his care for their needs. As the years went by Launcelot increasingly became his mother's favourite, the one child who had fulfilled all her hopes. Her devotion could be demanding and at times overpowering, but it won his loyalty and love to the end of her days.

In 1913 Launcelot's portrait was painted by Paul Croeber, a distinguished German painter of children. He had been a fellow student with Robert in Dresden and he remained a close friend of both Robert and Eleanor. While the portrait was being painted the artist asked Launcelot to sing to him in the hope of keeping him relatively still. The only songs of which Launcelot was really sure of the words were "Rule Britannia" and "God Save the King". These he sang with patriotic fervour, totally unaware of the rapidly deteriorating relations between Britain and Germany. The charming portrait, which Croeber gave to Eleanor, shows a slightly defiant Launcelot dressed in the kind of smock which Eleanor remembered the peasants wearing years before in Riga.

By now Launcelot had grown into a strong and healthy child and there was no reason why he should not be sent away to school.

STUBBINGTON HOUSE AND RUGBY

1915 – 1925

In September 1915 Launcelot left home for Stubbington House
School near Fareham in Hampshire. It was a long way to send a boy,
but Archie was already there. He had been sent south partly to get
rid of slight chest trouble caused by the Edinburgh climate, but
chiefly because he had set his heart upon a naval career and the
school had a high reputation for getting boys into Osborne, which
they then entered at the age of thirteen.

Life in a preparatory school in the early years of the century was
Spartan in its discipline and lack of comfort. The idea that children
learn more quickly if they are happy had not yet been understood by
any save the stranger "progressive" schools. In wartime, however,
discipline was inevitably more capricious, because the teaching staff
was made up of men who had either retired or were medically unfit
to serve, and of women. Furthermore, Stubbington's headmaster,
Major Montagu Foster, had been called up in 1915 and had handed
over his school for the duration of the war to a fat, red-headed and
red-moustached Welshman, David Hugh-Jones, known to his
pupils as Jonah.

The teaching was probably no better and no worse than in other
preparatory schools in wartime. Among the masters were two good
teachers, notably the men in charge of Classics and French. The
Classics master was a fine teacher who was thought by the boys to
have been sacked from a famous public school because of his
addiction to the bottle. Even darker suspicions were entertained of
the French master, Monsieur Guilmaut – 'Mr Gillymo'. It was
rumoured that he was really a German spy who used his electric
torch to flash signals to enemy agents from the playing fields after

dark. Those were the days when boys' imaginations were excited by magazine stories in which sinister foreigners were unmasked by heroic schoolboys. Apart from a sarcastic tongue and an unpleasant habit of lifting a boy up from his desk by twisting the hair above his ears, he was a competent teacher.

Of the other masters one was kind but incapable of keeping order, one or two others were mildly sadistic and one, imported to tighten up the discipline, achieved his purpose by encouraging informers. He was supposed to teach General Knowledge of which his own store was severely limited. 'Where is the Bridge of Sighs?' 'Venice, sir.' 'Wrong. St. John's College, Cambridge.' In reply to protests he conceded, 'Well, there may be one in Venice but the famous one is in Cambridge.'

At the end of the war "Monnie" Foster returned to his school and proceeded to restore the discipline which he felt appropriate to a school which prided itself on being a nursery for future naval officers. One of his methods was the occasional public flogging, and Launcelot has a vivid memory of being forced to watch the execution in the gymnasium. A contemporary of Launcelot's has described what happened on those occasions, known to the boys as "pubs". 'There would be a sudden cry of "All on parade" and when we were assembled Monnie used to deliver a long rambling talk, while we tried to discover what it was all leading up to. One I remember was on the supreme value of cricket as an instrument of moral training, and how anyone failing to take cricket seriously was a creature unfit for decent society. I felt very uncomfortable as I was no kind of games player and cricket bored me to tears. But as Monnie worked himself into a real or simulated fury, terrifying to behold, the diatribe became less general and more particular, and we learned that the object held up for our detestation was a boy on quite a junior game, a keen butterfly hunter, fielding at longstop. He suddenly spotted a White Admiral, a fairly rare butterfly, and left his "post of duty" to chase it, knock it down with his grey felt sun-hat and bring it back in triumph. Suddenly Monnie shouted out the offender's name and the wretched boy was seized by the gym instructors, Petty Officer Gilmore and Sergeant Harvey. He was thrown across the vaulting-horse, one holding his arms and the other his legs, while Monnie flogged him'.

These were rare occasions but the use of corporal punishment for most offences was frequent, though possibly less unpleasant than being made to drill with a "backboard", a heavy wooden board with a handle at each end which had to be raised up and down for a considerable length of time.

In retrospect Launcelot remembers being always cold and slightly frightened, but never seriously unhappy. The same is true of the contemporary who described the flogging, '. . . though I had times of great misery, overall I wasn't unhappy and a lot of it I actively enjoyed'. Another contemporary, who became a highly decorated admiral, believed that there was much to be said in favour of Foster's rule. 'A significant proportion of the boys had ambitions to enter the Senior Service, and this atmosphere pervaded the whole life of the school. I would not dispute that life became pretty rough at the end of the war, but I am sure that no school can boast of such a large proportion of its pupils having reached Flag Rank (nearly a hundred I believe).'

Few preparatory schools then believed in the need for any form of heating in the dormitories during the winter. The water in the two basins for evening and morning ablutions was often frozen when the boys woke, and their sponges were so stiff that they scratched away the night's sleepiness. However, this mattered much less to small boys than food. It was a very difficult task to feed children in schools in the closing years of the war. Food was scarce everywhere, and rationing was far more severe and less efficient than it was in 1939. Much less was known about what constitutes a balanced diet.

The food provided was inadequate and unpleasant. Tapioca puddings ('frogs' eyes'), margarine which bore no resemblance to its modern equivalent, and a strange substance called "cocoa butter" remain in the mind from those war years. Each boy had his own named jam jar containing his weekly ration of sugar, and theft of somebody else's jam jar was not unknown. Launcelot maintains that they were given ships' biscuits, (appropriate to a "naval" establishment), which at times contained live maggots. However, if the biscuits were unappetising the maggots provided welcome entertainment when set to race against each other. An undated letter to his father – probably written in 1916 – shows how insufficient feeding could be made to appear patriotic. "Just now we are having a small chunk of bread in an envelope for each day, it is supposed very economical and it is what Lord Devonport told us we must do".

Occasionally, at the end of term or on Sports Day, there was something of a feast. At the end of term there was the "grub tea" with cakes which boys tried to carry away for a dormitory feast that night. This was not easy as Eton jackets were not designed for concealment. One summer Launcelot wrote home: "We are going to have strawberries and ices to-day". The preceding sentence is only very thinly scratched out and reads: "I have finished the chocolates and pretty quickly too". He was lucky to get them as most sweets sent from home were usually confiscated. Food sent or brought by parents had to be handed in, and could also be confiscated as punishment for misdeeds.

In 1916 Robert, though over age, volunteered to go to Salonika. A base hospital, staffed by the Edinburgh Medical School, had been set up in a former orphanage for the small Allied force stationed rather pointlessly there after the Dardanelles failure. It was unhealthy country, and Robert's letters to Eleanor show that most of his patients were suffering from malaria and dysentry. Just before he left home Robert received this letter from Launcelot:

July 15 1916

"Dear Daddy,

I am rather sorry that you are going to Salonika. But do you know when you are going there? I suppose you will soon be made a major. We are going to have the competitions today I think because Miss Foster said the glass was rising to fine. I think there are fifty seven parents of different boys coming up to-day. A few days ago a master left to go out to India his name is Mr. Sassoon the one I used to hate. I think I am going to write to him to see what he will say. He might write and say Dear *Piggy 2* because when he played cricket with me he used to call me *Piggy 2*". (Then follow the sentences already quoted about the strawberries and the chocolates).

With love from
Launcelot".

Both his father and mother were naturally closely interested in Launcelot's progress. Like most other people they failed to detect the ability which for the moment lay dormant. It was his hard work which they applauded. "Lance has done magnificently for him and must have worked like a brick", wrote Robert to Eleanor in December 1916. A little earlier poor Launcelot had written to his father: "I am very sorry to say I am tenth in my class this week. I only wish I was higher up but I will still go on trying my best". However, in a rather curious letter in November 1916 his mother told Launcelot how well she thought he had done:

> "My dearest Launcelot,
>
> How splendid your half-term report – I'm sending it to Daddy – I think 5th is a very good place – and 5th doing *honourable* work is much better than 1st and cheating. Daddy *will* be pleased to know that when he is working so hard at Salonika his sons are doing their best at home. You are really helping the war by doing your school work well – for after the war when it comes to your turn to be a man – you'll be able to work for your country and show all of those who are giving their lives for you that your life and what you do in it is really worthy of their great sacrifice".

Robert felt very lonely away from his family, and Launcelot dutifully wrote to him the kind of letters which preparatory school boys write home so laboriously on Sundays when there is little to say.

Sun Feb 11th (1917)

> "On Sunday we did not go to church nor did we put on eton collars I do not know why. In the afternoon we had walks which is very dull."
>
> (Clearly this was too short and the letter was continued on the next two days).

Monday 12th

"On Monday we had General Drill instead of Tuesday. In the morning some of the boys had football but the rest went out for a walk and the same with the afternoon."

Tuesday 13th

"On Tuesday the boys who were going to join the navy went to the admiralty for their examination. I think there were five or six boys. We had Dancing in the morning. (I am learning dancing this term) and the boys who were not dancing went for a walk.

I must stop now

With love from
Launcelot."

Launcelot was an affectionate child who sent the threepenny piece which he had drawn out of the Christmas snapdragon to his father. Once on packing his trunk for school Eleanor came across a packet of sweets which he had saved to give to his friends. Robert greatly valued the trouble which Launcelot took in writing regularly, probably well aware how tedious a burden letter writing can be to a small boy. In his letters to Eleanor from Salonika Robert frequently remarked on "Lance who is a brick at writing" and his pleasure at Launcelot's hard work. One letter to her gives a rather charming picture of the relationship between them. "What would I not give to see you for 10 minutes even or to have 10 days at home even with the voyage both ways, submarines and all and every other objectionable element!! P.S. I would even *welcome*!! a scolding if I could get it from your own dear lips and should simply bask in it!"

Launcelot continued to make steady if unspectacular progress up the school and to enter into the games and other activities. One contemporary remembers him playing the part of an innkeeper in a form play, dressed in a striped apron and being thought 'frightfully good and howlingly funny'. Nevertheless, in March 1920 he left Stubbington with few regrets, and in the following term entered Rugby School, a school to which many parents living in Scotland sent their sons. Stubbington had been something of an ordeal for a small and sensitive boy, and he must have had moments of wondering whether the Rugby of Tom Brown still existed with its bullying and cruelty. His fears were rapidly to be proved groundless.

In that most perceptive of books about school life, *The Lanchester Tradition,* G. F. Bradby, a master at Rugby, told the marvellous tale of the running battle between the Reverend Septimus Flaggon, a progressive headmaster, and Mr Chowdler, a hidebound and reactionary housemaster. The two protagonists in the prolonged struggle are thinly disguised portraits of the Revd. A. A. David, headmaster of Rugby from 1910 until 1921, and Robert Whitelaw, an overpowerful housemaster to whom all change was sacrilegious.

When Launcelot arrived at Rugby David was nearing the end of his headmastership. At the start he had successfully faced the need to modernise the school, which had inevitably entailed overcoming considerable opposition from entrenched senior masters, like Whitelaw. The strain of this, followed by the problems of the war years and then by the anxieties of the dangerous influenza epidemic of 1918–19 had tired David, who was now ready for a change of work. It was a sign of a less firm hold on the reins that he had recently come under the dubious influence of a self-taught American psycho-analyst, Homer Lane. David had been convinced by Lane that in the new techniques of psycho-analysis could be found the cure for all the moral difficulties of adolescence. Senior boys soon found it all too easy to persuade their sympathetic headmaster that they were suffering from a "complex" which only a trip to London to consult Homer Lane would cure. This became more than his staff could accept, but their loyalty was not put to the test for in 1921 David left Rugby to become Bishop of St. Edmundsbury and Ipswich.

As a small boy Launcelot can have known little about David's slackening grip in the last year of his headmastership. He does, however, remember with gratitude David's regular visits to the school sanatorium and the friendly charm of his smile. During the summer term of 1921 Launcelot became seriously ill. He first

contracted scarlet fever and then developed a mastoid, which led
Robert to come down to Rugby to consult with the school doctor,
Dr. Simey. Although he recovered well and avoided any operation
on his ear, the period of illness left a permanent mark in that for ever
after he was unable to perspire on one side of his body. This was to
be a nuisance when playing a vigorous game of squash or hockey,
and a matter of some concern when preparing for his Arctic and
Antarctic expeditions. It may also have been the original cause of
the illness which affected his legs later in life.

David was succeeded by W. W. Vaughan, a cousin of Virginia
Woolf and married to a daughter of John Addington Symonds. He
was the first layman to become headmaster of Rugby, and at the age
of fifty-seven he returned to take charge of the school at which he
himself had been a boy, having already been both headmaster of
Giggleswick and Master of Wellington. In his *Rugby since Arnold*
J. B. Hope-Simpson said that Vaughan's pupils "saw a big, rather
clumsy figure, dressed in untidy secular garments, his hair a little
longer than was usual and wearing a full moustache. Someone
described him as resembling a huge shaggy dog with a
disconcertingly loud bark". He was a formidable figure to masters as
well as to boys, but it was quickly clear that he had the well-being of
the whole community at heart. To Virginia Woolf's annoyance this
meant expecting his wife to play a full part in the school life and
thus frustrating a potential literary career. Vaughan was not a great
scholar, nor was he a particularly inspiring preacher or teacher, but
he was alive to the educational needs of the post-war world. The age
old domination of the Classics was challenged, and modern
languages and science won a respected place in the curriculum.
Although not a musician himself, he encouraged music as an
important part in a boy's general education. Launcelot, to whom
science was to become his field of university study, was fortunate to
grow up in the early years of Vaughan's reign.

After a term in E. L. D. ("Beaky") Cole's waiting-house Launcelot
went into what is now known as Whitelaw's House, but was then
called by the name of its housemaster, the Revd. J. M. Hardwich.
Whitelaw, after his defeat by David, had left his House in 1913 and

Hardwich, then a bachelor, had taken over. For Launcelot's parents the choice of House was obvious. "Polly" Hardwich had been a great friend of the three Holland brothers, and Eleanor used to join in their games of cricket played in the Monks' Garden at Durham. Hardwich was an earnest and conscientious housemaster, an exacting teacher of the Classics and the possessor of a pleasant tenor voice. It cannot be said that under his guidance the House was particularly distinguished. To the complete surprise of his boys Hardwich returned at the start of one term having married his Scottish housekeeper. He became noted for the way in which he drove his car, a Standard, around corners at the then daring speed of twenty miles an hour, explaining as he did so that in this way he 'got over them quicker'. It is interesting to speculate on how far Launcelot's own driving habits were inculcated by his housemaster.

"'Is there any point to which you would wish to draw my attention?'

'To the curious incident of the dog in the night time'.

'The dog did nothing in the night time'.

'That was the curious incident,' remarked Sherlock Holmes."

In a sense this famous exchange between Holmes and Watson summarises Launcelot's Rugby career. After the rigours of Stubbington House he was, as he recalls, blissfully happy, but he made very little mark academically or athletically. *The Meteor,* the school magazine, barely mentions his name. In view of his later achievements it is curious that he rose in the school no higher than the "Twenty", a form just below the Sixth Form. It should be said that from the Twenty boys took the old Higher Certificate and so the form was comparable to the Sixth Form in other schools. He was in his House given "Sixth Power", which meant that he became a House Prefect. He enjoyed rugger but was no great player; he loathed cricket and fielded unimpressively at longstop in a game known as the "Remnants". It was a relief half way through his time at Rugby to be allowed to give up cricket and play tennis. Squash rackets he took up at Rugby and continued to play well for many years. In the O.T.C. he reached the rank of Sergeant, which to him was 'to rise to the giddiest heights of fame'.

As a young boy he possessed a good treble voice, and was the treble member of a house quartet which performed well in the music competition. He also learned the piano with a Miss Dukes, commonly known as the Duchess, and was one of her favourites. The trouble about learning the piano for Launcelot was to remember to clean his finger nails in advance of a lesson for it was embarrassingly difficult to hide them when his hands were on the keyboard. He was never likely to become much of a pianist, but the Duchess remained a friend of the family and Launcelot always made a point of going to see her whenever he was in Rugby. Within his House he had many friends, chief of whom was Eric Harding, his study companion and future stockbroker, but none of them retains a vivid impression of him. They recall a 'quiet' and 'serious-minded' boy whom they all liked but who did little of note.

Launcelot was clearly an example of what has come to be known as a "late developer". To some extent his illness must have affected him in his younger days. He himself says that by the time that he reached the "Twenty" he had gained the necessary "Credits" for entry to Cambridge and there seemed to be no obvious reason to work excessively hard to get into the Sixth Form. He was not a candidate for a university scholarship. Moreover, in George Riding, the form master of the "Twenty", Launcelot found a great teacher who was opening his eyes to the joys of literature. Whatever explanation may be offered for his comparative lack of achievement and for the failure of his friends to recognise "a budding bishop" in their midst, the time had not come when, in his own words, 'the point of doing some particular work is seen'. Vaughan, in a striking phrase, had once described the essential work of a teacher. 'The object of education through all its stages,' he said, 'is to release the imprisoned splendour'. That release for Launcelot came at Cambridge.

TRINITY HALL

1925 – 1929

On the subject of Cambridge and, above all, of Trinity Hall, Launcelot has never been wholly rational. Few men have ever had a more burning and lasting love for their College and all its members – dons, undergraduates and College servants – than he.

The College of the Scholars of the Holy Trinity of Norwich, or Trinity Hall, had been founded in 1350 by Bishop Bateman of Norwich for a specific purpose. Bateman was no pastoral bishop but a man who moved on the national and international stage and, as he saw the business of government developing, he realised the need for a steady supply of qualified lawyers, diplomatists and administrators. Such men would have to be trained in civil and canon law, and it was to this end that he founded his College in a hostel previously used by the monks of Ely when studying at the University. The foundation was timely for in the two previous years bubonic plague, the Black Death, had killed off a third, perhaps even a half, of the population of England. It had taken a particularly heavy toll of the clergy as they bravely but vainly tried to minister to those struck down. Of the six hundred and forty-eight clergy in the diocese of Ely, in which Cambridge lies, at least three hundred and fifty died. Since it was the clergy who then alone were in any sense educated, there was now an added reason for replenishing their ranks. The College soon began to flourish and in 1366, together with Pembroke College, was granted papal permission to have its own College Chapel. While developing in much the same way as other colleges, Trinity Hall has remained through the centuries renowned for its legal training, as its Founder must have hoped.

Launcelot was entered for Trinity Hall on the advice of the
Principal of Westcott House, Canon B. K. Cunningham, whose
sister, Mrs. Richardson, lived in Edinburgh and was a great friend of
Launcelot's mother. Through her she was in touch with
Cunningham who, although a Trinity man himself, felt that
Launcelot would be much happier in a smaller college and one in
which the dons had a reputation for the interest which they took in
the undergraduates. Cunningham could not have given better advice
for the Hall proved to be the ideal college for Launcelot. It was
sufficiently small for all its members to know one another and there
were no barriers to friendship between dons and undergraduates. As
in every Oxford and Cambridge college at that date the majority of
undergraduates came from public schools, though there was only
one other Rugbeian, but it was not such a socially exclusive college
as Magdalene then was. Launcelot's home and school background
ensured his quick acceptance into a singularly happy "club" in
membership of which he found an abiding joy.

Cambridge contributed to Launcelot's development in three
ways: he came alive intellectually, he made a wider and more lasting
circle of friends than in Scotland or at Rugby and, as part of his
intellectual development, he began to think seriously about his own
religious beliefs.

Launcelot had always been a hard and conscientious worker at
school but he had never shone academically. There was never any
suggestion that he should follow the strong Hall tradition and read
Law. His interest in Natural Science had been aroused at Rugby and
it seemed sensible to develop this by reading Physics and Chemistry
as two of the three subjects offered in Part I of the Natural Sciences
Tripos. It was his supervisor, Frank Potts, who made the far-seeing
suggestion that the third scientific subject might be Geology. It is
often a stimulating experience to embark upon a course of study at
university without any previous teaching at school. This certainly
was true for Launcelot. At the time the Professor of Geology was
"Johnnie" Marr, whose deteriorating sight caused him when
lecturing to start a new illustration on the blackboard without fully
rubbing out the previous drawing. 'The resulting chalk diagrams',

said Launcelot, 'provided a fascinating subject for detective interpretation.' He became a great friend and admirer of Marr, not least perhaps because Marr encouraged him to row, and he began to enjoy greatly his new scientific work.

The release of the "imprisoned splendour" did not take place all at once: the intellectual awakening was gradual. At the end of Launcelot's second year his efforts won him a safe "Second" in the first part of the Tripos, though it is probable that had the second class men then been divided, as now happens, he would have been awarded a 2(1). He did not take the second part of the Tripos for another two years, during which he became increasingly fascinated by Geology. This interest was in part due to his Supervisor, Gertrude Elles, Vice-Principal of Newnham and aunt of Launcelot's rowing friend, Robin Elles. There was an unforgettable day when she said to him, 'You know, Launcelot, I think that you are going to get a "First"'. This distinction he achieved in 1929. It had been worth sacrificing his place in the First Boat. All kinds of opportunities for the future seemed now to be opening. During his final year he himself had had a pupil, and the possibility of remaining at Cambridge as a don, lecturing in Geology, became very attractive.

Launcelot must have more friends than any man alive, and it is through them that his life has very largely been lived. As a Fellow of Trinity Hall wrote of Launcelot's years there: "Everyone knew Launcelot; everyone loved Launcelot". There had been good friends at Rugby, but his lasting friendships began to be formed at Cambridge. His rooms on E staircase soon became a magnet to which the most widely differing members of the College were drawn. The Boat Club provided the surest introduction to College life for him.

Launcelot had enjoyed playing most games at Rugby but had not played with any great distinction. Thus when the Captain of the Trinity Hall Boat Club, Frank Carr, later to become Librarian to the House of Lords and Director of the National Maritime Museum, knocked on the door of his rooms, he found an easy victim for his persuasive blandishments. Rowing was to give Launcelot the vigorous exercise which he always needed, close companionship and the knowledge that in whatever boat he rowed he would be representing his College. He joined the Boat Club at a moment when its membership embraced a large proportion of the undergraduates. Although not then as successful on the river as it later became, the Club flourished in other ways. It was a happy Club, free from internal dissensions, tremendously enthusiastic and one of the main centres of undergraduate activities. Its members, with pardonable bias, liked to claim that in the late 1920s the Trinity Hall Boat Club *was* the Hall.

Launcelot was too light to become a university-class oarsman but he was a much better oar than the bare record suggests. He got his oar in his second term in the Third Lent Boat. This Boat was stroked by Robin Elles, who had never rowed at school, and who in the following year made a sensational rise to be Stroke of the Blue Boat. In his third term Launcelot was with the Second May Boat at Cambridge and at Henley. The thrill of his first appearance at Henley was an unforgettable experience and ensured that in later years attendance at the regatta took precedence over all save the most pressing engagements. He rowed in the First Lent Boat both in 1927 and 1928, and would certainly have rowed in the Hall First Boat in 1929 had he not reluctantly decided that to row in Maay would seriously interfere with the work for his Tripos. For his weight he was an excellent oar, quick, lively and hard working. As a good "boat-mover" he was an asset to any boat. He usually rowed Bow and, typically, never said that it was the hardest place in the boat in which to row.

As his influence began to pervade the College, his value to the Boat Club became more than just a useful oar. It was his ability to resolve personal differences, to keep the Club the happy place which he found it and to be available to the many who sought his advice, which was so important. Rowing for Launcelot was an enjoyable sport but, above all, a means to companionship. Yet his friendships were in no way confined to members of the Boat Club. To have been at the Hall in any capacity was sufficient to ensure that a lasting bond would be formed.

Among the Fellows Launcelot came first to know his Supervisor, Frank Potts, a biologist and, like his pupil, a man who married late in life. Potts had been a Fellow for nearly twenty years when Launcelot arrived at the Hall. He was a man of great charm, much loved by those whose studies he directed. Three other senior Fellows became his friends and influenced him in various ways: Robin Hayes, a life-long bachelor and an engineer to whose rooms Launcelot used to go for gramophone concerts; Franklin Angus, a Classical scholar, whose friendship was not easily won; and the man who was to exercise the most profound influence on his future career, George Chase, later to become Master of Selwyn College and Bishop of Ripon.

A wise Freshman relies much on the advice of his gyp. George Langley had begun his life as a College servant in 1902, and for forty-five years he was in full time service and for another fifteen years continued to help. His sixty years at the Hall were only broken by the First World War when he became a Sergeant in the Rifle Brigade. He was a short little man with exacting standards who could make the life of the bedmakers working under him hell. Nothing was too much trouble if it helped the men on his staircase, and he and Launcelot were devoted to each other. For about twenty-five years Langley looked after him, not only in Cambridge but during some summer vacations in Scotland. One of Launcelot's pupils when he was Dean of the Hall was a woman, and on the day of her tuition Langley would wake him with words of encouragement to make him leave his bed: 'Little ray of sunshine this morning, sir'. In later years when Launcelot visited the Hall Langley, who by then was only working part time as a waiter at High Table in the Combination Room, insisted on seeing that he was properly served or supervised the unfortunate junior servant who was nominally doing so. Whenever one of Launcelot's friends came back to the College Langley's first words would be, 'Seen the Bishop lately, sir?' Langley's sole failure, which he shared with many another, was his inability to see that Launcelot was neatly dressed when occasion demanded. He died in 1974 at the age of ninety-three and it was only right that Launcelot should conduct his funeral service.

One of the advantages of a university education is to give a man
three or four more years before making a final decision about a
career. That Launcelot would in due course be ordained seemed
obvious to many of his friends, but certainly not to him. A scientific
career seemed much more probable and, as Cambridge took
possession of him, much more attractive but without seriously
undermining his faith.

Launcelot's whole upbringing had led him to accept, more or less
without question, the strong Christian belief of his parents. His
Confirmation at Rugby, for which he had been well prepared by his
Housemaster, had meant much to him. On arrival at Cambridge he
attended Chapel regularly and in his first term joined the Student
Christian Movement. At the same time he began to think critically
about the religious teaching which he had hitherto accepted largely
without intellectual difficulty. There was no long period of
agonising doubt, no sudden Damascus road revelation, but a
careful thinking out of his own beliefs for the first time. In this
process the Student Christian Movement helped him greatly and
with, as yet, little or no thought of Ordination. Launcelot's religious
probings became an important part of his whole intellectual
development.

Tempermentally he has never been very sympathetic to what
eighteenth century divines denounced as "enthusiasm". He says
that at this time his Christianity was hardly strengthened by the
well-meaning but misguided efforts of a Rugbeian from another
college. Launcelot had invited him to lunch unaware that his
friend was an arden member of the extremely Evangelical
Cambridge Inter-Collegiate Christian Union. 'I was quite
unaware that he was C.I.C.C.U. until near the end of lunch he
asked me if I was saved. I parried the question by asking if he
was and he said "Yes". Then as we got up from the table he
asked if we could pray together. I was embarrassed but said "Yes".
We both knelt at the sofa. I prayed fervently that none of my
Boat Club friends would come into my rooms. He, presumably,
prayed that I might be saved. My prayers at any rate were
answered.'

Early in his first summer at Cambridge the harsh realities of the world outside its four walls forced themselves upon University life, for in May 1926 Britain for nine days experienced the challenge of the General Strike. Members of the Trinity Hall Boat Club volunteered to act as special constables during the emergency. This in the end was to prove less exciting than having to drive buses and trains with enthusiastic lack of skill. Launcelot and his friends were not called upon to emulate the probably legendary exploit of the young man who drove his express train into Waterloo Station twenty minutes ahead of time despite the additional burden of the gates of two level crossings on his buffers.

The Boat Club volunteers were sent up to London in a convoy of cars and billeted in the barracks of the London Scottish Regiment, where they slept on the Drill Hall floor. After listening to a pep talk which hinted at the dangers lying ahead of them, they were taught how to make a baton charge. Unfortunately the authorities had run out of batons and so axe handles were issued instead, together with an armband as their authority for keeping the peace. Soon they were moved for the purpose of sleeping, to the more distinguished but not notably softer floor of Lord Howard de Walden's London home. A day or two later they were allowed to be guests of London friends provided that they were within easy call. For Launcelot this meant meeting for the first time Sir Anthony Bowlby, a famous doctor who had been head of the R.A.M.C. and who was a relative of his mother.

The day of action arrived. Launcelot and his friends were summoned early one morning to assemble at Tower Hill Police Station. Here they learned that a convoy of bacon was coming out of St. Katherine's Dock, which it would be their duty to guard as it passed the street corners. As they marched to the docks groups of five were deposited at each vital street crossing, and Launcelot recalls not feeling particularly brave in his cap, raincoat and armband, with only an axe handle to defeat the ominous-looking thugs, supposedly waiting to seize the bacon. The convoy appeared. At the head of the column were mounted police; then followed the lorries containing the bacon; and finally a body of armed soldiers.

The volunteers were totally unnecessary. So with feelings of relief or disappointment they were marched back to base.

Apart from the amusement of the experience in retrospect, what now dismays Launcelot is the ignorance of himself and his fellow undergraduates of the social and political implications of the strike. Of the genuine grievances of the miners, whose wages had been lowered and their working day lengthened by the mine owners, little was understood nor had any effort been made to find out. Certainly at that stage of his career Launcelot showed none of the burning desire of many modern undergraduates to set the world right. For the moment it was the needs of his friends which called forth his total devotion. People mattered more than causes.

In 1928 Robert Fleming bought the Innerhadden estate at Kinloch Rannoch in Perthshire. For some years he had had shooting in Glen Lyon but Innerhadden gave him and the whole family a country home which they adored. For Robert it provided an escape from work in Edinburgh at weekends and for longer holidays. Ultimately it was to Innerhadden that he retired and where he was to die. Eleanor was always a country woman who never liked city life, and at Innerhadden she could indulge her passion for gardening in a way which was impossible at Chester Street. She loved growing flowers in great masses, and she could now show herself a true granddaughter of Canon Tristram as she grew rare shrubs and plants from seeds given to her by two close friends, Bailey Balfour, the Regius Professor of Botany at Edinburgh University, and Sir Herbert Wright Smith, the Curator of the Botanical Gardens in Edinburgh, which she and Robert regularly visited. Her great work of creation in the Innerhadden garden was the glade. Here she planted rhododendrons and other shrubs amidst the beech trees and turned the rough hillside behind the house into a beautiful flowering wilderness.

In this work, and in much else, she was assisted by a remarkable character, Roddy MacLean. He was more or less a contemporary of Launcelot and had begun life on the estate as an under-keeper. In the Second World War he fought with distinction with The Lovat

Scouts and was awarded the Military Medal. For nearly half a century he served the family with devoted loyalty which never prevented the frequent employment of a Scottish directness of speech nor quenched his bubbling sense of humour.

Innerhadden is an attractively simple house in appearance. It dates in part from the sixteenth century but the present front of the house has 1747 inscribed over the doorway. Legend has it that Bonnie Prince Charlie escaped through a window at the back from those pursuing him after the failure of the second Jacobite Rising. The house stands a mile from the eastern end of Loch Rannoch, protected at the rear by hills which ultimately lead on to the towering form of Schiehallion. The cottage by the side of Innerhadden burn was built by Robert for his chauffeur a short way from the house. Another cottage was later given to Launcelot, and it was here that so many of his friends have stayed with him.

In the season shoots would normally be on Mondays, Wednesdays and Fridays. On other days there were long expeditions and picnics, fishing in the loch and for both Robert and Eleanor a full part in the life of the village. One of the many friends of the family who came regularly for the shooting recalls the wisdom of timing one's arrival toward the end of a Sunday morning if the austere form of Sabbath observance at the local kirk, which Robert regularly attended, was to be decently avoided. Although Innerhadden was a holiday home some of the formalities of Edinburgh life were maintained and it was usual to dress for dinner each evening. The domestic staff from Chester Street came with the family to Perthshire. Being on holiday did not stop Eleanor from good works. She was a power in the local Scottish Women's Rural Institute where, among other things, she taught the members the special stitch needed for Church embroidery. She sat on committees concerned with district nurses and other important local needs, and despite what she described as 'tiresome' opposition she usually got her own way.

Innerhadden has meant more to Launcelot than any of his other homes. He enjoyed the stalking and his father's shoots, but his chief pleasure came from walking the hills with his friends. Many a Trinity Hall man has climbed Schiehallion with him or, when really

energetic, has accompanied him on the thirty-two miles from
Innerhadden to the top of Ben Lawers and back. When in training
for rowing Launcelot would run along the loch side, sometimes
persuading Roddy MacLean to pace him; to this Roddy had only
assented provided that he was on his bicycle.

In later years, after he had left Cambridge, he would often take
Ordinands or young priests with him – how often they were Trinity
Hall men – who, as they panted in bad training to the top of
Schiehallion, saw preferment within their grasp. The loveliness and
magnificence of the countryside became very much a part of
Launcelot as he roamed the hills in his disgracefully tattered kilt
which Roddy's wife, and many another woman over the years,
vainly tried to keep in repair. Years later when he faced retirement
he thought of returning to Kinloch Rannoch. Only the realisation
that he would be too remote from friends and from his varied
interests prevented him from going back to the place where he had
always been so supremely happy.

Before his father bought Innerhadden Launcelot had spent part of
his summer vacations abroad. An Austrian Countess Czapary
owned a castle at Burg Finstergrunn near Salzburg into which she
was forced by financial necessity to admit a certain number of
carefully recommended paying guests. The Flemings were
considered worthy of this honour. In 1928, although Innerhadden
had by then been bought, Launcelot was again in Austria, this time
in the Tirol.

A year earlier he spent part of the Easter vacation on a map
reading course at Austwick, near Settle, which was run by W. B. R.
King, later to become Professor of Geology at Cambridge. It was
during his time here that a total eclipse of the sun, visible in that
part of England, occurred. Most of the party rose early and climbed
a nearby hill to get the best possible view. Unfortunately cloud
obscured the sight completely, a disappointment made the more
bitter by discovering on returning to their hotel that the one lazy
member of the course, who had remained in bed, had had an
excellent view of the eclipse through his bedroom window.

1   2   3

5

1, 2 Robert and Eleanor Fleming
      at the time of their marriage

3   Robert Fleming's mother

4   Eleanor Fleming's father
      and mother

5   Robert Fleming with Bob,
      Archie, Jean and Launcelot

6, 7 Robert and Eleanor Fleming
      in later life

6

7

8   Chester Street, Edinburgh. No. 10 is the house immediately on the left of the archway

9 Eleanor Fleming with Launcelot and Archie in the Chester Street drawing-room

10 Launcelot in the school-room

over

11 Stubbington House School, Fareham

12 Rugby School

opposite

13   Whitelaw House, 1925. Launcelot is seated second from the right

14   Trinity Hall, Cambridge. The Front Court

opposite

15   Innerhadden Lodge

17 The Cottage by the Burn, Innerhadden

16 Launcelot with his first stag

As Launcelot entered his final year as an undergraduate the question of a career became more pressing. He had thought of entering the Colonial Service, and the Master of Trinity Hall, Dr. Henry Bond, invited him to meet the Governor of Northern Nigeria, who was staying in the College. However, the permanent effects of his illness at Rugby ruled out serving for any length of time in a hot climate, and it would have been impossible to have worked only in the cooler districts. Geological surveying was an obvious opening and there was thought of working for the Burmah Oil Company. At times he thought of teaching and also of farming. The Innerhadden estate had its own farm, which may have influenced him. As his interest in geology and his scientific ability developed during this final year the thought of continuing to work as a scientist in some capacity became increasingly attractive. It might even enable him to remain in Cambridge if he did well enough in the Tripos.

It was at this time, when he was very uncertain about his future, that Launcelot received a letter from the Tutor of Trinity Hall, George Chase. Ostensibly the letter was written about fixing up rooms for him at 42, Sidney Street for his final year. The letter, dated 13th August 1928, is sufficiently important to quote at length.

"There is one thing I want to say, which is very difficult to put; but I think I can do it better by letter than by word of mouth. You write about your plans for the future. At one time I know you said you would like an academic life. Of course this would depend a good deal on how you did next year in Part II. But even if you got your 1st geology is not a crowded subject and few Colleges can afford to give a person a Fellowship for that alone. But if it could be combined with another office it might be quite different. Quite apart from this question I have sometimes wondered whether you would ever think of taking Orders. I believe you are well fitted for it. If you were Ordained, you might well get the position of Dean, either here or elsewhere. Don't laugh – or swear at me. I know it sounds as though I were suggesting Ordination as a means to a Fellowship. That I am sure you would despise, and so should I. But I do honestly think you are fitted for it and could do

really good work among undergraduates. And it is a possible
way of combining pastoral work with geology in a way which
is hardly possible anyhow else. Now it is a fact that we have
been keeping an eye open for someone who could be Dean.
We can't afford to take anyone who could do no teaching: we
don't want another Theologian, Classic or Historian, and it is
difficult to find a man who is suited to be Dean (the first
consideration) who has taken any other subject. Of course I
can't guarantee it, but I do think you would stand a very good
chance for a Fellowship here as Dean, whereas we frankly
could not afford a geologist, pure and simple. I won't say
more. Think it over and, if you like, come and have a talk
about it next term. I know the way I have put it makes it look
like an ulterior motive; but I know you don't want to drop
your geology; so I thought I must put the two in combination".

This letter made a decision about a career even more difficult for
Launcelot. Here was a virtual offer to remain in Cambridge,
probably at the Hall, but only at the price of Ordination. As Chase
feared, Ordination now appeared to be a useful way of staying in a
place which he loved but must never be his chosen career for this
kind of reason. There were strong family traditions which made
Ordination a natural step for him and he knew how much it would
please his mother. Here again were not the right reasons for
Ordination. At the same time he must have become aware, even if
subconsciously, of his influence over his friends. As a contemporary
wrote of him: "Boat Club types don't take kindly to 'goody goodies'
but Launcelot, though no prude, never allowed his personal
standards to fall whatever the company and no one ever set out to
shock him; he was too much liked and respected for that". A very
old friend, asked many years later to write a private testimonial
about him, summed up what so many contemporaries instinctively
felt when he wrote: "I always feel that by the incompetence of some
demon original sin was missed out of his composition".

In a strange way this man who was everyone's friend in College
was also different from others, a man set apart by an attractive
naivety, almost an innocence. Yet what was clear to his closest

friends was far from clear to Launcelot. Ordination was a possibility but, as yet, nothing more. The "First" which he was awarded in 1929 only strengthened his hopes of an academic life as a scientist. Fortunately for him the final decision could be postponed for a further two years because even before the results of the Tripos were published he was awarded a Commonwealth Fund Fellowship at the University of Yale.

When this was announced in May 1929 congratulations poured in. Two letters from Chester Street must have given him particular pleasure. His father, who once had admired Launcelot's 'determination' but had never thought him very clever, wrote to express his delight. "I am sure you will find Yale the very best College (after Trinity Hall). The go of an American is a great point in his favour and I learnt a lot from the Yanks I had as students. They enlarge your mind . . . "

A day later from "below stairs" came another letter showing the affection which Launcelot inspired among the family servants.

"Dear Mr. Lonclot,

"I am writing to congratulate you in the name of Helen, Jenny, Mabel and Margaret. We are all greatly pleased over the news of your success you have earned Your Laurels by Hard and Steady Work and we rejoice that you have been successful I need not say that your Father and Mother is both proud and Happy for you know they will be Perhaps the enclosed wi'll help to celebrate the Happy event The oat Cakes should remind you that Scotland is proud of her Successfull Sons so we count you as one of them.

"With warmest good wishes for your future as well as sincere Congratulations for the present

I remain
ever yours respectfully
Georgina Anderson. (Better known as Cook)

YALE AND WESTCOTT HOUSE

1929 – 1933

On the 15th of September 1929, after a cheerful send-off from
Innerhadden, Launcelot joined six other Commonwealth Fund
Fellows at Greenock, where they board the *S.S. Albertic*, bound
for Boston and New York. The party consisted of Geoffrey
Crowther, the future editor of *The Economist,* with whom
Launcelot shared a cabin; Eric Ashby, the future Master of Clare;
Leslie Lickfold, recently the organ scholar at Trinity Hall; James
Puxley who, despite coming from Oxford, became one of
Launcelot's closest friends; Norman Goodier and, the only woman,
Nora Mallinson from Girton. Of these all except Ashby and Miss
Mallinson were going to Yale. In spite of rough weather followed by
dense fog as the ship neared the American coast it was an enjoyable
voyage. In the evenings there were concerts and other forms of
entertainment, though most of the Fellows fought shy of the fancy
dress dance. Launcelot's first impressions of the Americans on
board were not wholly flattering. 'Some rather hearty and "fast",
some extremely practical and soulless business men and quite a
number of charming people . . . The children surprised us most:
they were all extremely bad mannered and their parents seemed to
be quite indifferent to their behaviour'.

After ten days at sea the ship reached New York. Here Launcelot
spent two days before going on to New Haven, Connecticut, where
Yale University is situated. The variety of nationalities whom he
saw on the main streets fascinated him and he enjoyed an evening at
the theatre watching a London company playing in John
Drinkwater's *Bird in Hand.* The high price of the indifferent seats
which had been booked rankled slightly. Before leaving for Yale the

party was entertained by Edward Harkness, who had founded the
Commonwealth Fund and whose munificent gifts to Harvard and to
Yale had enabled both universities to adopt a collegiate system.
Launcelot found him 'an extraordinarily modest and delightful
man, with the manner and speech of an Englishman, coupled with a
typically American generosity'. At the same time 'It was curious
having a formal luncheon with nothing but iced water to swill it
down with, and the absence of liquor made a considerable difference
to the atmosphere of the meal'.

Yale, the third oldest university in the United States, had been
founded in 1701 to train "learned and godly ministers" for the New
England puritan churches. Towards the end of the seventeenth
century some of the leading professors at Harvard realised the need
to move with the times and to rid the curriculum of the Aristotelian
doctrines which were still being taught. However, many still clung
tenaciously to the old ways but realised that their beliefs could no
longer be taught at Harvard. So they decided to found their own
university and ultimately settled at New Haven. Yale got its name in
1718 from its first great benefactor, Elihu Yale, a merchant who
came from Boston in Lincolnshire and who at one time was
Governor of Madras.

Launcelot was given rooms in the recently built Harkness
Quadrangle which, on the lines of an Oxford or Cambridge college,
consisted of a series of courts with lawns surrounded by flagged
paths and attractively planted with shrubs, trees and creepers. At
the corner of the largest court stood the tall Harkness Tower built, a
tribute to the first benefactor, as an imitation of the Boston
"Stump". Launcelot's rooms were in a nearby smaller tower
designed as a copy of Wrexham church tower. They were
attractively panelled, with a large stone hearth for a log fire in the
main room but, after Cambridge, he at first found it hard to become
accustomed to the noise from trolley cars rumbling day and night
along the road outside his window. He at once proceeded to make
these rooms as comfortable and cheerful as possible. "I have ordered
some cushions and a tablecloth of a very pretty material (and by
Jove they are expensive over here)", he wrote home. All his life

Launcelot has been worried about his finances, as those friends who have helped from time to time to sort out his affairs and persuade him that he is not on the verge of bankruptcy know well.

Living in the Harkness Quadrangle made easy contact with the student body possible. Doctor Edward Bliss Reed, who looked after the Commonwealth Fund Fellows, purposely arranged that their rooms should be in undergraduate "dormitories" There was also a senior member of the academic staff to act as guide and counsellor for each Fellow. Launcelot felt himself to be supremely lucky to have Professor R. S. Lull as his guide. Lull was a charming elderly man whose deafness had prevented him from entering the United States Navy as a boy. He had become a distinguished scientist whose Yale lectures on Evolution, reflecting his own deep Christian conviction, were extremely popular despite an old-world style of delivery. Launcelot was also much indebted to Lull for recommending him to bank with the Second New Haven National Bank, one of the smaller banks in New Haven not to go smash in the Wall Street collapse of October 1929.

Commonwealth Fund Fellows also had the privilege of membership of the Elizabethan Club, which met in a charming building originally designed to house a collection of rare books. As Launcelot wrote to his parents, the Club had been founded for "those people who would appreciate the books. It is a club of people who are by way of being Highbrows of Art (and very delightful people despite that qualification!) . . . Tea is served every day at 5.0 p.m. and each member has a Churchwarden pipe – of the Raleigh design". It may be hoped that Launcelot remained fairly silent over his pipe when the talk turned to painting, for at that time he claimed little knowledge about pictures as is clear from a letter to his mother. "I loved hearing about all the things you saw in Rome – although I did not know the names of all the artists whom you mentioned. However, Verocchio and Boticelli conveyed something to me and so did some of the others".

Launcelot had originally applied to go to Harvard but, as it turned out, Yale suited him better. At that time it had the better school of geology and the Peabody Museum of Palaeontology, which had

recently been built, was outstanding. His original intention was to
study petrology under Professor Adolf Knopf, but a lecture given by
a young and dynamic professor of geomorphology, Richard Foster
Flint, turned his interest to glacial geomorphology, and he decided
to make the geology of Long Island the subject of his research. "I am
studying the geology of the coastal regions east of here", he told his
parents, "where there are at least three granite intrusions – some of
them showing peculiar features and they have a somewhat complex
relation to the rocks into which they were intruded. The problem is
difficult and the region delightful country – both good points."

He bought an elderly Model A Ford car and often took Jim
Puxley with him on his expeditions. They became very close friends
and Puxley recalls those days together. 'Launcelot was always an
earnest scholar; I had quite avowedly applied for a Commonwealth
Fund Fellowship because I wanted to get to know Americans and
their ways and it was only in my second and third years at Yale that
I buckled down seriously to my research work. Launce, on the other
hand, really worked hard from the word Go. He used to drive out
along Long Island Sound with his geological hammer and would
frequently take me with him. I would lie on the shore and read or
write while he went exploring with his hammer.'

Apart from his geologising, Launcelot delighted in the
surrounding countryside and the small New England towns. The
colonial style houses, with white clapboard facing and green
shutters, and the white painted churches with their delicate spires
on the Central Green, gave him great pleasure. He was amused by
the Green at New Haven itself where the only buildings were 'three
churches, one of them modelled on St. Martin-in-the Fields, which
stand in a line separated from one another by a hundred yards or
more. These are churches of three different Protestant
denominations, and legend has it that each vies with the others to
possess the highest spire – a contest whose latest phase was extended
to include weathercocks.'

Launcelot's remarkable gift for getting on quickly with everyone
he meets, especially with young men, was shown at Yale by his

election to membership of a Junior Fraternity – the Beta Theta Pi. It had been contrary to custom for Fraternity Houses to admit graduate members on the grounds that a man who was worth anything would have been already admitted as an undergraduate. This had naturally been impossible for Launcelot, who was delighted when John Haas, living in the adjoining set of rooms, thought that it would be 'cute' to have an Englishman as a member of Beta Theta Pi. "It will be the very best way to get to know some of the undergraduates," he wrote, though "it adds somewhat to the cost of living but is well worth it." Typically he was distressed at the thought of enjoying this rare privilege alone and he persuaded his Fraternity colleagues to break their rules for a second time and elect Jim Puxley. "Launcelot was always immediately popular," Puxley wrote years later. "While the rest of us 'expatriates' were crying the blues because we weren't getting to know anybody, Launcelot somehow managed to pick up friends . . . He never grudged my muscling in on his preserves; it wouldn't have been in his nature to do so. He just liked me to have as many friends as he. There were times when I *felt* the role of second fiddle. Frequently when we went together to stay with some mutual friends, Launcelot, simply because he came from north of the Tweed (although his accent was identical with mine) would be shown straight into the prime guest room; while I, as a mere Englishman, would be left carrying in the bags! Such is the prestige of the name of Scotland!"

Almost in the first week of arriving at New Haven Launcelot had the good fortune to meet Jack and Meredyth Whiting, he an artist and she a poet. The Whitings made their house a second home for him and today four of Jack Whiting's paintings hang in Launcelot's home. There was only one Yale student, Charlie Janeway, to whom Launcelot had an introduction. A memorable winter vacation was spent at the Janeways' holiday home in the Adirondacks in New Hampshire. About five Yale men, including Jim Puxley, spent some days learning to ski. Launcelot had never been on skis before and he found his attempts frequently painful but exhilarating. 'I have always maintained that to be out of control on skis is about the most exciting experience for man.'

To get sufficient exercise in other ways during the winter was a problem. Graduates had no share in the athletic activities of the undergraduates. There were a few squash courts available and it was possible at times to row with the Senior Class crew; cross-country runs with Puxley were another way of keeping fit. Early in 1930 Harold Cooper, a Davison scholar from Sidney Sussex College, suggested that the Englishmen at Yale should form a rugger team and challenge the Englishmen at Harvard. Nothing much could be done until March as the ground was frozen hard, but Launcelot approached Dr. Grant Noble, then Episcopal Chaplain to the University, who recalls what happened. "Launcelot came to me one day and asked me if I would help him and a few Englishmen to start Rugby Football at Yale. Inasmuch as I was a freshman coach of the football squad, I said I would be happy to. I persuaded some of my football students to help. We got a team together [Cooper, Launcelot and Bullock were the only three Englishmen in the official Yale team] and played the first Rugby game in this country for fifty-five years. We played the Philadelphia Marines, who were just back from China and had learned the game there. It was written up in the *New York Times.*" Other games followed and at scrum half Launcelot got all the exercise he needed.

From his American friends it was inevitable that Launcelot should pick up certain American turns of speech which, to his mother's strongly expressed disapproval, kept slipping into his letters home. "I feel rightly admonished," he replied, "for having already started to use Yankee expressions. I hate them myself but it is extremely difficult in conversation not to use them. Already the word 'guess' has slipped into my vocabulary by the back door and I expect a few others. However, I really think I shall be able to avoid getting a strong accent (touch wood) for that is what I mind about most."

Commonwealth Fund Fellows were expected, in addition to their research, to see as much as possible of the American way of life and of the American scenery, and the Fund helped to defray the cost. So towards the end of his first term at Yale Launcelot, with Crowther,

Puxley and Goodier, set out in Goodier's car on a tour of the Southern States. The four met at Norfolk in Virginia, which Launcelot was to see again under very different circumstances some fifteen years later. They drove south to Charleston, a town which struck him as having 'a delightful atmosphere of newly-acquired shabbiness' and where they had a moonlight bathe. (Launcelot has always been ready to swim on the least provocation). They went as far south as Savannah, after which they began the journey back. At Sylvania they decided to inspect the local gaol, whose white inmates greeted them and assured them of a warm welcome if they cared to join them. The Appalachians fascinated Launcelot because of their geological formation and they were all struck by the marvellous scenery of the Blue Ridge. They reached Charlottesville on the twenty-third of December, after bumping down a road consisting of ruts and pot holes at the end of which they discovered a notice "Closed for Reconstruction".

Here Goodier had to leave them, while the other three spent Christmas at "Estrontreville", a plantation house belonging to the Randolph family. "Mr R is quite an English country squire type (perfectly charming) – Mrs R is more American and rather old for her age but very nice – and the two sons aged about 21 and 19, both of whom are very good fellows – the oldest is small, cheerful and very amusing, while the younger boy has much more charm but is a little bit spoiled by virtue of his good looks – and, last, the daughter who was dreadfully ugly and lacked humour, but was otherwise well meaning." Such was Launcelot's impression of his kind hosts.

The journey back to Yale was made by train, with a break of a week at Washington. Here Launcelot, Jim Puxley and another Englishman at Yale, Felix Greene, stayed with Coleman Jennings in his vast house in Massachusetts Avenue. Jennings was a remarkable man, who for a time had studied at Edinburgh University and had there got to know Launcelot's parents. He became a very successful business man but at an early age decided to devote himself and his wealth to good causes, one of which was the founding of a boys' club in Edinburgh, visited annually by him until his death in 1979. In the Jennings' home everything possible was done to make guests

comfortable, from the loan of one of the cars to the services of a
footman, who insisted on changing Launcelot's cuff links into a
clean shirt every morning. With insufficient shirts to last out the
visit, Launcelot used surreptitiously to change the links back to the
previous day's shirt. One evening Jennings took the young men to a
dinner which was being held in honour of a newly appointed Justice
of the Supreme Court. In the course of the dinner, to Launcelot's
surprise, a superb Sauterne was served although the Eighteenth
Amendment prohibiting the sale of "intoxicating liquors" and the
Volstead Act, which defined "intoxicating" as more than one half of
one per cent of alcohol, were still in force. Strictly speaking the law
had not been broken, for the wine had been purchased before the
Volstead Act came into force, but it seemed a strange way to honour
the newest interpreter of the American Constitution.

Launcelot's longest and most adventurous American tour took
place in the summer of 1930. Seven British, two Americans and a
Japanese naval officer, all studying at Yale, set out in four cars on a
journey of nearly 17,500 miles. Despite the generosity of the
Commonwealth Fund such as long tour made it necessary to watch
the cost carefully and to sleep, in the early weeks, in "tourist cabins"
or cheap hotels and later, whenever possible, in the open. Parents of
Yale friends also offered hospitality.

Driving south through Virginia and the Carolinas they made for
New Orleans before heading west into Texas to Houston and San
Antonio, where they faced Mexican food for the first time – 'either
quite tasteless or very hot'. Two more days of driving west brought
them to El Paso on the Mexican border. Here Leslie Lickfold,
unaware that it was an offence to photograph "soldiers, policemen
or poor people", was arrested and taken off to a cell on suspicion of
being a revolutionary. Luckily Felix Greene managed to persuade
the police that Lickfold was only an innocent, if somewhat
absent-minded, Limey, and he was released having only suffered the
confiscation of his film. They beat a hasty retreat from Mexico and
followed the valley of the Rio Grande to Santa Fé where they spent
six days on the ranch of a Yale friend. On the final two days
Launcelot got the chance of riding over the Sangre de Cristo

mountains up to a height of over 11,000 feet. Their route now took them north to Denver, near which another Yale friend lived close to Rocky Mountain Park. Leaving their cars, they rode to Lost Lake beside which they camped and next day walked up the Hallett Glacier. The indefatigable Launcelot with Geoffrey Crowther went on to climb one of the nearby summits.

From Denver they crossed the Rockies and then struck south-west to the Grand Canyon. The geology of the area fascinated Launcelot, as did the extraordinary colours of the bare rocks with their bands of red, yellow, white and black. Nevertheless he found the long ascent from the bottom of the canyon to the top of the cliffs more strenuous than he had expected. Leaving the Grand Canyon they drove across the Painted Desert to Los Angeles where they visited the Huntington Library and Mount Wilson Observatory. It was impossible not to spend a day at Hollywood. In his diary of the tour Launcelot described walking through acres of studio scenery representing "the Swiss Alps (ten feet high), French streets, Nôtre Dame, oriental bazaars ... and many other fakes. The artificiality of the scenery was typical also of the people involved. It was like being in a topsy turvey land with everything, including human values, distorted and changed."

They now drove northward to San Francisco, a city which particularly delighted Launcelot, though a visit to the Chinese Theatre where "the orchestra was the most trying part of the performance" might well have been avoided. They saw Yosemite Park before returning to the coast road running up through Portland to Seattle. Further north they saw the geysers in Yellowstone Park, and it was here that Launcelot "was woken up by two bears carrying on a noisy argument as to the rightful ownership of a bun". The final stage of the tour took them south to Salt Lake City and back again to Denver before starting on the long monotonous drive to Minneapolis and Chicago. At Detroit there was a chance to see the Ford works before moving up to Niagara Falls and back to New Haven.

It had all been a wonderful experience. Launcelot's diary of the tour shows how he revelled in the constant changes of scenery, the flowers, the strange and varied geological formations, but above all in the companionship. The large party had remained friends, partly thanks to the decision to avoid always having the same men in the same car. However, able men travelling for long distances in close contact with each other can become awkward at times, and even with changes of car Launcelot's skill in smoothing out minor personal conflicts was occasionally needed. He found the brilliant Geoffrey Crowther "the most remarkable character and perhaps the most difficult". As always with Launcelot he saw the good side of his friends more clearly than their shortcomings and he added to his diary the comment: "His attractiveness is directly proportional to the temperature and when it is cool he is delightful".

By the autumn of 1930, the start of Launcelot's second year at Yale, the decision about a career was becoming ever more pressing. It was no easy decision to take. George Chase's letter had urged him to consider Ordination very seriously. He knew how much this would please his mother, though she would not try to influence him. Probably he inherited from his paternal grandmother a touch of her Calvinistic outlook, for he feared that if he were to offer himself for Ordination it would be because the prospect of returning to Trinity Hall as Chaplain was too enticing. Throughout his life he has always had slight feelings of guilt if his material surroundings or his work seemed to be too comfortable. Moreover there was always the pull towards a scientific life. His researches were important and he had become a very able geologist. There was no danger of his scientific work undermining his Christian belief but he was as yet far from certain whether his life would be that of a priest or an academic.

Soon after arriving at Yale he had joined the Dwight Hall Association, a society connected with the Student Christian Movement. The members met fortnightly in an old mill house some ten miles out of New Haven, and after a camp supper discussed religious questions round a large log fire. More informal were the Monday evening parties in the home of Grant Noble and his wife. Here after supper the guests either played games or, more frequently, just talked and sooner or later the discussion usually turned to religion. After his trip to the Southern States in 1929 he went up to St. Paul's School at Concord for a conference on "The Ministry as a vocation". "The conference itself was really very helpful," he told his parents. "As you know, I find the question of a career the most difficult thing on earth to decide upon and these last few days have been a great help for basing the questions at issue on motives of service rather than selfish interest . . . Although I got no really new ideas out of the meeting it did at least act as a reinforcement and as an incentive to be really honest about the whole thing.

Looking back, James Puxley, who was with him at the conference, feels that it was clear to his friends that Launcelot would very probably be ordained even if he himself was far from realising it. Like Launcelot's Cambridge friends, Puxley had sensed the rare quality in him. "I frequently used to complain to fellow students at Yale that Launcelot was one of those unfair people who were totally good and totally nice because they simply had no desires to be anything else. He was just good through and through without effort, while the rest of us mortals had an awful time trying to be half-decent . . . There was, of course, nothing priggish about Launce; he was boisterous and full of life but seemed to be free of all temptation to sin!" It is unlikely that anybody as human as Launcelot had as easy a life as Puxley half-humourously suggests. At the same time Puxley felt that Launcelot's natural goodness had its slight disadvantage in his general development. "Possibly Launce lost out mildly by his very purity. I was not debauched but I did royster occasionally and thus got to know a side of university life from which he was self-excluded. There was not much of enduring value in it, and I don't suppose Launce has lacked anything during his life's ministry from not having experienced it. But he *just might* have learnt more of life if he had occasionally joined me at the vingt-et-un tables over a glass of applejack!"

On returning from his long summer tour Launcelot was again in touch with George Chase. Another very long letter which Chase wrote to Lancelot on the 24th of October must have helped greatly to resolve some of his doubts and makes clear the importance of Chase's influence on Launcelot:

"I am still convinced that you are fitted more than most men for a 'pastoral' job among undergraduates, and further that your rather specialised subject of Geology would go with it particularly well. I think a person who is doing pastoral work here is much happier and also more useful if he has academic interests as well . . . 'Pastoral' sounds very parsonic, but I don't necessarily mean by it directly religious visiting: to me it means getting to know the men in a natural and friendly way, letting the religious side come in when it does so naturally. I think one of the functions of a Dean or Chaplain is to act as a 'social mixer' and that does take time; but it should have a religious background. Now, at the risk of seeming to flatter, I will say exactly how I think you fill the bill. It seems to me that you have quite an exceptional power of getting men to meet together happily: witness the heterogeneous crowds that used to meet in your rooms. Further, your particular study could be arranged so as to give a good deal of time, and another strong point with you is your capacity of arranging your time. Behind it all is a genuinely religious background. I do think you fit the bill rather exceptionally well.

"Now, one of the subjects which I am inclined to preach about *ad nauseam*, under the influence of B. K. [Cunningham], is that our strong points are a direct guidance from God as to our line of service. The proper thing is to make the most of these rather than make a set upon our weaker points and try to force ourselves there. We cannot all do everything and we do best when we work along the lines where we feel God has given us special powers. I don't want to preach you a sermon! But I feel that at the back of your mind is the feeling that such a job would be too pleasant as being in line with your own preferences; I believe on the other hand that that is clear guidance that it is the sort of job God wants you to do. For it is not a selfish job but a real bit of service. I felt that strongly in your case when I wrote before and I have not changed my mind in the least bit since. I think it would be tragic if you turned it down because you thought it likely to be too pleasant."

The letter goes on to hold out the distinct possibility of Launcelot being elected a Fellow of Trinity Hall and becoming Chaplain. Chase mentions the difficulty of Launcelot not having any parochial experience following Ordination but he did not think that the Bishop would have serious objections. Finally he advised Launcelot to get in touch with Westcott House with a view to going there either in October 1931 or January 1932.

Launcelot still hankered after a few months more travel during which he hoped somewhat optimistically to see his future course more clearly. Nevertheless he took Chase's advice and was in touch with the Principal of Westcott House. On Christmas Eve 1930 Launcelot wrote home: "I had a very nice letter from 'B.K.' saying that he could take me in January 1932 at Westcott. He advised staying in one country such as India for two or three months rather than travelling. I myself have rather given up the idea of just travelling round the world and am trying to sort out all kinds of other alternatives. So I may come home in June after all." In the end this is what he decided to do. He left Yale with his research work recognised by the bestowal of the degree of Master of Science and he returned to England with the promise of a place at Westcott House a term earlier, in October. Inevitably his doubts to some extent remained for he made his acceptance of a place at Westcott clearly conditional on not being finally committed to Ordination

In 1881 Bishop Westcott had founded a Clergy Training School in Cambridge which in due course became Westcott House, one of the most distinguished and sought-after of the theological colleges. During the First World War the stream of Ordination candidates had inevitably dried up and the House had been closed for the duration of the war. In 1919 when the House was to be re-opened a new Principal was needed and the Council of Westcott House had no doubt that the right man was Canon B. K. Cunningham, at that time an Army Chaplain in France. Before the war he had been in charge of Farnham Hostel, a theological college with comparatively few students but informed by a distinctive spirit. It has been described as being "rather like a perpetual reading-party organised by some human and deeply-beloved college don". 'B.K.', as he was universally known, brought to Westcott the ideals and spirit of Farnham, and since so much of what Westcott stood for appealed to Launcelot it is important to understand B.K.'s attitude to Ordination and the work of a priest.

In his first Embertide letter from Westcott House B.K. explained his hopes for the college. "I am most eager that this place should help the men to be not indeed like one another, nor like those on the staff, but to be each his own best self as God intended. I am anxious, too, that men ordained from this place, to whatever school of thought they may belong, should be above all else *real* in character and belief and worship. It is, as those of us who have been chaplains know well, the strong and wholesome demand of this generation. I hope, moreover, that we shall be able to have here the minimum of discipline imposed from without together with the maximum suggested and worked out from within." Furthermore, B.K. had an intense dislike of any idea of the priest as a "professional", set apart from his fellow men. "Now that our friend has taken Holy Orders and we put 'Reverend' on the envelope and his name is written in the Book of Crockford, we must not be so irreverent to his holiness as to think of him as human . . . if we drop a meaningless oath we will apologise even to his cloth." He loved quoting Oliver Quick's remark that "many people forget that Our Lord may be, in certain ways, much less religious than the curate of the parish."

Holding such views, B.K. was equally anxious that men trained under him at Westcott House should be free from all taint of clericalism, whether Catholic or Evangelical. To him the glory of the Church of England lay in its comprehensiveness, in its ability to hold together men of the most divergent views. Thus he took great care in the selection of the members of Westcott House, making sure that those admitted represented very different brands of churchmanship. B.K. himself was a High Churchman by inclination, though as a good Scot he had Presbyterian ancestors. He and Launcelot took naturally to one another and had a good deal in common. Both loved the Scottish hills, both enjoyed shooting, and B.K. was also a great fisherman. Above all both had a charisma when dealing with young men, though both were more readily at ease with men who came from the same social background as themselves. What B.K. stood for suited Launcelot perfectly and influenced him throughout his own ministry.

Like many other men coming to Westcott Launcelot had made no study of theology. Partly because of this, but probably more because he knew what lay ahead for Launcelot, B.K. advised him to stay at Westcott for two years rather than for the usual one year. He particularly enjoyed his studies in theology and attended the lectures on great scholars like Burkitt and Hoskyns. The latter, like so many speakers, had a word – in his case 'Theme' – which occurred with considerable frequency. At Hoskyns' final lecture there was a sweepstake on the number of times he would refer to 'the Theme' as opposed to references to 'the Ultimate Theme'. The 'Ultimates' won by ten to six. On a rather different level lectures in elocution were given by the father of Jack Hulbert the actor.

At the time that Launcelot was at Westcott the influence of Buchman and his Moral Rearmanent gospel was rife in Cambridge and for a while was a divisive influence among Ordinands. Some threw up all question of Ordination and went to work for the movement, others were repelled by Buchman's teaching. B.K. quite deliberately sat on the fence but his attitude was clear when Buchman visited Westcott. Sheltering behind his serious deafness B.K. remarked to the Sheriff, at that time Kenneth Carey, 'Ken, would you take Moral Uplift to your rooms. I shall be busy'. Launcelot remained largely uninfluenced by the emotional impact of the message. Probably his scientific training helped him to evaluate the worth of Buchman more accurately than could some of his friends.

It was natural that men contemplating Ordination should have doubts about their vocation. At that time there were no Selection Conferences to help. Launcelot's problems came not in the field of belief but in making the choice between two vocations. Despite George Chase's latest letter there must have been many voices telling him that with his Cambridge and Yale qualifications he would have been wrong to turn away from Geology and the life of a scientist. Although Chase had shown how the scientific and the religious life might be combined Launcelot knew that if he were to be ordained science must increasingly take second place. The decision was not made easier by Launcelot's close links with Trinity Hall while a member of Westcott. He fully shared what B.K. called the 'Common Life' of the House but he was also slightly detached from it. He began to coach the Hall boats and he had dining rights in the College. Not until the start of his second year at Westcott was the conflict finally resolved. The pursuit of might-have-beens is always fascinating but seldom very rewarding. Had Launcelot decided that his vocation was to be a scientist he would have done well but, in the opinion of scientific friends of university stature, it is unlikely that he would have been elected to the top university posts. For basically Launcelot is not a single-minded academic. He has integrity of mind carried to a high degree but he is not exactly an "intellectual". However in the life to which he was at last whole-heartedly committed is scientific knowledge and training were to prove invaluable. No theological proposition could be acceptable to him if he felt that it were in conflict with scientific truth.

So on Trinity Sunday, the 9th of June 1933, Launcelot was ordained Deacon by Bishop White-Thompson, the Bishop of Ely, in Ely Cathedral. Five days earlier he had been elected Fellow and Chaplain of Trinity Hall.

EXPLORATION IN THE ARCTIC

1932 – 1933

Early in May 1932 Sir Vivian Fuchs stopped Launcelot in Sidney Street and told him about an expedition to Iceland which was planned for the following month. The aim was to cross Vatnajökull, the largest ice-cap in Europe, and a geologist was needed to join the party. At that moment Launcelot was at Westcott House but its members did not usually keep the Long Vac term. He went at once to seek B.K.'s approval and was delighted when his Principal wholeheartedly supported the idea. Part of Cunningham's genius in training young Ordinands was his insistence that they must never become professionally cut off from the laity whom in due course they would serve. So with great excitement Launcelot found himself welcomed by the five other Cambridge men who had already been selected for the expedition. The party were due to leave Hull at 8 a.m. on the 22nd of June. As with so many of his journeys Launcelot cut the time he needed to rush to Hull to the minimum and drove through the night from Innerhadden.

The leader of the expedition, Brian Roberts of Emmanuel College, an ornithologist, had decided that the cheapest way of reaching Iceland was to travel by trawler. As they boarded the *Lord Balfour of Burleigh* it became clear that she had not been designed for passenger comfort. All six members of the expedition had to share his cabin with the skipper. The smell on board was nauseating and came from the barrel, still lined with the remnants of fish livers from the previous catch, which was tied on the outside of the smoke stack for the fire in the captain's cabin. Added to this was the smell of diesel oil for the engines and the curious smell of coal dust. The combination of smells was enough to turn anyone's stomach on the calmest voyage. As it was, the voyage was extremely rough and the motion of the ship became really bad as they steamed through the Pentland Firth. Seasickness quickly took its toll.

At lunch on the first day out a sweepstake was arranged upon the order in which the members of the expedition would succumb. Every diabolical effort was made to upset the man whose name one had drawn. On reaching the Pentland Firth Launcelot was triumphant when his 'horse', Vaughan Lewis the seismologist, bolted from the room as the first victim. His triumph was shortlived as he only survived for another half hour himself. He recalls two youths, wearing immaculate suits, whom the skipper incongruously described as 'pleasurers' and who were, if possible, even more seasick than the Cambridge men.

The party disembarked at Hornafjordur and travelled on ponies along the south coast of Iceland as far as Stadadalur. In the course of the journey several rivers had to be crossed and, as Launcelot later pointed out, it was important to have a pony which swam high. Most ponies swam at a level at which the water flowed directly into the thigh-high Wellington boots which were essential to wear. As each river was crossed a stop was necessary to empty boots. The ponies were also needed to transport men and gear up on to the ice-cap, which involved a climb of some 3,300 feet up a precipitous route.

On reaching the ice-cap the Icelandic guide took the ponies back, as it had been decided that sledges and not ponies had to be used. With no grass in central Iceland, and even if some fodder were added to already heavy loads, it would have been impossible to remain on the ice-cap for any worthwhile length of time. So the plan was to haul two three-man ridge tents, equipment and provisions for a month to six weeks on two eleven foot Norwegian sledges. Launcelot, who because of ten days skiing in America was regarded as the expert at this method of travel, has nevertheless a vivid memory of what skiing is like when you are also hauling sledges. 'Manhauling is very hard work and is apt to make one mule-minded, with a sullen suspicion that you are the only member of the team who is doing any work – until you discover that the others have exactly the same idea.'

Vatnajökull covers an area of some 3,400 square miles; it is ninety miles from east to west and sixty-five miles from north to south, approximately the size of Yorkshire. Even for an expedition lasting rather less than two months physical strength, powers of endurance and an ability to get on well with the rest of the team are essential qualities. The food ration for each man was 26 ounces per day. This was made up of 6 ounces of biscuits, 8 ounces of Bovril pemmican, 4 ounces of butter, 4 ounces of chocolate, 4 ounces of sugar and two drinks a day of cocoa. Malted milk tablets were available on special occasions. This diet ensured sufficient nutriment but did not satisfy the desire for a good meal. Launcelot bore witness to this in many a later lecture. 'Pemmican is advertised on the tin as "a meat extract rich in albumen, meat fibre and animal fat", which is exactly what it tastes like. You take it like soup and it is more palatable with pea flour added. A plateful in the evening after pitching camp gives you the impression you've had a five course dinner. The great thing is to go to sleep before you discover you haven't, because the sledge rations are deficient in roughage and though one gets plenty of energy vitamins – chiefly consumed as liquids – the result is that one's inside is astonishingly empty.'

Bad luck seriously affected the expedition's plans. One of the most important pieces of work to be carried out was the sounding of the thickness of the ice-cap but this had to be abandoned when the seismograph broke down. The weather at the start made progress difficult and at times impossible. It took fifteen days to cover the thirty-seven miles to Kverkfjöll, and for four and a half of those days a blizzard forced the men to remain in their sleeping bags. It is a great test of patience to lie for several days looking at the name of the tent maker stamped on the canvas above one's head and wondering if the rain will drip through. Perhaps it was to encourage the virtue of patience in adversity that Launcelot chose to regale his two tent companions with readings from the book of Job. Even when they were able to leave their tents progress was slow, for on the north side of the ice cap extensive thaw streams caused the sledges to sink deeply into pools of slush. Torrential rain had made the surface of the ice very difficult to cross and the great problem was to find something other than water on which to pitch the tents. Wet from above and below was the enemy, not the cold.

On the 14th of July the base camp was pitched on the marginal moraine close to the eastern scarp of Kverkfjöll overlooking a small ice-dammed lake. The surrounding prospect was bleak, a waste land of black sand and scoriaceous lavas. However, fifteen successful days were devoted to mapping the area, which proved to be very different from that shown on existing maps. Launcelot was mainly concerned with a geological survey of the district. On one day he went off to survey the area which the party had named the Gates of Hell. That Launcelot was happily at work was clear to two other members of the expedition who heard the sound of "The Bonnie Banks of Loch Lomond" coming across the desert. In camp bridge was often played. One contest was fought out between the "Patriarchs", represented by Launcelot and Anderson, and "Youth", represented by Angus Bennett and Vaughan Lewis. Bennett in his official account of the expedition describes the competition. "The stakes, to be paid on our return to civilisation, consisted of a bottle of Malt Extract (Icelandic beer) per thousand points. After three rubbers the 'Patriarchs', by producing an ace from the pemmican, finished the morning one fiftieth of a bottle to the good." Launcelot must on occasions have strained the goodwill of his companions. Having filmed a scree descent by Bennett and Anderson he saw nothing wrong in asking them to climb up to the top again and to scree down once more just in case his first shot had been a failure.

The return journey was slowed up by five days of continuous rain and snow. The surface of the ice had been so cut up that it became necessary for the gear to be carried on each man's back until the higher ice was reached. Fortunately perfect sledging conditions followed but by then food was running short and the original plan of reaching the edge of the ice-cap some sixty miles further west had to be abandoned. Instead it was decided to return to the starting point by the shortest possible route. Three days later they reached the edge of the ice-cap where an incredible thing happened. To their astonishment they were met by the guide who had brought them up

five weeks before. He had a local reputation of being psychic and he
claimed that he had dreamed that the party were returning to their
original camp rather than to the point agreed and that they would be
there a week early. So far as could be ascertained he could in no way
have known about the movements of the expedition. Whatever the
explanation the reunion was hilarious. The descent on firm ice
meant that the sledges moved so quickly that they could only be
slowed by the prostrate bodies of the expedition entangled in their
skis and their harness. The men could only shake the guide's hand
with difficulty, being unable to get up.

It had been hoped to return to England by trawler from one of the
fishing stations on the east coast, but the fish had moved further
north and the trawlers had followed them. A small and leaky motor
boat was chartered to take the party two hundred miles along the
coast to the Westermann Islands. It was a terrifying voyage. A
serious storm blew up and it soon became clear that the skipper, the
worse for drink, was completely lost and the boat was dangerously
near the lee shore. After a night of vicious wind, by good luck the
Westermann Islands were sighted and a landing made. A horribly
seasick Launcelot bravely offered to give a talk to the local
inhabitants about the expedition. A steamer bound for England
from Reykjavik picked up the party, and on the 22nd of August they
were once more in Hull.

A year later, one week after being ordained Deacon, Launcelot
was off again. Once more he was fortified by B.K.'s approval of
this way of filling the four months before starting work as Chaplain
of Trinity Hall. His appetite for polar exploration had been whetted
in Iceland and now he was invited to join a much larger expedition
of eighteen men, organised by the Oxford University Exploration
Club which had been founded in 1927. At this time university
expeditions were playing an important part in accumulating
detailed information about the Arctic. They tended to be informal
affairs, with the leader believing that rigid discipline should be
unnecessary when he could rely on every man making his full
contribution. Thus the choice of personnel was all important and

members of an expedition were selected equally for their scientific qualifications and for their ability to work together as a team.

The purpose of the 1933 expedition was to explore the virtually unknown New Friesland ice-cap in the far north of Spitzbergen. The leader was A. R. (now Sir Alexander) Glen, who had just completed his undergraduate years at Oxford. He had done most of the planning for the three months expedition with no thought of leading it. At the last moment the leader designate, James Martin, who had contracted severe frostbite in the Canadian Arctic, was told that he would not recover in time to join the expedition. Glen took over, proving as successful a leader as he had been an organiser.

Launcelot was to be the chief scientist and leader of one of the two sledge parties. The task of his team was to cross the ice-cap, to survey as much of the area as possible and ultimately to return across the glaciers to the main base at Petunia Bay in the Ice Fjord. It proved to be an extremely arduous assignment, physically more demanding than the much longer journeys which he was later to undertake in the Antarctic with dog teams. As one of his sledge team testified, Launcelot had all the necessary qualifications for this expedition. He was an excellent geologist, 'incredibly tough', yet very sensitive to the importance of personal relationships. Glen was always surprised that such a slightly built man should have such remarkable stamina and powers of endurance.

On reaching Bergen the party sailed in a mail boat up the coast as far north as Tromso, where they and all their gear were transferred to the M.S. *Isbjorn*, a Norwegian sealing boat specially constructed to withstand pack ice but with consequent lack of stability. Seasickness kept most of the men below until anchoring on the 6th of July at the head of Ice Fjord, opposite a hut built by the Scottish Spitzbergen Syndicate and let as the expedition's base. Eight members of the expedition were to work in and around the base whilst the other ten were to be taken round to the north coast, there to form three parties: three men would go by boat down Widje Bay and then overland to the base; Launcelot in charge of "A" party with three companions, and "B" party with three men, would travel by different routes over a mountainous region known as Garwood

Land, surveying and geologising in this largely unknown territory, to the base.

After being landed at Treurenberg Bay it quickly became apparent to the two sledge parties that with nine weeks' food supply and heavy gear they had a much greater load than they could possibly manhaul by sledge. It was decided that before serious scientific work began Launcelot, together with Binny, leader of the "B" sledge team, and Carrington Smith, should leave at once on a sledge journey south so as to make a depot of part of the food near the southern end of New Friesland, somewhere above the Lomme Bay Glacier. The remaining four men would take the rest of the gear as far up the Duner Glacier as possible and do any scientific work they could fit into the time.

On the 13th of July, with a load of about 1000 pounds distributed between two Nansen sledges lashed together one behind the other, some 17 feet long in all, Launcelot and his two companions set out. It proved to be a gruelling task. The warmth of the sun made the surface difficult for hauling and the exhausting haul on to the Duner Glacier at first reduced progress to one hundred yards after an hour's struggle. Soon it became easier to travel by night, hoping that lower temperatures would make the surface harder. "The first two hours sledging went quickly enough", wrote Launcelot, "but at the end of each day, when the heavy loads began to tell, the last half of each hour (before the agreed ten minutes rest) dragged out into an eternity of effort. We generally sledged from six to eight hours a day, covering a distance which varied between three and fourteen miles according to the surface and gradient."

Conditions gradually improved but once after a nine hour day of sledging the men almost fell asleep over their supper. In fact Launcelot did briefly doze off while smoking, only to be rudely awakened by feeling his shirt burning. At moments it seemed as if they would never reach the head of the Duner Glacier and that New Friesland must be "all uphill". At length their efforts were rewarded with the magnificent sight of the Stubendorff and Chydemus mountains standing out clearly against the greenish-blue sky. Nevertheless four more days of arduous work separated them from

Mount Poincaré where they had decided to make their depot.

Inevitably the diet on this journey was monotonous. It "consisted of two courses – pemmican and porridge, or, if we wished to vary the menu, porridge and pemmican. We ate our ration of sugar and margarine with the porridge. A spoonful of dried yeast added flavour and the necessary vitamins to the pemmican. We were well satisfied with this diet, though we always felt the need of something to chew." One evening a hazardous attempt to remedy this deficiency by making scones was disastrous. "A mixture of Plasmon powder, oatmeal, sugar and margarine resulted in a peculiar brown object, at least double the weight of the largest scone we had ever seen." Twelve hours of acute indigestion followed and no progress was possible the next day. Lack of lemon juice and the physical strain of each day's work led to feelings of lethargy, and at night in their sleeping bags the three men recalled the Spitzbergen legend of the Old Hag and the eleven virgin sisters, some of whom spent their days in spreading scurvy through the island.

However by the 22nd of July the depot of food had been established, and with a much lighter load Launcelot, Binny and Smith retraced their steps. At first the weather was good but two days of thick fog, blinding snow and impossibly soft surfaces delayed them it was not until the 29th of July, nineteen days after leaving the *Isbjorn*, that they rejoined their other sledge companions some eight miles up the Duner Glacier. Not only had these men relayed some 2500 lbs of food and equipment to this camp but they had successfully carried out valuable scientific work.

Next day Launcelot and his three companions were at last able to start out on their main journey. Since their work was to be concerned mainly with geologising and surveying, J. M. Edwards, a research geologist from Oxford, and Carrington Smith of the Royal Engineers, an Ordnance Survey expert, were two of his team. The other member was A. S. Irvine, a famous Oxford oar, whose brother had died on Everest with Mallory in 1924 and "whose capacity for hard work", in Glen's opinion, "was to be rivalled only by his repertoire of stories".

They remained in the Duner Glacier for three days and then

moved up the ice-sheet where they were completely shut in by fog for the first few days of August. Even geologising was impossible; a search for rock proved vain and there was a great danger of tracks back to camp being concealed by drifting snow. The fog lifted on the 5th of August and Smith and Irvine were able to set out for Hecla Hook with all their heavy surveying equipment. After a long day geologising, Launcelot and Edmonds scarcely noticed that a storm was blowing up. They were seven miles from camp and were soon engaged in an involuntary game of "Where the Woozle Wasn't", trying to retrace their outward tracks which had often been obliterated. It took five hours before they stumbled on their tent. They could do nothing but label rock specimens, mend ski skins, read, eat and sleep. Fortunately they had plenty to read including Doughty's *Arabia Deserta*, "which Edmonds had brought as a psychological antidote to the cold". They were worried about what might have happened to Irvine and Smith but could do nothing to help them.

Early on the 8th of August a yodel announced their safe return, and that night the reunion and Launcelot's twenty-seventh birthday of the previous day were celebrated with a special menu which read:

Ivory guils à la Valhall (beurre and pemmican)
Porridge, butter and raisins (Valhall pudding)
Biscuits and syrup
Crystallised fruit
Tea

They found that "a little Worcester sauce goes excellently with the pemmican".

Not until the 10th of August could they strike camp, and before they could move on it took them seven hours to disinter boxes, sledges and tent from under the drifts of snow which had almost completely buried them. For the next fortnight they journeyed south on the high ice, carrying out their scientific work when possible but too often forced to remain in the tent playing bridge. Because of the persistently bad weather they decided to do their surveying and geologising on the fine days and to sledge on bad days,

often in fog and sometimes in a blizzard. Bad visibility made it
difficult to keep to a compass bearing and it was necessary to keep
their route by noticing the angle at which the snow was driving
across their skis or the wind struck the cheek and nose. As their
rations would be exhausted by the 21st of August it was essential to
reach the food dump by then. Three days of dense fog made it
impossible to find the cairn. Fortunately at the critical moment
when rations had run uncomfortably low the fog lifted and the
supplies were found. Throughout the journey they had made sure of
having sufficient lemon juice to keep the Scurvy Sisters at bay, but
cod liver oil became increasingly nauseating. "For six weeks we had
one teaspoonful of this per day until on the Lomme Bay Glacier we
felt that we could bear with it no longer." The tin, along with other
unnecessary and heavy boxes, was left in the middle of the glacier to
make its infinitely slow but stately way to the sea.

Ahead of them now lay sixty miles of sledging along glaciers and
through the mountainous Garwood Land. Launcelot piously
christened one glacier 'Trinity Hall' but later fell into a crevasse
where luckily his sledge held him up. The surfaces soon deteriorated
seriously and the sledges stuck in the snow; there was no alternative
but to carry all the equipment on their backs. Even so when goggles
became clogged with snow progress was impossible. If they were not
again to run dangerously short of food it was essential to try to keep
to the timetable and Launcelot daily exhorted his companions to
make a punctual start, though not always the first himself to be
ready to move. The most anxious moment came when they feared
that they were on a track which seemed to be becoming impassable
and must retrace their steps a long way. However, with luck and
skill they found "carriage-racks" of smooth ice which greatly eased
their journey. At last on the 10th of September they reached the
base in safety where "roast pheasant . . . letters from England, the
weekly *Times* and dance music from Daventry" awaited them. It
had been a fine achievement.

Sixteen years later Glen read the news of Launcelot's
appointment to the bishopric of Portsmouth, and wrote to him.
"Everyone who has had the privilege of knowing you, Launcelot,

has had no doubt that you were cast for important duties. This I remember feeling so clearly as your party was coming down Ebba valley after crossing the ice-cap. One of these odd striking moments one never forgets."

THE BRITISH GRAHAM LAND EXPEDITION

1934 – 1937

Launcelot was back in Cambridge shortly before term began, eager to begin his work as Chaplain of Trinity Hall and with no thoughts of further polar adventures. Early in the following year John Rymill, who had been with Gino Watkins in Greenland, called on him with an exciting proposal. Rymill planned to undertake the expedition, which Watkins had hoped to lead before his tragic death, to that part of the South Polar region which lies to the south of South America, officially known as the Falkland Islands Dependency. At that time it was the largest stretch of unknown country in the world, with an unexplored coastline some two thousand miles long. Rymill explained that the expedition would concentrate on Graham Land and he invited Launcelot to join it as geologist and Chaplain. He planned a two winters' stay in the Antarctic in a region in which many ships had been lost when trying to reach it.

Launcelot's immediate reaction was that he must refuse. He had been wonderfully fortunate in being chosen for the job which above all others he had wanted after leaving Westcott House and he had barely served his college as Chaplain for half a year. To ask now for about a three year leave of absence seemed out of the question. Nevertheless he agreed to discuss Rymill's offer with his colleagues. He consulted the Master, George Chase, the Dean, and several others including, as ever, B.K.. All gave him the same answer: it would be right to accept. After much heart-searching he agreed to join the expedition, making clear that he regarded his work as Chaplain as being as important as his work as a geologist.

The British Graham Land Expedition of 1934-37 was the first

major expedition to leave Britain since Scott's last journey in 1911. In the story of Antarctic exploration it lies midway between the heroic age of Scott and Shackleton and modern highly scientific surveys equipped with every possible aid. Despite generous financial support from the Colonial Office, the Royal Geographical Society and a number of private donors, the money raised was limited and this compelled rigid economy. No member of the expedition received a salary. Two naval offices, Lieutenant R. E. D. Ryder and Lieutenant E. H. M. Millett, who acted as Captain and Chief Engineer on the voyage, had been seconded by the Admiralty, as was Surgeon Lieutenant-Commander Bingham, whose medical skills were supplemented by invaluable experience in handling huskies. Two soldiers, Lieutenants I. F. Meiklejohn, the wireless operator, and L. C. D. Ryder the Second Mate, a brother of the Captain, had been released from other duties by the Army Council. Rymill's ten other members had all obtained leave of absence to continue their various scientific researches in meteorology, surveying, ornithology, biology and, in Launcelot's case, geology and glaciology.

The chief means of travel in Antarctica was to be by dog sledge. Mechanised travel was to be limited to a small three-seater de Haviland Fox Moth, which would be used for aerial survey and reconnaissance, a 19-foot motor boat and a small tractor. The combination of dog sledging and air survey was to prove very successful. Limited funds dictated the method of reaching Graham Land.

Rymill had found and bought a three-masted topsail schooner with auxiliary engines, 112 foot overall and 24 foot beam. She had been built in Brittany in 1908 to serve as part of the Breton fishing fleet on the Grand Banks. She later became a training ship for Breton girls and when Rymill bought her she had been fitted out in England to be an American's private yacht. Rymill had her sheathed with greenheart and her forefoot was strengthened with oak and iron to withstand the pressure of the Antarctic ice. He rechristened her *Penola*, the name of his home in Australia. Before any exploration or scientific work could be carried out it was to be the task of fourteen totally inexperienced but willing members of the expedition, under the command of the two professional seamen, to sail *Penola* from Tilbury to Graham Land.

Two winters in the Antarctic meant being away from home and friends for the greater part of three years. Launcelot preferred to part from his family at Innerhadden and not to bring them south to see the ship sail. As he wrote a year later: "I hope you feel as I do that the last au revoir to me was like seeing me off to school – always rather a beastly wrench; but the term however long it seems at the time comes to an end and there are always the holidays to look forward to!" It mattered greatly to him that both his father and mother supported him in his decision to join the expedition. In an undated letter written a month or two before sailing he expressed his gratitude. "One of the most precious blessings which God has given me, and is giving me, is your love and understanding." To his mother he had submitted the special prayers which he had composed for use by the expedition and for those left at home.

On the 10th of August *Penola* was due to leave Southampton for Tilbury. Three days later Launcelot wrote home: "I'm feeling fed up with everything connected with the sea and ships. *Penola* was launched today and evidently she had something wrong with her, so she's had to go back on the stocks." It was frustrating and the delay revived his worries about leaving Cambridge, "though the College are quite clear that I did the only right thing." However there was now time for a final medical check-up, which removed any serious fears that his "defective heat-controlled mechanism" might cause him trouble when experiencing extremes of temperature. There was also time for a brief farewell party at the Criterion restaurant in London which his eldest brother and brother-in-law helped to organise. Minor matters like arranging for life insurance coverage during a period of possible danger had barely occurred to him and were left to Cambridge friends to sort out. Soon *Penola* was ready to sail round to St. Katharine's Dock at Tower Bridge, though her final departure was again delayed until some parts needed for her engines arrived from the German manufacturers.

Now began the immense task of loading the ship, and no time was left for worries or vain regrets. Stevedores helped the members of the expedition, and friends, like Alexander Glen, came down in the evening after a day's work in London to assist. Food to last for three years had to be stored. Hundreds of cases of flour, sacks of sugar, tins of bully beef, boxes of sledge rations and crates of wines and spirits had all to be taken on board and stowed away. Rymill had consulted the eminent French explorer, Dr. Charcot, who had once sailed in the *Pourquoi Pas* to Graham Land, about supplies. Charcot had commented: 'Of course it is all right for you English because you need no wine!' *Penola's* store of wine had to be somewhat restricted from lack of space, but room was found for enough sherry and port to provide about one bottle a week each of one or the other in the ship and at the base hut. Some extra wine and spirits were taken for special celebrations such as Christmas, midwinter and birthdays. Four thousand gallons of diesel oil, sacks of coal and coke and the tractor, which Robert Fleming had presented, together with the cumbersome clutter of scientific equipment had all to be found a place. In addition, livestock in the form of two pigs and eight fowl, whose expectation of life was short, were embarked, as were two huskies from a recent Greenland expedition which had spent the last two years in the London Zoo. As the amateur crew were soon to discover, it was only possible to reach some of the belaying pins by diving head first between oil drums or coal sacks and the bulwarks. The response to an order to pull on a rope was an obstacle race, especially hazardous at night.

Fortunately an advance party consisting of W. E. Hampton, the Vice-Leader who was also the aviator, and Bingham the doctor, had taken the plane, its oil and the huskies, in the whaling research vessel R.R.S. *Discovery II,* which was maintained by the Colonial Office. She went ahead of *Penola* to the Falkland Islands and then on to Port Lockroy, an anchorage on the west coast of Graham Land formerly used by whalers.

On the 10th of September *Penola* began her long voyage. Launcelot's uncle and godfather, Prebendary William Holland, was among the party of relatives and friends at the dock, and he sent his sister Eleanor an account of the ship's departure. "I ran about sending off wires for him [Launcelot] and then turned up at 2.00 for the blessing of the ship by the Bishop of Gibraltar; Launcelot being robed behind him. They both stood on the top of the companion, the Bishop in cope and assuming his mitre for the actual benediction. He spoke a few very homely and unemotional words and followed with a *beautiful* prayer of commendation of the ship and all who sailed in it . . . Launcelot had his robes on over his *very* dirty blue shirt and torn flannel bags . . . The *Penola* moved out of dock on her own steam: no tugs at all: excellently done. On board were two pigs running about and 2 huskies from the Zoo tied up . . . There was very little time to talk to Launcelot. All of them were hard at it, loading up the last things to come on board . . . Three of them were sawing up an ox into chunks to be put into a zinc tub with ice: not scientific dismembering! . . . All on board were very cheery and busy and practical. Launcelot all smiles. [Many relatives remained on board until 7.00 p.m. when they disembarked at Gravesend]. Then we watched the tiny *Penola* slowly out of sight . . . Canon Marshall, ex-naval commander, was most explicit that he would rather have a crew of educated men, whose heart was in it, even if amateurs, than ordinary sailors. He says one week will teach them everything."

For a young naval lieutenant of twenty-six the responsibility carried by Ryder as *Penola's* Captain was heavy. "At sea I was inescapably responsible for the safety of the ship and the lives on board. *Penola* was a very unhandy vessel and this together with an amateur crew required an added vigilance. Among all these undisciplined members from the university I endeavoured to maintain what was essential in that respect." The next few weeks were to provide a very tough schooling for them all.

Launcelot's own words best describe the early stages of the voyage. It was a 'grim first week'. Acute seasickness, tiring hours on duty and total ignorance of sailing left most of the party very exhausted. "We were on watch from 8.00 p.m. till midnight . . . and slept soundly and very comfortably till 4.00 a.m. when we were turned out. To be disturbed from an all too brief sleep whilst it is still dark is most trying . . . on watch again at noon." Two days later:

"I have always wondered how on earth people fill in their time at sea even if they are in a sailing ship. I shall wonder no longer." The Bay of Biscay lived up to its reputation but the crew had to carry on somehow. Norman Gurney, the youngest and least experienced member, was sick every day from leaving England until the ship reached Montevideo.

The strain must also have been considerable for the two officers who were responsible for implanting the elements of seamanship into the heads and hands of their men. During the storm in the Bay of Biscay it was necessary to shorten sail with all hands on deck. "I was given a rope by the second mate. When he said 'Let go' I paid out the rope round the belaying pin. He got a bit agitated and shouted, 'Let go, let go'. So I took the rope off the pin and let it go. Up shot the rope into the inky skies above and down came the top yard on the cross trees with an almighty crash. It then transpired that one of my shipmates was somewhere aloft in the vicinity of that yard. I never ventured to ask whether he was on the yard, dodging underneath it, or doing the fireman's greasy pole trick down the mast. All I do know is that when he got back on deck he said a lot of things which were not at all proper for a parson to hear."

Martin, the First Mate, was professionally a hard task master, who held "the theory, which he has been trying to put into practice, that fear is the dominant motive in making people work. He has always dealt with people of less intelligence than himself and he has been trying to treat us (at least afloat) in the way he treated them." He also believed that "seasickness was caused by the imagination and so always sent Gurney aloft when he was looking ill. We resented this as much as he did. It wasn't the more obvious dangers of his position relative to our own but the fact that he invariably shed a marlin spike or a knife as a sign that all was not well."

However they gradually learned their tasks. In spite of leaking ventilators during bad weather, *Penola* proved a sound though very slow ship. The engines had to be used more than the Captain wished, but even so an unplanned call at Madeira to order wireless parts together with the effect of weak trade winds made the voyage to Montevideo take sixty-eight days, with a further twenty days to reach Port Stanley in the Falkland Islands. As Colin Bertram, the biologist, later wrote: "Could we have walked alongside our course we would have got there quicker." At least by the end of the voyage the members of the expedition had learned to live together, recognising each other's strengths and weaknesses.

Throughout the voyage Launcelot had held Services on board which Gurney described in a letter to Eleanor Fleming from the Falkland Islands. "The Services we have are a great joy and are often held under trying conditions. When it is fine we have Matins or sometimes Evensong on deck and it occasionally rains during the sermon; then we scuttle below and finish the Service in the saloon." Bertram described Launcelot preaching one Sunday on the final stage of the voyage. "Wearing what we rudely called his 'balloon spinakers' – an apt description for a surplice when worn preaching on deck in the Southern Ocean – he was in full voice when we sighted the first penguins swimming alongside. They naturally squawked loud comment at this extraordinary apparition met suddenly far from land, and the attention of some of us wandered from the intricate web of the sermon." For some of these Services Quintin Riley, the meteorologist, accompanied the hymn singing on his piano accordian, though, as Launcelot described it, "the speed at which he played would have put even the slowest Presbyterian organist to shame."

To be Chaplain to the expedition after little more than a year in Orders gave Launcelot much anxious thought. About a fortnight after leaving England he wrote home, perhaps a trifle wistfully: "One thing makes me feel extremely happy – that I think a good many members of the party do really appreciate the fact of having a priest with the expedition . . . I really am beginning to settle down to the life and beginning to feel my way towards an idea of what my job should be." By the time that they neared the Falkland Islands he had discovered that "several of the party have the most extraordinary (to my mind!) views of God and the world. John [Rymill] has some very odd views and he is a much finer man than the beliefs which he maintains he holds. It is not always easy to make one's talks suitable for people like him and for others whose beliefs and aims are more clearly Christian. If nothing else my job is a very humbling one and I am learning more than I thought I would!" Christmas was spent in the Falkland Islands where Launcelot became very friendly with Dean Lumsdale and his wife. When he left for Antarctica the Dean commissioned him as the first priest in charge of the largest parish in the world – five and a half million square miles – but with no parishioners save his fiteen companions.

Shortly after leaving the Falkland Islands on the final stage of the voyage it was discovered that as a result of storms *Penola's* engine beds were moving relative to the hull. To repair them properly would entail wintering in the Islands and thus seriously curtail part of the expedition's purpose. The only course was to return briefly to the Islands and there take aboard some tons of cement to bind the engine beds until proper repair work could be done after reaching Graham Land and to complete the voyage entirely under sail. Fifteen days of alternating storm and fair weather brought *Penola* to Port Lockroy. It was a voyage memorable for bad seasickness and long hours on watch. Even Launcelot's kitten, christened Aula (Hall), was "sea sick on New Year's Eve before we had even left Port William. I am trying to educate him to grow up as a brave seaman cat but at present his chief interest in life is his food and his second concern that of keeping warm. He sleeps coiled round my neck, though he occasionally goes for a midnight stroll on my tummy."

Without engines it was impossible to drive *Penola* through the ice and Rymill was reluctantly forced to alter his plans and to build his base camp on one of the small group of rocky islands known as the Argentine Islands, considerably further north than he had hoped. The site for the camp alongside a safe anchorage for *Penola* had been found by air reconnaissance from Port Lockroy, and the double task of building the base hut and making *Penola* safe for the coming winter occupied all members of the expedition for some weeks. Nine men, including Launcelot, formed the shore party to build the hut and the aeroplane hangar, the wood for which had been brought out in sections from England. The remaining seven men stayed on board *Penola,* now moored by steel cables, and began the heavy task of repairing the engine beds and of strengthening the ship against the pressure of the ice. In addition an old galley and one of the cabins in the ship were converted into a scientific laboratory and photographic dark room. On the 11th of February 1935 Launcelot was able to cable home: "Hut built. Comfortable, warm. Magnificent scenery. Seals good eating." Before leaving England he had been appointed Special Correspondent to *The Times* and also to the *Glasgow Herald* and in a despatch printed in *The Times* on the 12th of April he described the hut.

"The hut is a two-storeyed building with an enclosed porch in one corner, where stands the electric generating plant for wireless and lighting. The two rooms are built with a double thickness of boarding and are insulated on the principle of a vacuum flask, metallic paper being placed within the inner and outer walls. The lower room measures 22 feet by 15 feet. This serves as a workshop, kitchen and dining room, and one corner is partitioned off to form the wireless room.

"Just inside the door a ladder rests against an open hatchway leading to our sleeping quarters. Before occupation this room, with its bare wooden bunks ranged round the walls and separated from each other by wooden partitions, looked as if it might be used for a dog show. But now that it is furnished it makes an attractive and comfortable bedroom. A stove, table and six canvas chairs stand in the middle of the room. Near one of the windows there is a bookcase and an excellent collection of gramophone records.

"Meiklejohn has fitted loud speakers in both rooms and after tea we listen to the news. Wireless is our only material link with the outside world. Since there is little likelihood of mail till we return in the Spring of 1937 it means much to us to be able to receive occasional messages from home."

A man's bunk was his sole place of privacy. Here he kept his personal possessions, his photographs of home, his books and his clothes. Each man adorned the walls of his bunk according to taste. Launcelot had brought with him a water colour of Schiehallion and a Dutch print to hang alongside his sledge flag. On a shelf stood the silver Celtic Cross which his mother had given him and which was placed each Sunday on a work bench or whatever served as an altar

for the Communion Service. He has never been the tidiest of men
and, according to Colin Bertram, his bunk was a chaos of bibles,
prayer books, the Cross, letters, papers, geological hammers and
specimen rocks. Launcelot admitted that he found it hard to confine
his belongings to his alloted area and that from time to time they
escaped down the hatch into the lower room. The copy of *War and
Peace*, which he had brought with him to pass the time remained
unopened.

Sixteen men, forty dogs and their expected pups all needed meat,
For the next two years, save on sledge journeys and on special celebrations, they ate seal meat twice a day. Well cooked, they found it
more pleasant than they had expected, and by the end of the expedition 550 Weddell and Crabeater seals had been killed to provide
nearly a hundred tons of meat and blubber for the men and dogs. At
first Launcelot disliked having to kill and butcher the seals for "they
are attractive creatures with very large childlike eyes and they lie on
their backs in the snow and look at you with most benign expressions." Since meat would be scarce in the winter it was necessary to
kill more seals than were needed for immediate use and these dead
seals were stored in an ice cavern dug out close to the base hut.

Scientific work soon began in earnest. Bertram had already found
the seal killings very helpful in his study of the species. A
meteorological station was set up; accurate map making of the
Argentine Islands began. Brian Roberts, the ornithologist, made
interesting and important observations of penguins, gulls, shags and
especially of the smallest petrel, the Wilson petrel. He found near
the base the nesting site of these birds in patches of moss into which
they burrow to lay their eggs. This species is only known to nest in
the Antarctic but their migratory flights extend well north of the
Equator. By ringing some of these birds Roberts found that the
parent birds returned in the following season to the same mates and
burrows. As for Launcelot, he was immersed in a series of studies of
rock and ice formations. He was particularly fascinated by the fringe
of glaciers, often only a few score feet thick, skirting the Graham
Land shore and terminating in a continuous band of ice cliffs a
hundred feet high.

Only Rymill, the leader, who was mainly intent on discovering hitherto unexplored territory, was disappointed that his plan to spend the first winter further south had been thwarted. The enforced delay was even more frustrating for a man who had little or no interest in the scientific work of the expedition, which he undervalued. In the early months Launcelot found him "the most difficult person to understand . . . and it is strange how little he appreciates the feelings and sympathies of other people. He is a queerly lonely person and though very kind he has an almost impenetrable reserve." Any early criticism of his leader was confined to his private diary. "As you can imagine, it's very relieving to one's feelings, when one is a bit pent up, to loose off steam by writing it down in one's diary." Nevertheless Launcelot came to appreciate Rymill's considerable qualities as a leader. He had excellent judgement of situations and, to a slightly lesser extent, of men. He won the confidence of the expedition's members by his skill, for instance, in judging whether it seemed justifiable to travel across newly found sea-ice or whether it was wiser to wait. He was not, however, a good communicator, even making allowances for a leader to keep certain things to himself. To someone like Launcelot for whom personal relationships meant so much Rymill's aloofness, especially in the early months of the expedition, was distressing.

A house-warming party for the new hut on the 13th of March was combined with the celebration of Rymill's birthday, an occasion marred for Launcelot by one or two men very much the worse for drink. Rymill tried to persuade him that an occasional 'blind' was necessary for men living in difficult conditions and under pressure. The celebration on the 21st of June of the Antarctic Midwinter Day was a far happier occasion. The hut was decorated with flags and a small Christmas tree. Invitations were issued to the ships' party to join the base party at "7.30 for 8.00" in the upper room of the hut where schnapps and sherry were produced. Then followed a dinner of roast chicken, sausages, celery, mashed potatoes and plum pudding with rum butter, all washed down with wine and beer. After dinner presents from the Scott Polar Research Institute in Cambridge and from one or two friends were distributed and the evening ended with dancing to the gramophone.

Later that evening, sitting beside the Aga stove, Rymill talked to Launcelot and R. E. D. Ryder with unwonted freedom about his plans for the long sledge journey to be undertaken in the Charcot Land area during 1936 when the whole party had moved south. He paid them the compliment of saying that he believed that they had the necessary strength and powers of endurance to be chosen for the sledge party. To his private diary Launcelot confessed his pleasure at having won his leaders's confidence and also his very natural anxiety lest the task proved too demanding for him. It had been a "rather awe-inspiring" end to a cheery evening. He could not then know how often circumstances and fresh ideas would change Rymill's plans in the next two years.

Before undertaking even short sledge journeys, not only had the dog teams to be trained but several of those in charge of a team needed basic instruction in this difficult art. First it was essential to master the way to use the 22-feet long whips. "My first efforts were not very promising. I succeeded in whipping most parts of my anatomy – sometimes quite hard – and at other times I would get the whip entangled round itself like one does when one tries to cast too long a fishing line." Ten minutes practice each day for several weeks enabled the novice to learn enough to drive a following dog team but to drive the leading team on a long journey demanded much experience. Launcelot had a very soft spot for the huskies and at times secretly wondered whether his more kindly approach did not get better results than the firm handling by the experts.

By July there were fifty-four fully grown dogs, sufficient for six teams. They had to be trained to obey the four commands – go, stop, turn right, turn left. In Launcelot's opinion "they display in an extraordinary way the varied temperaments of human beings. Their response to sledging must in some ways resemble the reaction of schoolboys to their work: some immensely conscientious and no trouble at all; some sly and only working when the driver is looking; some with a hearty and boundless energy frequently misapplied; some languid and apparently self-pitying. You can, of course, turn their susceptibilities to good account. If Ginger hates Hero and Hero is afraid of Ginger, then put Hero immediately in front of Ginger and you have two dogs pulling their best. But they are almost without exception affectionate and loyal." Their two most tiresome habits were fighting among themselves and gnawing their harness or any part of sledge equipment within reach. This could be serious on a long sledge journey and the team driver had to sleep "with one ear awake and be ready to go out at any time of the night if you hear suspicious noises."

Life on the expedition was infinitely varied and by the time that he had been away from home for a year Launcelot could boast that "I have taken part in the following occupations – priest, scientist, photographer (still and ciné), journalist, seaman, carpenter, slaughterer and butcher, cook, char, housemaid, boatman and stevedore." As for cooking, the usual rule was for one man to be responsible for a week's meals. On the outward voyage to Montevideo a cook had been found by Rymill, prepared to come unpaid just for the experience. Unfortunately Rymill omitted to find out if he could cook, and it at once became apparent that his "most resistant bread it has been my lot to chew" proved his total ignorance.

Launcelot's first spell in the galley came on the voyage from the Falkland Islands to Graham Land. It was no easy task in a heavy swell when feeling seasick. "You must never fill a pan too full or allow it room to slide or a catastrophe will undoubtedly take place. This morning we heeled over especially badly and everything started to come adrift. At the time Norman [Gurney] was also in the galley frying mutton chops and there was a pan of potatoes boiling on the other oven. The dripping and water that spilt made a bad enough mess and added to that some pieces of raw meat came out of their basin and distributed themselves on the floor. Then all the enamel dishes clattered about to give appropriate noise effects." However, he had made doughnuts and baked a cake before his week was over, even though his flapjacks were "a thin layer of charred cinders". With greater experience he grew more confident and sought ways of varying the diet from the rather limited supply of raw materials. The bread began to rise properly and Cornish pasties ("minus the onions and potatoes") followed by an orange trifle testified to his prowess.

As the months went by each cook in turn realised the need to modify the recipes to the raw materials available. "The cherry cake," Launcelot confided to his diary, "is quite good when made with a little Birds' egg substitute in place of eggs, lard or mutton fat instead of butter and minus the cherries." He discovered that "a shepherd's pie served in a dish with greasy dirt round the edges looks most uninviting," and he came to the conclusion that "cooking in fact is not just a technical matter but an art." It is to be hoped that in moments of stress he took fresh courage from St. Teresa of Avila's reminder to her novices, who complained that kitchen work was unspiritual: 'The Lord walks among the pots and pans'.

The second Christmas away from home was a very happy occasion. A Communion Service in the hut at 8.30 a.m. was followed by the formal dressing of *Penola* over all. The evening Service to which nearly all the expedition came was held in the ship and the traditional Christmas hymns were sung. "After the Service there was a cocktail party in the ship. The cocktails were made of lime juice, sugar, a little absolute alcohol and water – most unpleasant stuff and I confess I hid my glass behind a boot on the floor after the first sip." Dinner was eaten in the hut and the evening ended with eightsome reels, which Launcelot had taught the party.

By now it was Antarctic midsummer and everyone eagerly awaited the move south to a new base once *Penola* was free to move. On the 3rd of January 1936 she sailed northwards to Deception Island where there had once been a whaling station. Here the ship's party found enough old timber to build a new base hut, sheet metal to roof it and coal to supplement the expedition's limited supply. Even a few pounds of still edible bacon and a giant can of marmalade were valuable finds.

Most appreciated of all was the mail which Lincoln Ellsworth, the American explorer, had left there in November and which *Penola* brought back on the 29th of January, the first letters which the expedition had received for thirteen months. Some of the men fingered their pile of envelopes, pondering their possible contents, and leaving them unopened to another day to enhance the thrill of reading. It was a strange experience to receive news from home written over a year ago when only nine days earlier the party had learned from the wireless of the death of King George V half an hour after it had occurred. In the first bag of mail which the aeroplane had brought ahead of the ship Launcelot had sixty-five letters and there were more in the next bag in *Penola.* His only anxiety was that since he had received more letters than anyone else the rest should be "jealous of my good fortune".

While *Penola* was at Deception Island Rymill, Stephenson and Launcelot set off on a sledge journey aiming to penetrate directly inland on the mainland of Graham Land. They hoped to travel up to the backbone of the peninsula which they thought might be some seven or eight thousand feet above sea level. As the weather was warm they travelled by night but after only three nights of difficult progress they were held up by deep crevasses. Roped together they made a reconnaissance which showed that further advance was impossible.

On return to the base the packing up started, and on the 16th of February *Penola,* with every inch of space crammed and with eighty dogs, sailed south to Marguerite Bay. The two men left at the base with the aeroplane waited for the message to fly south. When this was received the hut was boarded up and on the door a notice was painted: "This House To Let, Season 1936-37". The new base was sited on one of the six tiny islands at the south of Marguerite Bay, which were formally christened the Debenham Islands after the six children of the Cambridge Professor of Geography, who had been one of Scott's companions and was one of the principal advisers to the expedition. By mid-March all the stores and building materials had been unloaded and the porch of the new base hut built.

Penola was now free to sail back to the Falkland Islands for a much needed refit before she returned in the following year to take the party home. Among other things she carried with her over a hundred letters from Launcelot, as well as his photographic negatives. The nine members at the base had every inducement to work hard in completing the hut. The porch was occupied by

Launcelot and Bertram, while the other seven men had to sleep in tents on the beach until the hut was ready. Here they experienced a foretaste of the strength and persistence of the winds on this small group of islands at the mouth of a long fjord-like arm of the sea.

The first year had been unavoidably disappointing as far as the exploration of new territory was concerned. Now hopes ran high of exciting discoveries of which air reconnaissance had given some indications. However it was not until May that the ice was sufficiently strong to justify beaching the boats for the winter and training dog teams for the long sledge journeys ahead. Rymill's original plan for a thousand mile expedition, which he had divulged to Launcelot and Ryder that night in the hut, had been altered in favour of a shorter but much more thorough exploration of the land to the south. Launcelot had been hoping for this change, not from fear of the likely dangers of the original plan, but in the interest of scientific work. For on a very long journey "there is rarely time for anything except getting there and getting back at the greatest speed possible."

On the 11th of June most of the party set out to lay a depot of stores some seventy miles to the south from which a further advance could later be made. Launcelot was unable to join this expedition as his dog team was insufficiently trained. The journey was a nighmare. Midwinter is not ideal for sledging as there are only four hours in each day when the light is good enough for safe progress. Winds of up to one hundred miles an house were encountered and it was at times doubtful if the tents would survive. Worse still was the discovery in the middle of one night that the ice around the camp was breaking up within six feet of each tent. There was only one course open. Two tons of stores and the tractor were piled in heaps, marked by tall bamboo poles and abandoned. The party found refuge on an island which they thankfully named Terra Firma, where they camped until new sea-ice had formed to a thickness to enable them to start back to the base. With only ten days of food for men and dogs they moved in and out of the ice-floes, sometimes guided only by the light of an electric torch, until soaked through from falls into ice-cold water they struggled back to the hut. It was a disappointing start to the season's work.

On the 14th of August Launcelot and Bingham set out in search of the abandoned depot. Recent heavy falls of snow made the going slow and especially difficult for the dogs, who often sank in up to their shoulders. Four days later they had a piece of very bad luck. Launcelot and his team had started off first from camp and after forcing his way ahead for a quarter of a mile he stopped to wait for Bingham to catch up with him. It was soon apparent that Bingham was not following and, fearing that his knee which had previously caused him much trouble had again let him down, Launcelot went back to find out what was wrong. "I found Doc's team lying quietly in their place and Doc standing disconsolately beside the tent which had two or three bad tears in it. Apparently when Doc had turned his team to follow me he managed to drive the dogs well clear of the tent but forgot that the sledge would cut the corner and the sledge charged straight into one side of the tent. Doc had an awful job turning the dogs back and extricating the sledge from the tent. The damage looked rather alarming but after both of us had sewed for the best part of two hours the rents were mended. It was very cold sewing outside without gloves on but anyway we got it done." Recalling the incident, Bingham contrasted the language he would have used to Launcelot had their positions been reversed, with Launcelot's sole concern that Bingham's knee might once again be causing him serious pain. Ultimately bad visibility and thick snow made any hope of finding the depot vain and they were back at the base before the month ended.

The long sledge journey south began on the 5th of September. Rymill, Bingham, Stephenson, Bertram and Launcelot set off with forty-five dogs and a load of 6,000 pounds of food for themselves and the dogs, tents, sleeping bags, wireless time-signal sets and scientific equipment to explore and survey the land so far only seen from the air. The plan was that after about three weeks Rymill and Bingham should return to the base with light loads, leaving the other three men with full loads to last for about ten weeks and thus to extend their range. From the start it was heavy going as deep snow made it impossible for the dogs to pull more than half their loads at a time. Eighty miles of sea-ice, followed by a 2500-foot climb up a glacier, lay between them and the Sound which the aeroplane had sighted. Moreover Launcelot had been having trouble with his dog team. "Rosie is still in season and causes any amount of trouble especially among the three front dogs – Imp, Pie and Cyclops – who have more to interest them behind than in front."

Before long hopelessly bad visibility forced the men to lie idle in their tents for eight days, consuming their rations without making any progress. All of them suffered from severe headaches caused by the fumes from badly designed stoves. There was little to do save to remain optimistic, to talk and to read. In addition to his Office Book and Prayer Book Launcelot had taken with him *Pilgrim's Progress*, Readings from von Hügel and Kingsley's *Ravenshoe*, a somewhat formidable choice. When it was possible to move Launcelot and Bingham worked out "a very smooth running routine in the tent. We take it day about to do the cooking and when travelling the one who is not cooking is the outside man. At the end of the day's sledging the cook feeds and ties up his dogs as quickly as he can, the tent is pitched and he gets inside to lay out the interior of the tent and light the primus, whilst the outside man puts the snow on the tent flaps and finishes all the outside jobs. Then by the time he gets inside some snow is generally melted for him to have a drink. In the morning I generally light the primus and put the pots on, since I like to have time to read my Office and say my prayers."

On the 24th of September, after further progress had been made, Rymill decided that the time had come for him and Bingham to return to the base where they could replenish their stores and set out again to meet the other three men on their return journey.

So Stephenson, Bertram and Launcelot continued with heavily loaded sledges through poor light, which made it hard to distinguish crevasses from safe ground as they threaded their way through the icy maze. They found that the best plan was for one man to ski ahead, using the lash of a dog whip to explore the ground. When the end of the lash disappeared there was probably a crevasse. Even so on one occasion Bertram found that he was advancing unknowingly along a narrow wall of ice between two chasms. At night there were two tents for the three of them and they arranged that each man in turn should have a tent to himself for three weeks. Usually the man on his own would join the other two for tea or supper, and on a Sunday Stephenson and Bertram joined Launcelot in saying Evensong.

Soon there came spells of colder clearer weather which enabled them to cover over twenty miles in a day. By the 3rd of October they had reached the Sound, which proved to be a long channel some fifteen miles wide, floored by shelf-ice and flanked by mountains rising to 8,000 feet in Alexander I Land. It was a magnificent sight and the channel clearly continued much further south than had been thought. By the 8th of October the men were convinced that they were making an important discovery. In 1926 Sir Hubert Wilkins had flown over the western seaboard of Graham Land and had interpreted the depressions running east to west as straits, concluding that Graham Land was an archipelago of islands, detached from the main Antarctic continent. Wilkins had never seen into the Sound and it became increasingly clear that his conjecture was wrong and that Graham Land was in fact a peninsula jutting out from the continent.

They now had to decide how much further to advance and when it must be wise to turn back. The progressive lightening of the loads and the slight deterioration of the dogs' strength seemed to cancel out. They agreed to continue until half the rations for themselves and the dogs had been used up. But when that day came they still had not discovered where the Sound was leading. The two shorelines – the eastern shoreline of Alexander I Land and the western shoreline of Graham Land – still continued in a southerly direction. They felt that they must continue for a few days longer but on shortened rations. Their reward came a few days later when the Alexander I Land coastline clearly ended in a cape, showing that Alexander I Land was an island, though much larger than had previously been presumed. On the 19th of October a little south of latitude 70 degrees they decided that they must turn back. Thanks to a brilliantly clear day they could see some sixty miles ahead, the first travellers in that part of Antarctica.

The return journey began well. For the only time on the seventy-four days expedition four consecutive days of travel were possible. On the outward journey through the Sound Launcelot had become increasingly excited about the rock formations. All the rocks of the Graham Land mainland were either igneous or metamorphic, but during their southward journey he noticed that some of the cliffs on the western side were distinctly stratified and it was decided to reserve at least two days on the homeward journey to examining them. On the 23rd October Launcelot was delighted to have his hopes fulfilled. The stratified rocks yielded fossils of bivalve shells, fragments of primitive plants and a shark's tooth. These fossils gave in general terms a clue to the dating of these formations – middle Jurassic – and proved that millions of years earlier the area had enjoyed a much warmer climate.

Unfortunately as October drew to its close the weather deteriorated. Drifting snow through which although it was possible to ski blinded the dogs and compelled the calling of a halt. "On lying-up days we always postpone breakfast to as late an hour as possible for in that way the pangs of hunger are less keenly felt." On good days they might travel for twenty miles, though insufficient food made them tire more easily and feel the cold more intensely. Despite taking all possible care Stephenson and Bertram fell over a thirty foot ice cliff while reconnoitring a route but very fortunately landed unhurt in deep snow. Launcelot later confessed to a moment of wondering how he would complete the journey alone had there been a tragedy. By the 1st of November six dogs had to be destroyed as there was insufficient food for them all. Philosophically optimistic they struggled on towards the point where they knew that a depot of food awaited them. On the 11th of November, after observing the two minutes silence of Armistic Day, they suddenly saw what at first appeared to be two lone penguins in the distance. The penguins turned out to be Rymill and Bingham coming towards them. They camped together that evening to exchange news, and next day Stephenson, Bertram and Launcelot, still very hungry, started on the final stage of their journey. On the 21st November they were safely back at the base, justifiably pleased with their geographical and scientific discoveries. As Launcelot wrote in his diary: "The hut seemed curiously comfortable."

Addressing the Royal Geographical Society in February 1938 Launcelot and Stephenson ended their lecture with these words: "The most vivid and enjoyable days in Graham Land were not those spent at the base, not even after a long journey when one was revelling in the luxuries of a hot bath and a shave, of scrambled penguins' eggs and the comforts of a warm bunk. The best days were those of sledging in unknown country – untouched, unspoiled, as God had made it. The interest of wondering what is round the next corner, the stimulus of discussing the origin of newly discovered land or glacial features, the companionship of the dogs and most of all the close friendship which sledging establishes amongst the members of the party."

Meanwhile Rymill and Bingham had turned east in an attempt to cross Graham Land and reach the Weddell Sea. The journey involved a climb of 8,000 feet through a pass in the mountains, always twisting and turning across heavily crevassed glaciers. All the while they were facing a sea of cloud which prevented them from being absolutely certain that they had reached the eastern side. Eventually diminishing food supplies forced them to turn back. Travelling by night they made rapid progress over crusted surfaces and they were safely back at the base early in January 1937, just before the sea-ice broke up.

The work of the expedition was now over and its members could boast of three important additions to the map of Antarctica. First, Graham Land had been proved to be part of the continent; second, Alexander I land was found to be an island of more than two hundred and fifty miles in length; thirdly, Alexander I Land is separated from Graham Land by one of the most impressive features of the earth's surface, namely the great Sound on which Launcelot and his two companions had been the first human beings to tread. On the 15th of January 1938 it was announced that King George VI had given permission for the Sound to bear his name and two years later he decorated the members of the expedition with the Polar Medal.

All thoughts turned towards getting home. *Penola* was known to be on her way to fetch the shore party but ice would make it impossible for her to reach the base much before the end of February. Launcelot filled in this frustrating period of waiting by working on his geological specimens and by winning a £2 bet that he would not swim across the creek where the ice was breaking up. On the 18th of February "shortly after midday I got my £2. Unfortunately there were several fairly large bits of ice drifting through the creek and I had to wait for a clear run. In actual fact after the first few strokes, which I felt intensely cold, one becomes used to the feel of the water and the last few yards I found quite pleasant swimming." The previous day he had recorded in his diary the friendly barrage of taunts on what a Scotsman would do for a mere £2.

On the last day of the month *Penola* was back. Launcelot was in the aeroplane taking a film of her return and so excited that he could scarcely hold his camera steady. The final departure was delayed by such a severe storm that for a week all communication between the ship and the shore had to be by semaphore. At one moment there was grave risk that *Penola* "would be cast up on our doorstep." At last on the 12th of March she set sail for South Georgia. "This morning they closed up the Base . . . Oddly enough I do not much regret leaving, in fact I am so heartily looking forward to home and Cambridge that the parting from the Base was in no way a sorry business."

A month later Launcelot was thankfully on shore at the whaling station of Grytirken in South Georgia where he held a Service for the small community. Plans were made for the shore party to return in a whale-oil tanker, which would travel far more quickly than *Penola*, and by May he was home. To have been away from all that he held most dear for nearly three years was a long absence. That it had been abundantly rewarding and that it had been one of the most formative influences in his life he never had a moment's doubt.

After six months with the expedition Launcelot wrote in his diary: "It does seem at least that a man has the chance to re-adjust his values and to learn to know other people and himself with deeper insight than before." When it was all over and he was home again he was convinced that the most important lesson which such an expedition taught was the doctrine of acceptance. "You just have to put up with certain physical conditions. You have to put up with the stores you have got with you; it is no good complaining about what you have left behind. You have to put up with the limitations imposed on your activities by the weather. But far more important you have to put up with your companions and they with you because there is no escaping them for the next two or three years."

A small incident which occurred during the last tedious weeks at the base illustrated the need for acceptance of one's companions. One man was angry with Rymill on some matter, lost control of himself for a moment and, snatching the barograph off its shelf, smashed it on the ground and swept out of the hut in a furious temper. A moment later he was back again for there was nowhere else to go; the temperature was not conducive to staying outside. The man apologised privately to Rymill and no one referred to the incident.

On the whole the members of the expedition got on well. There were times when the shore and ship's parties became critical of each other and then it was, as *Penola's* Captain recalls, that Launcelot "really more than anyone else acted as a moderating influence and prevented criticisms from becoming acrimonius." It was said that towards the end of the expedition he was the only member on speaking terms with everyone else. Nevertheless even the kindly Launcelot, being only human, found it necessary from time to time to exercise the discipline of tolerance. It was a relief to him that more of his companions preferred to listen to classical music on the gramophone than to jazz. A much greater strain was the meal time conversation, especially on the long outward voyage. "It is curious why men of apparently high moral calibre will join in foul talk which is essentially foreign to their nature."

He was in a difficult position. He had no wish to set himself up as a model of virtue and thus appear to cut himself off from his companions: at the same time he felt that he would be shirking his duty were he to remain completely silent when talk was especially crude and hard swearing unnecessarily frequent. Looking over his diary years later he commented: 'I get the impression that I really was a pretty insufferable prig in Graham Land with so much emphasis on a dislike for bad language and getting drunk at a party, etc. I think I did dislike these things then and don't much like them now, but I don't think that these were the really difficult things to come to terms with in accepting my companions.' On this two further comments can be made. First, the diary, as he said, was a place in which feeling could be relived and was not meant for publication. It certainly recorded, often quite critically, what he felt at the moment but not his considered opinions. Secondly, the remarks of a man in his late twenties are bound to appear naive and slightly embarassing when read forty years later.

Nor is there any evidence that Launcelot's companions thought him a prig. "He was always very welcome on board," wrote Captain Ryder, "and stood up to all of our ribald jokes with the greatest good humour. I was the first person to nickname him 'The Bish' and The Bish he remained." What impressed members of the expedition, as Ryder said, was "his sincerity, sound judgment and a combination of good humour and unselfishness." In fact, partly out of respect to him, the cruder talk grew noticeably less. Bingham at any rate accepted Launcelot's occasional reproof in good part. 'It seems to me,' he once said, 'that you are a pillar of the Church and I a buttress of Hell!' Launcelot, who had a high regard for Bingham, used to admit that 'Doc Bingham's language, though hardly suited to the drawing-room, had about it a certain style, largely because he did not repeat himself.'

It was what his companions thought of him as a priest in their midst, however much he won their respect as a scientist and sledging partner, that caused Launcelot the greatest concern. He had no easy task with only the limited experience of a College Chapel to give him assurance. No curate serving his first title ever had a more severe testing. At the end of his first year in Graham Land, in a letter to his mother, he summed up what he had so far learned. "I have been very careful not to press people in the least bit to come to our

Services and for this reason I think they really do appreciate them. Sometimes I feel impatient and anxious about my job as Chaplain to the party but that I know is fruitless as in any case it is God and God alone on whom one can rely . . . As you can imagine my job as Chaplain is not an easy one. The outlook of the party is so very mixed in things religious I find it difficult to know where to begin! Every Sunday we have Holy Communion before breakfast. We use the work bench as an altar. Quintin Riley made a scarlet frontal – the fair linen cloths are the right size – and we use the Communion set which Chase gave me and the Cross you gave me. Generally only two come to this, though at intervals one or two others come and at Easter time we had ten. Most of the party at the base come to the evening Service and some come from the ship – there are generally nine or ten. Every other Sunday I give an address at this Service . . . My chief difficulty is to find a form of Service which will meet the spiritual needs of a very staunch and argumentative Anglo-Catholic, a keen Weslyan, a Presbyterian, a Christian Scientist (by upbringing) and one or two others who do not quite know whether they would call themselves Christians or not and of whose prejudices and ideals I am aware . . . I am really learning a great many things that are absolutely vital to a padre in his job – people do say what they think – and one realises all too fully that the ultimate test of religion is judged by the kind of character it produces."

His companions certainly said what they thought about Launcelot's addresses. Few other parsons can have undergone the searching experience of preaching in a small hut to those with whom he would be sitting down to supper a few minutes later, knowing that all his words and his logic would be subjected to a kindly but detailed "post mortem". Never before had he been brought so starkly face to face with the task of dealing with men to whom Christianity meant little or nothing. "It is desperately difficult to preach Christ to those who have had opportunities to learn of Him and have been left relatively indifferent in their attitude to His way of life. Even if one has seen a vision dimly and failed adequately to live up to its demands, it is bewildering to live

with others who care little for the 'music' of that vision . . . This
attitude makes me realise my own inadequacy." However depressed
he might become at moments, there were signs that his care for his
tiny parish was having an effect. That thirteen out of the fifteen
came from time to time to his Services, that constant religious
discussions took place in the hut and the growing realisation that the
kind of talk which so distressed him was often largely superficial,
redressed the balance and gave him continuing faith in the value of
his work.

The British Graham Land Expedition had been for Launcelot an
enriching experience which had broadened his outlook and had
deepened his own religious life. "To live like this with fifteen
excellent fellows gives one an amazingly keen insight into human
nature – one's own included. It has made me realize, sometimes
with almost painful yearnings, the truth of all that Christianity
involves and the very great need for living in communion with God
and by His Power. It is dangerously easy to use grand phrases and
more difficult and more exacting to live them. Here I do seem to
have found my neighbour and myself as they are; we have little in
the way of artificial disguises and we are free from the dangers of
trying to win popular credit or pandering to public opinion. A man
sees himself here as he really is and not as he wants other people to
believe him to be. It comes as a bit of a shock and a bit of stimulus to
most of us, anyway to myself. I think this is the real appeal (to those
who have experienced them) of expeditions such as this one: it is a
if one drew away from the world to lonely places, there to see
oneself stripped naked before the eyes of God and one's small
community of fellow men and there to have the chance to strive
afresh, knowing and convinced that God knows and God cares."

Bishop Hensley Henson, speaking of Ordination, once said that
nobody can be respected as a priest who is not first respected as a
man. The years of polar exploration ensured that Launcelot had
won respect as both.

Chapter 7

DEAN AND CHAPLAIN (i)

1933 – 1940

One of the strange facts about Launcelot's Cambridge career is that while he was officially attached to Trinity Hall in one way and another from 1925, when he first came up, until 1949 when he became Bishop of Portsmouth, he was only in actual residence for less than half of those twenty-four years. What is remarkable is not his absence in the Antarctic or on war service but the strength of the influence which he exerted in the College over a comparatively short and interrupted time. Something of this influence had been felt in his undergraduate years, which in some measure accounts for the readiness of the Governing Body to elect him to a Fellowship as Chaplain of the College five days before he had even been ordained and before he could ever prove his quality in direct experience of pastoral work. This position he only held for a year and a Long Vacation Term before being granted three years leave of absence to join the Graham Land Expedition. Doubtless the Master and Fellows realised that these three years in the Antarctic would be a far more valuable training for a College Chaplain than serving a term as a curate in a parish. When in 1934 the Dean, George Chase, became Master of Selwyn College, Launcelot was appointed Dean as well as Chaplain, but he could not exercise this double office until his return to Cambridge in 1937. It was thus between 1937 and 1940, when he joined the Navy, that as a don he first became a force in the College.

There was a remarkable group of dons in the College at this time. Owen (later Sir Owen) Wansbrough-Jones, the scientist, had succeeded Chase as Senior Tutor and in that position could greatly influence the life of the Hall. Among others were Charles Crawley,

later to be the historian of six hundred years of College life; Tom
Ellis Lewis (known to all as 'Tel') and Trevor Jones who together
looked after the budding lawyers; Robin Hayes, who was in charge
of the engineers, and Franklin Angus, the classical scholar, who had
a profound influence on a varied if rather small number of
undergraduates. Over them Professor Dean, a noted pathologist,
presided as a much loved and respected Master, whom probably in
his heart of hearts Launcelot would have given much to succeed. As
the years went by Launcelot's influence grew steadily until there
were some who maintained that, if such things can be measured, it
was second only to that of the Master.

   The intermittent periods of residence prevented Launcelot from
being the kind of Fellow interested in guiding the College into new
ways or in actively pursuing some particular line of policy. Even
had he been in continuous residence this would not have been his
way of contributing to College life. Looking back on his years at the
Hall it is clear that his influence was the cement which bound
everyone together – dons, undergraduates and College servants
alike. Something of his nature affected all whom he met and helped
to make the Hall a wonderfully happy and united society. At the
weekly meetings of the Governing Body, held round the
crescent-shaped table in the Senior Combination Room, he was a
conciliator when necessary, not an innovator and never a College
politician. His contribution to a discussion was always valuable but
he was not a man who believed that he would be heard for his much
speaking.

   He knew that his real work lay in the College Chapel and in being
available at all hours to those who sought his help. He knew, or
quickly discovered, that one of the obvious problems for a College
Chaplain is that young people are unlikely to discuss or seek
guidance about the deeper and more personal issues of faith and life
until they come to know the Chaplain well. This requires not only
sympathetic understanding and sensitivity but takes a great deal of
time. Most of a man's deepest hopes and fears cannot be discussed in
groups, which means even greater demands upon a Chaplain's time.
There are some young men who delight in baring their souls in

public but this was not an approach to religion which Launcelot could ever encourage. So it was that he threw himself as fully as possible into College life – as a Supervisor of undergraduates sent to him, as a Boat Club coach, as a man whose rooms were even more of a magnet than they had been in his days as an undergraduate himself. To him, as a Christian, there should be no rigid distinction between the sacred and the secular. His love of God made inevitable his love of humanity, and these twin loves were the driving force throughout his life.

As in so many Oxford and Cambridge colleges the Chapel at Trinity Hall was in a central position physically, and Launcelot was determined to make it also 'the centre of our life as a community'. At the start of each term every man in the College received from him a card with details of the times of Chapel services and of the preachers, together with a short personal letter reminding him gently of his obligation to worship. "The Chapel services," he wrote, "are voluntary and by that is meant, not merely that there is no rule compelling members of the College to attend, but that there is no underlying thought that those who come will thereby acquire merit . . . The object of this letter is most emphatically not to try to persuade you to come to Chapel services; it is to ask you to think over the matter and to be honest with your own conscience in regard to it. I would particularly suggest that you do not allow yourself to stay away if the only reason is slackness." With this approach Launcelot gradually made the Chapel a place of great spiritual influence in the life of the College.

On week days every morning before breakfast, except on Thursdays and Saints Days when Holy Communion was celebrated, there was a shortened form of Matins, and every evening, except on Saturdays, there was a Service between the two sittings in Hall. On Sundays those who had made their communion used to breakfast together in the attractively furnished room known as Doctor Eden's Room. In his letters to Hall men Launcelot was at pains to stress the importance of the "principal act of Christian worship" and he had no hesitation in welcoming members of all denominations to take part. "The Church," he wrote in one of his circular letters, "is a

Family and the Communion Service is essentially the Family
Service of the Church. Attendance is therefore not only a personal
matter but one which concerns the life and effectiveness of
Christians as a whole. There is no suggestion that a man must feel
'good enough' before he attends. No one is good enough for what
God provides but that is no reason for refusing His gifts. What is
required is the intention and desire to receive what Our Lord has to
offer, namely a closer relationship with Himself."

For many members of Trinity Hall Sunday Evensong, slightly
tailored to meet the needs of men of all denominations or of none,
affectionately known as 'Flemingsong' and at which there was
usually an address, was the occasion when the corporate life of the
College seemed more fully expressed. Launcelot's invitation to
"disengage yourself from the river, tennis court or tea-party" and to
bring relatives and friends often led to the small Chapel being
uncomfortably crowded. It had been designed in days when
although Chapel attendance was compulsory the number of
undergraduates was far fewer and it met the needs of the time. There
were only two rows of seats on either side facing inwards and as
numbers grew benches were placed on both sides of the aisle with
nothing in front as a support during the prayers. Here late comers,
somewhat self-consciously, had to sit. Soon after Launcelot's return
from the Antarctic the decision was made to construct pews which
could be pulled out when needed, the concertina effect being
invisible when not in use. However there was always one way of
being certain of a seat, as Launcelot pointed out in a circular letter
written after the war. "I would quote the comment made by a Chief
Petty Officer at Portsmouth in another connection: 'Them that's
keen gets fell in previous'".

One or sometimes two of the addresses would be given by
Launcelot each term. Probably no preacher has ever agonised more
than he over the composition of a sermon. Unfortunately for him he
did not inherit his father's natural gifts as a speaker, and every word
was laboriously written down and corrected again and again. There
can be few of his friends who have not been subjected to the slightly
embarrassing experience of being asked to listen to the draft of a

sermon and to comment on it. His extraordinary humility makes it impossible for him not to expect valuable improvements to his script from the least qualified to listen. This practice he has never abandoned.

He has never thought of himself as a great preacher and, while interested in theology, he could never claim to have been an original thinker. He has in fact always been a quite shameless borrower of other people's ideas and phrases. When it come to writing a sermon he hasa magpie ability to pick up thoughts and quotations from his friends' writing and conversation and to weave them into his own text. At times, totally untroubled by any question of copyright, he has been known to borrow and preach an entire sermon. This could lead to an awkward situation. Once as Bishop of Portsmouth he borrowed a New Year sermon from the Archdeacon of the Isle of Wight, who intended to preach it himself shortly. Since it was the Bishop who was preaching in the Island church, a reporter was sent and the sermon duly appeared in the local paper before the author of the sermon had been able to use his own work.

When he preaches Launcelot uses no tricks to hold the attention of the congregation; there is seldom any attempt at humour. Despite this he is a compelling preacher, for it is the man himself who shines through, relying entirely on presenting the truth about God, as he has come to understand it, with reverence and simplicity. A distinguished Cambridge theologian wrote about Launcelot's powers as a preacher: "I value his sermons; but that is not because they say much to my head but because they always spring from the heart and cast a sort of reflected light upon the preacher's own sensitive, delicate and affectionate understanding of human nature." This is why the impact of his sermons is so much greater at the time of delivery than if the text is read at a later date. It is also the reason for his success in preaching to young people in school or college Chapels. For while they can enjoy oratory they can often see through it if it is false; what they demand of a preacher above all else is sincerity.

Launcelot himself described one of his most successful experiments as Chaplain. "I initiated, I think in my first year as

Chaplain before going to Graham Land and certainly in the periods
before and after the War, some talks under the general umbrella of
'Personal Religion'. These took place once a week in the
Michaelmas and Lent Terms and in the first half of the Easter term.
The talks were normally given as a series, such as talks on prayer or
on ethics etc. I would personally invite a member of the College
after explaining what these talks were meant to do – and I did not
only invite Chapel goers or the religiously committed but people
whom I thought would be interested. I asked them to come once or
twice and then if they found the occasion of value and wanted to
come regularly I asked that they would honour that intention by
making this a first call on their time on that evening of the week.

"The talks were timed for 10 o'clock when the College gates were
closed to men living in digs. There was first a cup of tea and biscuits
and then, about 10.20, I would ask people to sit down. After a
moment's quiet the speaker would start and talk for fifteen to twenty
minutes. There was no general discussion and the party dispersed. A
few men generally stayed behind but not necessarily to discuss the
subject of the talk. These evenings enabled those who came to
reflect seriously on all sorts of personal issues without the
embarrassment of a general discussion, which could obviously
better take place in a much smaller group. I used to give the talks in
one of the terms and would invite others to do so in other terms –
Charles Raven, Owen Chadwick, Alec Vidler or C. F. Angus, whose
talks on 'Some unsuspected Christian virtues' were especially
memorable and helpful. One merit in this plan was that it did not
monopolise a whole evening.

"These 'Thursday Evenings' did really seem to meet a need. Large
numbers came regularly – about as many as there was room for on
the chairs and floor of my larger sitting room. They were never
advertised on the College noticeboard but there was nothing secret
about them and I would ask those who came to let me know of any
whom they thought would like to be asked."

It was not only on a Thursday evening that Launcelot's rooms
were filled to overflowing. Of his work at this period a
contemporary wrote: "Among the undergraduates he was perhaps

18   Commonwealth Fellows on board
      S.S. *Albertic*

19   Harkness Quadrangle, Yale

20   Launcelot in Iceland, 1932

21   Members of the Spitzbergen Expedition. The leader (A. R. Glen) is sitting in
the centre. Launcelot is sitting on the extreme left.

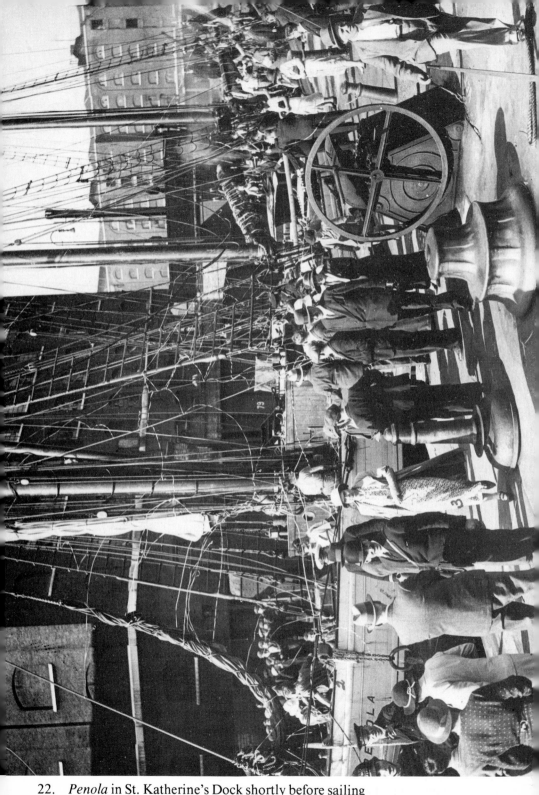

22. *Penola* in St. Katherine's Dock shortly before sailing

23   *Penola* under full sail

24   *Penola's* first anchorage at Port Lockroy

25　Building the Southern Base

26　Launcelot does his share of the cooking

27 Interior of the living room

28 The changed map of Graham Land

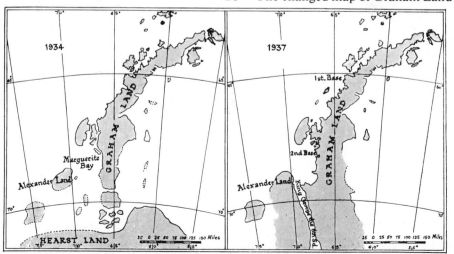

29   Digging a pit for geological investigations, 1935

the leading influence. His familiar rooms on E Staircase were hardly ever without visitors at any hour of the day or night. I can remember being mildly exasperated once at my inability to find him alone! And the conversation ranged over an astonishing variety of subjects from the serious to the absurd. Everyone loved him, everyone looked up to him, everyone listened to him eagerly." Yet it was his presence in the room which created the atmosphere which drew men there rather than what he said. For unlike many dons he was never a brilliantly exciting and provocative talker. In fact he has always been in conversation a hesitant speaker, whose sentences never quite finish and are left hanging in the air.

Joan Hopkins, Launcelot's indefatigable secretary, whom he must many a time have unconsciously overworked, tells of the stream of people who poured through the outer room in which she worked into his inner sitting room. Boat Club officials, knowing that Launcelot never interfered in Club politics, still came to talk over their problems and departed somehow aware of what they ought to do, although little direct advice had been proffered. Men came with their personal problems and with their good news. Potential Ordinands found their paths clearer and their entry to Westcott House – always Launcelot's first choice for his friends – made easier by his influence. One man, proud of his atheism, ended as a priest, thanks to Launcelot. "He never strove to win an argument," this man wrote. "He would listen and appreciate what *you* had to say. Often I left him in the small hours after a marvellous night of talk and happy that I had made *my* points so well, only to find a day or two later that somehow mysteriously I had come round to agreeing with him. This method of winning an argument by allowing himself to be defeated was not guile on his part. I think it was his genuine interest in the person he was dealing with that was so winning – plus, of course, his intelligence!"

However it was not only the solving of personal problems which brought men to Launcelot's rooms. It was the sheer fun of an evening with him and one's friends, the gossip over endless cups of tea, the companionship of healthily relaxed young men which remains in the memory of so many old Hall men. The man who

could listen with sympathy and understanding to a friend's worries
and difficulties also had a bubbling sense of fun and a delightfully
dotty sense of humour. The evenings were not always wholly
devoted to talk. On occasions his rooms would be packed to
suffocation for informal music. His enjoyment of music, which he
inherited from his mother, was genuine though never profound. On
one of these evenings the grunts and heavy breathing of an
unaccompanied violinist, struggling to perform in the confined
space, were more memorable than the music. While the evenings
were the time when most men dropped in on Launcelot, he
regularly invited undergraduates to breakfast, though at this hour of
the day his guests had to accept his greater interest in his
correspondence than in them.

Much of this devotion to the needs of undergraduates is not
peculiar to Launcelot. Any good College Chaplain does the same,
though perhaps few can have devoted such a high proportion of
every twenty-four hours to them. What is remarkable about
Launcelot is his continuing hold on those who have once come
under his spell and had become friends for life. They were never
able to cease from making demands on him. Old Hall men did not
fell properly married unless he performed or at least assisted at the
ceremony. One claims that his was the first marriage service which
Launcelot ever conducted and that one of his preliminary tasks as a
bridgegroom was to make Launcelot presentable by hiring a frock
coat for him. As the years went by requests to act as godfather were
difficult to refuse and weddings of his friends' children were a new
delight. Undergraduates who had been led to Ordination continued
to share their hopes and problems with him. Testimonials for
aspiring headmasters were readily forthcoming, and Governing
Bodies soon became familiar with the heavily corrected typescript
and with Launcelot's difficulty in hinting that the candidate might
not be quite perfect.

His correspondence became increasingly heavy as each year the
number of his friends grew and his interests widened. Joan Hopkins
struggled to keep abreast of the work showered upon her by an
employer who must be the worst dictator of a letter known to any

secretary. This inability to express himself clearly at the start is largely due to his being a perfectionist and to his scientific training: the word used must be exactly right. Because he worked to hard himself he never realised that he could be a very demanding employer, quite unconscious that the burden of work was unreasonable. Many a secretary came to know well the moment when a beautifully typed letter awaiting signature came back with so many corrections that it had to be typed again.

When a friend was in serious trouble Launcelot did not wait for the cry for help. At the time that he was Dean of Windsor a Hall man of this period was forced to serve a short term of imprisonment. Unknown to this man, Launcelot at the time of the trial had written to his Counsel testifying to the accused's good character. When this failed a series of moving and encouraging letters enabled the prisoner to surmount the experience without bitterness or self-pity and to emerge from his ordeal strengthened rather than broken. It was typical of Launcelot to have told this friend how much he himself had learned from the letters written from prison and that henceforth the intercessions at St. George's Chapel would contain one 'for those awaiting trial'.

Nobody welcomed Launcelot back from the Antarctic more enthusiastically than members of the Trinity Hall Boat Club. As an undergraduate member of the club he had been a valuable oar but he was too light to aspire to a place in a university crew. While he was at Westcott House he had begun to coach Hall boats and when he became a Fellow he normally coached two boats a day, relying on Bruce's Principles. On his return to Cambridge in 1937 he was down at the river on most afternoons. He was soon in the first flight of College coaches and had he had unlimited time to spare he might have helped to coach successful university crews. This he was to do in the post-war years. His success as a coach lay mainly in his ability to get people to do what he wanted them to do – a skill not confined to the river – and in having a clear picture of what he was trying to achieve.

Another reason for his success as a coach was that he continued to row actively when he was in residence. He was not a member of any

racing or representative crews; he rowed for pleasure and to keep
himself fit. Former members of the Boat Club revisiting the Hall
were pressed to go out with him in a pair, and one who had formerly
been a 'Blue' remembers how hard pressed he was to keep up with
Launcelot's energy. The cox of a university Trial Boat recalls seeing
a pair ahead, seemingly oblivious to two polite requests to move
aside. 'Get out of the way, you bloody fools,' cried the cox in
desperation. The pair shot into the bank with a charming apology,
but the cox has never forgotten his embarrassment at swearing at
the Dean of Trinity Hall.

Launcelot in a high-necked pullover and grubby flannel trousers
was a familiar sight on the tow path. Here he preferred to run rather
than to ride a bicycle. As a result he developed a keen sense of how
fast a boat was moving: if he could not keep up the boat was fast and
going well. His incompetence with a stop watch – as with other
pieces of mechanism – became notorious. He first appears in the
records as a coach with the successful Second Lent Boat of 1933 and
the May Boat of that same year. Thereafter there can be few Hall
oarsmen between 1937 and 1960 who were not coached by him at
one time or another; for whilst he was at Portsmouth diocesan duties
never completely prevented him from lending a helping hand with
novices or with experienced crews. The years when he ran shouting
along the banks of the river Cam, with occasionally a surprising
strength of language, were the years when the fortunes of Trinity
Hall Boat Club were at their zenith.

There was one inevitable casualty as a result of this life totally
devoted to the College – his scientific work in Graham Land.
Launcelot had returned laden with geological specimens and with
piles of notes, but unfortunately there simply was not the time
available to arrange for the specimens to be thin-sectioned and
studied in detail nor for papers to be written for scientific journals. It
was only possible to write a paper for the Royal Geographical
Society describing his work in the Antarctic in general terms. He
was absolutely certain that after three years absence his first priority
was his work as Chaplain. Accordingly his specimens were handed

over to other geologists and in the course of time some of his tentative theories about Graham Land and Antarctica were superseded by the work of Sir Vivian Fuchs. An unofficial suggestion that he should lecture for the Department of Geology had to be refused through fear that the work involved would prejudice his availability as Chaplain. The most that he felt it right to undertake was the supervising of men reading for the Geology Tripos. There was never any lingering doubt that his calling was that of a priest and not of a scientist.

Life in these pre-war days was gloriously full and rewarding. Like so many busy men Launcelot somehow found time for additional activities. Early in 1934 he had become a member of the Conference of Schoolmasters and College Tutors, familiarly known as Dons and Beaks, and in 1939 he took on the work of Secretary to the Conference, a position which apart from the war years he held until 1949. The Conference had been started towards the end of the previous century as a silent retreat for dons and schoolmasters. Possibly because its membership consisted of compulsive talkers the imposition of silence was relaxed. There was a period when those who wished to be silent wore a white badge and were not disturbed by their more vocal colleagues. Legend has it that the last man to wear the badge was Lionel Ford, headmaster of Repton. However the Committee eventually ruled that the noise which he made while drinking his soup was tantamount to speech and the Conference finally ceased to be a silent weekend. The meetings were held alternately in an Oxford or Cambridge college and the weekend programme consisted of the discussion of some educational topic followed by three devotional addresses, usually delivered by a well-known divine.

Membership had to be restricted to a number likely to fit into the usually rather small College Chapels. College Chaplains and a few dons represented the university side, while public school headmasters and some of their religiously-minded assistant masters were the 'Beaks'. It was, until recently when it came to an end, a Conference which aimed at being intellectually stimulating and spiritually refreshing, and both Dons and Beaks valued an invitation to belong to a very friendly body. The Secretary's task as the annual meeting approached was onerous. In January 1939 Launcelot wrote home to his mother: "I am now in the throes of making arrangements for the Conference. I have come to the conclusion that if I could impose two forms of asceticism, one, that they should go without any food, two, that they should say their prayers outside in the snow, then I should be a roaring success as the Secretary. But unfortunately the modern educators are not quite so Spartan."

In April 1953 Launcelot, then Bishop of Portsmouth, was invited to give the three devotional addresses at Dons and Beaks. He chose to interpret the Christian vocation of the don or schoolmaster within the context of Our Lord's prayer of dedication: 'For their sakes I sanctify myself'. This personal sanctification on behalf of schoolboy or undergraduate can come, he believed, through the cultivation of three great qualities – humility, courage and compassion. The addresses made a deep impression when delivered and at the request of the Conference were subsequently printed.

Dons and Beaks was far from being the sole commitment undertaken by Launcelot outside his College life. In August 1938 he ran a camp in Glamorgan for a hundred unemployed men. In the following year he was much involved as Chaplain with a camp run for members of newly formed boys' clubs in South Wales. The chief camp officer was David Carnoch-Taylor, a third year undergraduate at the Hall, and his assistants were all third year Hall men. Some unemployed men helped to pitch the camp on a beautiful site on the Gower peninsula. Launcelot's most vivid memory of that camp is of the first night. "As the camp was not quite ready the boys were encouraged to go out after supper. They arrived back for prayers and cocoa. I was presented with a novel problem as it became evident when prayers were started that a large proportion of the boys were drunk. Their singing was magnificent but the prayers were shortened in the attempt to bring the proceedings to some sort of orderly conclusion. That night it was decided that any tent making a noise in the middle of the night should be turned out to double barefoot round the field where the tents were pitched – the field being conveniently provided with a good many nettles and thistles. I can remember as late as 3.30 a.m. hearing the thud of feet and an occasional 'Don't cut the corners'."

Despite this somewhat untoward start the camp was a tremendous success. "A film was made on the sand dunes in which all the staff and boys were involved. The scene was set in a Pacific Island where a British colony was attacked by a neighbouring tribe in order to run off with the Governor's daughter. She was, of course, saved by the A.D.C. whom she later married. The fighting scenes in the dunes were enthusiastically acted, with bracken stalks being used as weapons. The film was shown during the following winter to the Clubs, with parents invited."

His work as Dean and Chaplain gave Launcelot a sense of complete fulfilment. He could not have asked for work bringing greater happiness. It was a joy to his father and mother to visit Cambridge and to catch such glimpses of their son as his busy life afforded. They became great friends of the Master, who shared Eleanor's love of gardening. Vacations were by no means free from work but there was usually time to go north to Innerhadden with a party of undergraduates and with the faithful Langley and one of the College chefs in tow. One such young man has a vivid memory of his week at Kinloch Rannoch: "If Launcelot personally was an eye-opener to my young atheist soul, Innerhadden was a revelation to my young Socialist one. There in Doctor Fleming was an old-style landowner whose household came in for morning prayers before the munificent breakfast; there was a small scale feudal system where everyone 'knew their place' but all were respected and it enchanted me. Mrs. Fleming simply bowled me over! Launcelot took us for an incredible walk one day from Innerhadden: up over the hills, down into Glen Lyon, up to the summit of Ben Lawers, and all the way back again. Total 33 miles across country, including 10,000 feet of total climb. His physical stamina was colossal."

In 1939 the shadow of the coming war could no longer be disregarded by even the most carefree young man. A great number of Hall men turned to Launcelot to discuss where their duty lay if war should come. There was much talk of pacificism in the air of Cambridge at the time though of those who consulted Launcelot very few became conscientious objectors. Nearly all who did refuse to fight named Launcelot as one who was willing to testify to their sincerity. For him personally the problem could not arise for by his calling he was debarred from combatant service. The question which he had to answer was where he could best serve. By 1940 it was clear that the handful of undergraduates left in Trinity Hall could not justify his remaining as Chaplain beyond the end of the academic year.

At the time of Dunkirk and the threatened invasion the Governing Body decided that it would be wise to disperse the College silver. The Founder's Cup was sent to Canada and Launcelot was deputed, with two strong undergraduates as his escort, to take six large tin boxes full of silver to a bank in Helston. They were seen off at Cambridge station by Charles Crawley and Robin Hayes and hoped that they would be undisturbed in their first class carriage. "Just before the train left two thuggish blokes got into the carriage. They used some of the tin boxes as a card table. I think we expected the silver to rattle at such an indignity. Our companions were bookmakers from Newmarket. I believe that the place selected for the safe keeping of the silver was a part of the coast which the Nazis had chosen for their invasion of England!"

About three days later Launcelot looked out of the window of his room one evening to see the grass in the First Court covered with exhausted soldiers, sound asleep with their rifles and packs beside them. It was time to make his choice about which of the three Services he wished to join as a Chaplain. The Navy had always appealed to him for two reasons. He liked what he had learned about the tradition of the naval padres and the absence of any badges of rank. There was also a natural bias towards the Navy in his immediate family for both his brother, Archie, and his brother-in-law, Daniel de Pass, were naval officers. It was the most difficult Service to enter for it was the smallest of the three and much sought after by young priests. His interview with the Chaplain of the Fleet, Archdeacon Crick, went off better than he feared and he was surprised to be asked: 'What ship would you like?' 'Well, sir,' Launcelot replied, 'I've always associated the Navy with the sea'. Crick remembered this when after a brief period ashore he sent Launcelot to sea.

Chapter 8

'A FRIEND OF ALL ON BOARD'

1940 – 1946

On the 9th of July 1940 Launcelot arrived at the Royal Naval Barracks in Portsmouth with a document in his pocket appointing him "Probationary Temporary Chaplain, R.N.V.R., additional to the Royal Naval Barracks, Portsmouth, additional". As he later wrote: "I felt in much the same frame of mind as when I had left home at the age of nine to spend my first term in a boarding school. The words of my appointment, and especially the insistence on my apparent superfluity, did nothing to alleviate the mood. When I got out of the taxi at Portsmouth and walked into the Officers' Mess, wearing ordinary civilian clothes with a clerical collar, the sentry at the gates presented arms with a smartness that seemed far more appropriate to an Admiral than to a very additional Chaplain. Anyway it took me completely off my guard and I was so embarrassed that, instead of acknowledging the salute, I pretended to study the plain brickwork on the opposite gateway." However his morale was restored when he found two former Trinity Hall men as fellow Chaplains in the Barracks.

After a week's indoctrination at Portsmouth, Launcelot took up his first appointment as Chaplain of H.M.S. *King Alfred,* the R.N.V.R. Officers' training establishment on the sea front at Hove. Today the building has become a sports centre but it still bears the name of the King who has some right to be regarded as the founder of the Royal Navy. Launcelot arrived less than a month after the evacuation of British and French troops from the Dunkirk beaches when the country awaited Hitler's threatened invasion. He was the first full-time Chaplain in the establishment. All R.N.V.R. officers had to undergo a short course here at the start of their naval service,

which involved turning them as quickly as possible into men able to
take charge of a small ship. Some found themselves taking
command at the tender age of nineteen, shouldering a heavy
responsibility but finding every chance of exercising personal
initiative and leadership. The atmosphere at *King Alfred* was one of
great seriousness of purpose, mixed with the high spirits of a
preparatory school. There were even occasional pillow fights at
night. To the great delight and amusement of the Chief Petty
Officers Launcelot went through the course himself.

Within twelve hours of his arrival Launcelot was shown the room
which the Commanding Officer thought might be suitable for a
Chapel. "Two days later at lunch time, when the notices are given
out, I asked if there were any who would help in planning its
decoration. I went up to my cabin after lunch and waited rather
nervously for the response. Presently there was a knock on the door,
which was followed by others, until there were squashed into my
small room three architects, three interior decorators, two artists
and one churchwarden . . . An appeal for the £120 required to meet
the cost of the furniture was very soon over-subscribed." Stanley
Bate, the architect chosen for the work, was later to design two other
naval Chapels and a new Chapel for Bishopswood, the official home
of the Bishops of Portsmouth.

So from the start of his first appointment Launcelot learned of the
importance which the Royal Navy has for so long attached to the
Christian religion. In the reign of Charles II, when Samuel Pepys
was Secretary to the Navy, the Articles of War had been framed and
the very first Article of all enjoined the worship of God in all ships
and the observance of Sunday throughout the Fleet. The same
insistence was enshrined in the King's Regulations and Admiralty
Instructions. Before any mention of the duties of a sailor and the
discipline imposed by the Admiralty, the requirement is laid upon
the Captain of each ship to take care that Divine Service is
performed each Sunday and to see that the Chaplain is treated with
the respect due to his sacred office. Further, the Chaplain should not
be required to do any executive work so that "nothing may interfere
with his being regarded as a friend and adviser by all on board." An

Admiralty Fleet order of November 1940, posted on the noticeboard of every ship, stressed once again the importance which Their Lordships attached to the practice of the Christian religion, even though under war conditions it would not always be possible to obey the old Admiralty Instructions about worship to the letter.

"I have just finished taking my first Church Service and giving my first address to the men here: an ordeal which was rather like my first sermon at Trinity Hall," Launcelot wrote home. He found himself very heavily committed. It was a demanding task to minister in any sense personally to a training establishment in which the turnover was "devastatingly rapid". Because he believed that ministering to the needs of the men was useless if it were not, as far as possible, personal, he "asked if I could give a lecture period to each new class in the first week's routine, and my request has been granted. One needs some means of getting to see everyone soon after their arrival." By the end of his five months at *King Alfred* he had come to know about fifty per cent of all the R.N.V.R. officers in the Royal Navy, but he found it "something of a problem to remain decently sober when invited to attend three passing-out parties each week". One task he took on but shared with the Liaison Officer was the editorship of the establishment's magazine. This proved more difficult than he expected for with the start of the bombing of London the printers "had neither electric light, gas, nor water and that has set us back a lot". As with his sermons, his own magazine contributions were sometimes submitted to his mother for her trenchant but constructive criticism before they were printed. In additon to his very full time job at *King Alfred* he preached from time to time in local churches.

The Chaplain of the Fleet had not forgotten Launcelot's belief that the Navy was connected with the sea. In November 1940, to his great delight, he was appointed Chaplain of the battleship H.M.S. *Queen Elizabeth*. She had been laid down in Portsmouth Dockyard on Trafalgar Day 1912, launched a year later and was ready for service in the Dardanelles operation in 1915. She had ended the First World War as the flagship of the Commander-in-Chief. When war was declared in 1939 she was undergoing an extensive refit at

Portsmouth and Launcelot visited her there after a brief leave, partly spent in his old rooms at Trinity Hall where "almost the entire 2nd and 3rd year left there came in to see me". He found the ship occupied more by dockyard mateys than by matelots and he had to pick his way over piles of "rubber tubing, compressed air drills, rivet hammers, red lead paint and a great deal of unavoidable rubbish".

Once again the priority accorded to the Christian religion in the Royal Navy was shown by the fact that the Chapel was the first place to be completed and in normal use. Stanley Bate has again been invited by Launcelot to design it. The Chapel held forty men and could be extended to take double that number. Many of the furnishings were a gift from former members of Trinity Hall. The Commander had chosen a cabin for the Chaplain within easy reach of the mess decks, and being a "named cabin" he could not be asked to make way for some senior officer. This "parson's freehold" Launcelot named "The Vicarage" on the cabin door. It was the to find that the right colour tone was "Celestial Blue", which he thought most fitting for the padre's cabin.

The refit was expected to be complete in about six months. Suddenly Captain Claude Barry was told by the Admiralty that Intelligence believed that the German Luftwaffe intended to launch a massive air attack on the ship in retaliation for the Fleet Air Arm attack on the Italian battle fleet at Taranto during the night of November 11th/12th. He was asked to report how quickly the *Queen Elizabeth* could put to sea and make for a Scottish harbour if a full crew were provided. Forty hours later, amid scenes of indescribable chaos, she sailed for Rosyth where the refit was completed.

When a new Chaplain arrives in a ship or at a shore establishment sailors will assume that he is a good man. This comes partly from politeness, partly from the belief that goodness goes with the job. However, it will take some time before the sailors give him their full confidence. Launcelot thinks that his first month in the *Queen Elizabeth* was the difficult period in his whole ministry. Never before had he been closely concerned with the welfare of men from a social background different from his own. Whenever he entered a mess deck there would be total silence; the moment that he left normal conversation would be resumed. Confidence is a plant of slow growth and there was much suspicion to break down. Sailors, like other people, do not immediately feel at ease in the presence of a parson whose "dog collar" is a very real barrier. Although a naval Chaplain holds no rank there is often a suspicion that he may be a spy from the wardroom. After a month, for no reason which he can give, Launcelot suddenly found that the sailors accepted him; an acceptance which, he thinks, might never have come about had he made a serious mistake, probably quite unwittingly, during those first cirtical weeks of testing.

Launcelot found his path eased both by the strong support given him by the *Queen Elizabeth's* Captain, Claude Barry, and Commander, Renfrew Gotto, and by the position which the Royal Navy accords its Chaplains. In the naval hierarchy a Chaplain's status is defined as being "superior and inferior to no one and a friend of all on board". He was thankful at not being compelled to wear the uniform designed for Chaplains as "the ensemble makes one look rather like a cross between an undertaker and a yachtsman and anyway I don't see why a person should masquerade as a sailor when he's not actually doing a sailor's job." He preferred to wander round the ship in a flannel suit and "a crushed and well-worn soft hat" (which became a vivid memory among the sailors) even in the heat of battle. The hat was essential for the acknowledgement of salutes. It was a great help to be the one man allowed to go to any part of the ship, and since shared danger makes for comradeship his task was in some ways easier than a Chaplain's task in the post-war years. Although he had many doubts about the wisdom of Church parades, which were then compulsory, they gave the Chaplain an obvious job in the eyes of the sailors.

At Rosyth everyone worked hard to get the *Queen Elizabeth* ready for active service. Many of the ship's company were unable to go on Christmas leave, so Launcelot agreed to run a dance for them, which would also help to raise money for ship's comforts. His chief problem was to find sufficient girls. There were only two main sources of supply, "Wrens" and "Waafs" stationed in Rosyth and girls working in the local Co-operative store. On the sound principle that it would be wise to have fewer girls than men so that no girl would be left sitting out, he managed to ensure that sufficient partners would be available on the night. The evening was disaster. The men were either too shy to dance or preferred to drink at the bar, with the result that the walls of the hall were lined with girls forlornly waiting to be asked to dance. In the middle of this very sticky party a crowd of drunken sailors from H.M.S. *Hood* tried to gate-crash the dance. The Royal Marine sentries guarding the door bravely prevented them from entering but the police and even the Chief Constable were needed to quell the riot in which some damage was done. 'Who is in charge here?', demanded the Chief Constable. Launcelot, emboldened by anger at the whole miserable evening, retorted, 'I am, and the sooner you take your drunken citizens away the better!' Next day, in some trepidation, he called on the Senior Wren to apologise for the failure of the dance. His apology was graciously accepted and he was rewarded with a drink. The ship's comforts fund gained nothing as all profits were swallowed up in paying compensation for damage done during the fracas. However the sailors all assured Launcelot that it had been a wonderful party. Fortunately the *Queen Elizabeth* soon sailed for Scapa Flow and her final trials.

Here another incident occurred which might have been much more disastrous but which ended by endearing the Chaplain to the whole ship's company. One evening during the last dog watch the men were listening to a B.B.C. programme relayed over the ship's public address system. Suddenly the broadcast stopped and in its place came the sound of church bells. At that time church bells had only one meaning: Hitler's invasion had begun. Many of the men came from the Portsmouth area and their immediate thought was for the safety of wives and relations as Nazi troops landed on the south coast. The sound of bells ceased as abruptly as it had started and was replaced by the voice of an abjectly apologetic Launcelot. He explained that he had just got hold of a record of church bells

which he thought was the ideal way of informing everyone that a
Service was shortly to be held in the ship's Chapel. He confessed
that he had totally forgotten that the ringing of church bells was
strictly forbidden except as a signal of invasion. As one man later
wrote, "the incident proved that he was at least human and capable
of making a bloomer as well as anybody else and having the guts to
admit it so apologetically." Captain Barry laughingly accepted
Launcelot's personal apology, and added, 'You know, if it had been
me I think I would have suspected that I was destined for the high
jump!'

Once at sea Launcelot's life became infinitely varied. Although
the Navy demands nothing of its Chaplains outside their formal
religious duties, he was determined to seize every chance of getting
to know his parishioners personally and to meet their needs. The
ship's company quickly became accustomed to seeing their
Chaplain in his civilian clothes wandering about in every part of the
ship. Every day he visited the sick bay and on one occasion he talked
for three hours at the bedside of a frightened young man who was
about to undergo an operation for acute appendicitis, staying with
him until the surgeon was ready. Each day he saw a number of Boy
Seamen individually in his cabin. Commander Gotto always kept
him informed about serious defaulters and every day he visited them
in the cells. His chief memory of the "criminals" is of a stoker who
had a passion for drink and who, when temptation was put beyond
his reach, was reduced to drinking Brasso which has a minute
alcohol content.

Launcelot's cabin was also visited by a stream of men wanting
help in every conceivable situation. One wanted an argument
settled which involved the ultimate disposal of several tots of rum.
A tongue-tied stoker eventually confessed to his bachelor Chaplain
that he did not know how to propose to his girl friend. Launcelot
agreed to draft a letter which the stoker would then put into his own
words. The letter was sent off unaltered and Launcelot's fame as a
matrimonial expert grew. Another man came to discuss with his
Church of England Chaplain the best way of joining the Roman
Catholic Church. At any time of the day he had to be ready to listen

to domestic tragedies – a wife had died, a girl friend had gone off with another man, a child was in trouble with the police. Often little could actually be done but it was a help for a man in distress to share his trouble with a compassionate listener. For some young men, coming from sheltered homes, life on the lower deck was often difficult, and Launcelot's cabin provided sanctuary from monotonous conversation and continual swearing. Launcelot sympathised with these young men's dislike of bad language. Once when hard at work in his cabin he was driven beyond endurance by a flow of obscene talk outside his door. 'For mercy's sake say "bloody",' he demanded. Within his cabin were books to borrow or gramophone records to play, or men could just sit quietly and chat. A mother of one of these young men wrote of her gratitude: "He made such an impression on my son that he wrote to him regularly after he left the ship until he was killed in action in 1944 and his letters were always answered."

A retired naval commander, who joined the *Queen Elizabeth* just before his nineteenth birthday, has written of his personal debt to Launcelot. "He could 'read' people from lofty Captain to humble Boy Seamen and he 'read' me. He saw where someone needed an encouraging word, where a rebuke, where a sympathetic ear. He knew instinctively when to be just a good reliable friend in a secular sense and when to be a priest. His touch was as sure as his energy was ferocious." This young man had not taken to Launcelot on first meeting but quickly found that his judgement was mistaken, for two months after their first meeting Launcelot "nudged" him into being baptised and later confirmed. This was no rare example of Launcelot's understanding of his calling. He was quite clear that he was not in the ship as "welfare worker, entertainments or sports officer, or as a liaison between officers and men, or as a means to bolster up morale"; he was there as a priest. Thus he was pleased that so many came to the voluntary Services in the Chapel and that even more appreciated the parade Services, men who would have been shy of attending had the Services been voluntary.

Launcelot always needed exercise and luckily there was no difficulty in getting as much as he wanted. "This afternoon," he told his parents, "I played deck hockey and then refereed a match and after that did P.T. with the younger officers and midshipmen and feel much better for it." His energy has always appeared to be inexhaustible. One encouraging sign of his acceptance by at least part of the ship's company was the invitation issued to him early in 1941 by the Warrant Officers to become an honorary member of their Mess. This enabled him "to have a meal with them without special invitation, as I do in the Gunroom". At about the same time Their Lordships decided that he was no longer on probation or "additional" but had earned the rank of Temporary Chaplain in the R.N.V.R. So he could write home: "Somehow these last few days I have felt that my job has been going better – why or in what way it would be hard to explain – but it has been encouraging, for this life is a singularly strange one and the job in one sense is rather lonely, though I am lucky in having some good friends on board." When his mother learned that Captain Barry's second name was Barrington, a family which appeared frequently in her pedigree, she told Launcelot that he was distantly connected to his Captain. "I imagine that you have a 62nd part of Barrington blood!"

For all who served in the *Queen Elizabeth* during this two and a half years commission it was a time of great activity and frequent danger. After completing her trials at Scapa Flow the ship joined the *Hood* and the *Repulse* in operational sweeps over the North Atlantic in search of the two German pocket battleships *Scharnhorst* and *Gneisenau*, which had escaped from the Baltic and were preying upon Allied shipping before being temporarily bottled up in Brest harbour. The *Queen Elizabeth* then moved south to the warmth of Freetown in West Africa preparatory to joining the Mediterranean Fleet. In the welcome lull before the storm broke Launcelot was able to take parties of Boy Seamen to a beach where they bathed and lay on the sand consuming large quantities of tropical fruits.

The Desert Army in North Africa was desperately in need of tanks and, despite the risks involved, it was decided to run a fast convoy of five large merchant vessels through the Mediterranean to Alexandria rather than to send them on the long haul round the

Cape. The *Queen Elizabeth* and two cruisers were to join what was known as Force H and escort this convoy as far as the Straits of Pantellaria. At the same time Admiral Cunningham's Eastern Mediterranean Fleet would move west to meet the convoy, taking the opportunity to deliver urgently needed supplies of oil to the beleaguered island of Malta and, for good measure, to bomb the Nazi army supply port of Benghazi on the way. Once the operation was over the *Queen Elizabeth* would continue with the convoy to Alexandria and there become part of Admiral Cunningham's fleet.

On the 6th of May "Operation Tiger" began as both fleets moved towards each other. Benghazi was heavily attacked and despite dangerous minefields the oil was safely landed at Malta. Up to this moment Force H had mercifully been protected by an unusual amount of heavy cloud and the two fleets met south of the island. The next day as Admiral Cunningham's fleet moved eastwards back towards Alexandria the weather changed and on a night of flat calm with a full moon, German bombers delivered a powerful attack on the convoy. The tremendous barrage put up by the *Queen Elizabeth's* guns – known as the Loch Ness Monster – together with the guns of the other protecting ships beat off the attack and by the 12th of May the tanks were being safely unloaded at Alexandria. Before the month was out the *Queen Elizabeth* was again in action in the closing stages of the battle of Crete. From the 1st of September, (since H.M.S. *Warspite* had been damaged) she became Admiral Cunningham's flagship in place of the damaged *Warspite*. She was based at Alexandria but was frequently at sea on operational sweeps and protecting convoys.

Memories of Launcelot during the times when the *Queen Elizabeth* was in action are vivid. The spare figure in his grey flannel suit and rather battered trilby hat stood on the bridge and over the "inter-com" broadcast a blow by blow account of the engagement, knowing that a vast proportion of the fifteen hundred men on board could see nothing and that this was an added strain on them. Then he would walk round the ship "with a kind word of encouragement to hard-pressed crewmen, many of whom, like myself [a nineteen-year-old Seaman-Torpedoman] were more than a little frightened and scared of the whole situation." It was at such moments that he became "our padre" and never more than on the 25th of November when H.M.S. *Barham* was sunk.

On the previous day the Commander-in-Chief had sailed from Alexandria with the battleships *Barham* and *Valiant* and eight destroyers to be within call if enemy heavy ships should be used to protect an enemy convoy making for Benghazi and which a lighter British force was intercepting. At about 4.30 p.m. on the 25th of November the *Barham*, immediately astern of the *Queen Elizabeth*, was hit by three torpedos fired from a U-boat. The ship rolled nearly over on her beam ends and her crew could be seen massing on her upturned side. A minute or two later one of her main magazines blew up and the ship became completely hidden in a great cloud of yellowish-black smoke. When it cleared away the *Barham* had disappeared and nothing could be seen but a bubbling, oily patch on the surface of the sea, covered with wreckage and the heads of about four hundred and fifty survivors. The Captain with fifty-five other officers and eight hundred and six men had lost their lives.

This sudden and ghastly disaster affected the men in the *Queen Elizabeth* and other ships profoundly. For those on deck who had witnessed the sight it was an unforgettable experience. Launcelot went to the Captain, who asked Admiral Cunningham for permission to say prayers for the dead and for the whole Fleet over the "inter-com". The Admiral readily gave his assent, provided that Launcelot realised that the prayers might have to be interrupted for urgent signals. Launcelot told the ship's company what he was about to do and he then read a few short prayers. When he went round the ship afterwards he was deeply moved by the number of men who thanked him. Never before had he felt so close to every man in the ship, nor had he ever before experienced a deeper sense of communion in prayer. In the ensuing weeks he got the impression that from this disaster had come a greater stability throughout the whole ship's company.

Less than a month later, on the 19th of December 1941, the *Queen Elizabeth's* turn came. She was seriously damaged in Alexandria harbour by a daring "human torpedo" attack carried out

by an Italian officer and a rating. Three of the boiler rooms were
flooded and it was impossible to raise steam. A hole about forty feet
square had been blown and the ship was completely out of action. A
similar attack on the *Valiant* was even more damaging and the
Eastern Mediterranean Fleet had temporarily lost all its battleships.
It is uncertain whether the enemy was fully aware of the success of
the attack, as every effort was made to give the appearance that life
on board ship was going on quite normally. Nevertheless both ships
presented a vulnerable target for some months until temporary
repairs had been completed.

During this anxious time and whenever before this the *Queen
Elizabeth* had been in harbour Launcelot was indefatigable in
organising ways of keeping up morale. Lectures, a concert party,
innumerable quizzes, darts matches in which he played for the
Warrant Officers, all helped to pass the time. Kim Peacock, an
R.N.V.R. Lieutenant in the ship, had been in civilian life a writer,
actor and producer. He it was who staged the revue, appropriately
entitled "Up Spirits", to which sailors from all the Fleet came. He
also produced a pantomime, "Cinderella Afloat", in which
Launcelot made a brief appearance. "I have only about three lines
to learn, the rest being Egyptian noises. I am supposed to be a gharry
driver demanding backsheesh from the ugly Sisters."

In a circular letter sent to friends towards the end of 1941
Launcelot summed up his impressions of his "parish". "One often
hears it said that a sailor is more religious than men of other callings
– but that is sheer fiction. Sailors are a great deal more sentimental,
especially about home which they see far too seldom, and they are
more superstitious than most other people. A sailor likes to come to
church as a sort of sweet memory of home or to indulge in community singing, without necessarily having any deeper sense of the
worship of God. But he possesses one spiritual asset, too often
squeezed out of people who live softer lives–namely a childlike simplicity; and I now realise why under the patronage of St. Nicholas
you find coupled together 'sailors' and 'children'." Two years later
he came to think that there were certain factors which should help a

sailor to see the need for religion. "The sailor lives closer to and is more dependent on the forces of Nature than most other people. He also lives under conditions where the artificial props of what is called civilised life cannot so effectively disguise his real worth from his own eyes and from those of his shipmates. These two factors are a promising soil for the growth of the seed of God's Word."

A sailor may or may not be naturally more religious than other men; his ignorance of 'the barest outline of what the Christian faith is' disturbed Launcelot. He learned in the Navy, even more than in Graham Land, the urgent need for elementary Christian teaching in simple language. He was worried that so many men and women are genuinely mystified and put off by the language of the Church. In particular he was concerned that the Sacraments appeared to have a pathetically weak hold on the minds of so many actual members of the Church and not just those outside it. In the Navy he found that the emphasis which a parade Service gives to Matins is apt to make Service men regard the Holy Communion as an optional extra. Yet there was one observation which gave him encouragement. "In a training establishment from each draft of new entries class leaders are selected. They are picked for their capacity for responsibility and their soundness of character. Over a considerable period of time it has been noticed that 80% of the men so chosen are practising Christian churchmen."

By May 1942 the *Queen Elizabeth* was pronounced to have been sufficiently repaired to sail by a roundabout route to Norfolk, Virginia, where she could undergo a thorough refit. It was an anxiously slow voyage as the ship still took in water but she arrived safety in harbour early in September. Now that there was no longer any danger from enemy action it promised to be a time when the sailors quickly grew bored and were a nuisance to everyone unless kept occupied and amused. As soon as the ship docked in Norfolk Launcelot went up to New York where he visited the Union Jack Club to discuss ways in which British sailors could be entertained. Then he went on to Yale where he stayed with Mrs. Edward Bliss Reed, widow of the former Director of the Commonwealth Fellows.

She arranged a party at the Country Club to which she invited a number of friends, including some with contacts in Virginia. It was as a direct result of this party that Launcelot set up an organisation through which about a thousand homes gave hospitality to the ship's company of the *Queen Elizabeth* and to a few men from other British ships which had put in to the Norfolk naval base.

The first batch of sailors to be sent to American homes during their leave were all men whom Launcelot knew well and was certain that he could recommend to their hosts. When they returned the news of this scheme spread like wildfire and Launcelot's cabin was invaded by practically every man from the next batch due for leave. Launcelot was worried that among this second batch were men whom he knew to be less reliable. He consulted the First Lieutenant, who brushed aside Launcelot's anxiety when he said, 'Padre, they're the best advertisement we've got.' And he proved to be completely right.

The position was soon reached when in response to a sailor who came to him for an address where he could spend his leave Launcelot could say, 'Do you want to stay with a millionaire and ride his horses? Or do you want to go to Washington or New York? Or do you want to browse in the country? Or where do you want to go?' The organisation of men's leaves meant a very heavy burden of work, especially over Christman and the New Year, but the response of the American hosts was magnificent. Some generous Americans also provided funds which helped to supplement the meagre reserves of a British sailor's pay to meet his travelling expenses. Furthermore scores of letters from hosts and hostesses to Launcelot testify the pleasure which they had gained from these simple acts of kindness. For their part, the men returned to the ship loud in praise of their hosts and full of the wonderful time which they had been given, "except for one solitary case – an old Chief Stoker who loves his glass of beer and was stupidly put with a family who proved to be teetotal and who dragged him off to church for the greater part of his leave."

Christmas Day was no rest day for Launcelot. There were four Services in the morning, followed by hectic telephone calls to fix

Christmas dinners for many who were allowed ashore for a few hours. After lunching in the Wardroom he visited the sailors who were in hospital, taking them presents. On returning to the ship he dealt with a package of two hundred presents for the ship's company given by a local school. Games followed and then an impromptu Carol Service at the men's request. The day ended after two hours of talks on the mess decks. Three days later he wrote home: "I was very much touched tonight. I was asked to go down to the Stokers' mess deck and there solemnly presented with a notecase, a pipe and the most lovely travelling case. I have never been so touched by anything. I believe it is quite against the rules for me to gain a combined present but there it is and I couldn't say 'no'. I feel all the more overwhelmed as they are men whom I respect so strongly and like so much." Shortly afterwards his grateful embarrassment was increased when the Seamen's mess deck gave him a fine wrist watch.

Not only did Launcelot arrange homes to which men could go when on leave but he himself organised a trip for about seventy men to Washington. During the time that they were in the city there was such heavy flooding caused by torrential rain that the men could not get back to the ship and were forced to while away the time on the top floor of the Y.W.C.A. He could also provide entertainment of a different kind. He rashly agreed to wriggle through a 15-inch gun from breach to muzzle, a distance of some fifty feet. He claims that when he was half way through somebody shouted 'Action Stations', which might have led to the insertion of a 15-inch shell into the breach and blowing him out. On this occasion there was no £2 reward.

On the 8th of July 1943 the *Queen Elizabeth* returned to England and the commission ended. Launcelot admitted that he never could have believed that he would have enjoyed his job so much. Captain Barry had left the ship before this and one of his final tasks had been the writing of reports on his officers. On Launcelot's form the various qualities listed had to be assessed by marking out of a possible ten marks. On the principle that no man can be perfect it was always understood that the highest permitted mark was nine. Launcelot was awarded nine marks on every count and the brief comment added: "My idea of a real Christian". Several American hosts had taken the trouble to write personally to his mother telling her about him. The letter from his friend Coleman Jennings, with whom he had stayed in Washington when a Commonwealth Fellow, was especially perceptive: "I really cannot describe to you what an impression he makes on everyone who meets him. From Lord and Lady Halifax down to the seamen on his ship I get the same glowing reactions. There is a particular quality about Launcelot which not only makes people admire him but gives them a sense that he is a man apart." A rather more terse comment was made to Launcelot by Captain Gotto, who had taken Captain Barry's place: 'If they gives the likes of me a fourth stripe for the little I did, you should be an Archbishop!'

In August 1943 Launcelot was appointed Senior Chaplain to H.M.S. *Ganges,* the naval establishment at Shotley near Ipswich. There were four Anglican Chaplains there, together with one Free Church Padre and one Roman Catholic. One of the other three Anglican Chaplains was John Phillips, who became Senior Chaplain when Launcelot left, and who was to follow in his footsteps in dealing with Service Ordination candidates and later succeeded him as Bishop of Portsmouth. At the height of the war there were nearly a hundred officers in the Wardroom and between four and five thousand men under training. This training lasted for just over ten weeks, which meant that each week there were nearly four hundred and fifty men joining and leaving *Ganges.* For many of the officers their time at *Ganges* was something of an anti-climax after having seen action all over the world. For the men under training shore leave was limited and even when granted the nearest town was thirteen miles away and the local bus service very restricted. The Chaplains realised that in the circumstances they had a great opportunity for giving the basic instruction in the Christian faith, which experience had shown them was so much needed. There was a daily celebration of Holy Communion at 6.30 a.m., and for the greater part of the day Launcelot and his colleagues were available to all comers until 10 p.m. On Sundays there was a parade Service once a month, attendance on the other three Sundays being voluntary. A choir was formed for Sunday Evensong drawn from all ranks, with the treble and alto lines entrusted to "Wrens" and nurses from the *Ganges* hospital.

In other ways activities organised to relieve boredom were much on lines which Launcelot had found successful in the *Queen Elizabeth.* Dances (less disastrous than at Rosyth), film shows and a series of lectures entitled "I was there" were popular. Launcelot gave the first of these talks on his Graham Land experiences and was followed by, among others, Lord Mountevens of Scott's last expedition, Noel Odell on Everest, Wing Commander Gibson of Dambusters fame, and the actor Esmond Knight, who had been blinded in the *Bismarck* action. Launcelot also launched out into theatrical management. His productions, of "Sweeny Todd" and a Grand Guignol show toured Suffolk, accompanied by the Royal Marines band, and were a riotous success. Not surprisingly neither Launcelot nor John Phillips could find time to take leave.

It was while he was at *Ganges* that Launcelot was first made aware that after the war he might not be left at Cambridge indefinitely. Late one evening he came into the cabin of an R.N.V.R. officer, a schoolmaster in civilian life, to show him a letter which he had received inviting him to apply for the headmastership of Loretto School where two close connections of his mother had formerly been headmasters. He wanted this man's opinion on whether he would make a good public school headmaster. 'I thought you were married to Cambridge' was all the help he got.

Launcelot's naval service ended officially on the 15th of December 1944 with his appointment as Director of Service Ordination Candidates. A week earlier in one of his circular letters to Trinity Hall men he had written: "I shall in many ways be very sorry indeed to leave the Navy, not least because it gives a Chaplain a wonderful chance to do his job and to set about it as he chooses – and I should have loved to have gone to sea again. Leaving *Ganges* is not so bad as it would have been a year ago, for the place has changed a good deal. Also in some ways a Training Establishment is an exasperating job. You just get to know people and off they go, and it is terribly difficult not to become mechanical when you are saying 'How do you do?' and 'Goodbye' to streams of fellows each week."

The concept of establishing Selection Conferences for Ordinands originated from the minds of Archbishop William Temple and the Bishop of Maidstone, Leslie Owen, whom Temple had appointed as Bishop with responsibility for the Armed Forces. The Central Advisory Council of Training for the Ministry (C.A.C.T.M.), as it was then called, and of which Bishop Owen was chairman, was appointed partly by the two Archbishops, partly by the Church Assembly and partly by the Principals of the Theological Colleges and Theological Faculties of the universities. It was set up to advise the Bishops about Ordination candidates though they are not bound by its recommendations. The Council had two Secretaries. Launcelot was responsible for candidates coming out of the Services after the war and his old friend, Kenneth Carey, who was later to become Principal of Westcott House and Bishop of Edinburgh, looked after the others. Their task was to do the considerable administrative work which the scheme entailed: the organisation and conduct of the Selection Boards, endless correspondence with Bishops and with candidates, and preliminary interviews with great numbers of possible Ordinands. Launcelot inherited from Kenneth Riches, who had become Principal of Cuddesdon Theological College, the names of about three thousand men in all three Services who were contemplating Ordination on release from active service. The headquarters from which all the work was conducted was at 2, Great Peter Street, Westminster. This meant that the secretaries must live in London. They decided to share a flat which, after much searching 'mostly by Carey', they found at 2, Abingdon Court, Kensington, and into which they moved early in January 1945. "The only trouble with the flat," wrote Launcelot, "is that it feels like the catacombs, being in a basement."

At first Launcelot was uneasy at the idea of working in a central Church office and he was apprehensive at the very thought of centralisation when it came to selecting Ordinands. It was all so different from the way in which he had worked as a College Chaplain and in the Navy and the new procedure seemed fraught with possible dangers. However, his experience at C.A.C.T.M. steadily led him to believe that the dangers which he had foreseen were more imaginary than real. He was impressed by the care which Bishops took in the choice of clergy and laymen to sit on the Selection Boards. Even more impressive and vital to him was the spirit which informed the work at Selection Centres both at home and abroad. The aim was to reduce bureaucracy to the bare minimum and "to discover through prayer and study and friendship what God's purpose is for each candidate".

What Launcelot had learned in Graham Land and in the Navy was the comparative unimportance of brands of churchmanship and the evils which could spring from party prejudice. He rejoined that the spirit of the Selection Centres seemed to kill any divisive differences. "If the genuis of the Church of England is her comprehensiveness, then Selection Centres have been truly Anglican, I believe that they have helped many of us to realise that the Catholic, Evangelical and Liberal traditions each embody truths of the Christian Gospel, which are not mutually exclusive but complementary," he wrote on returning to Cambridge in 1946. He was heartened to discover how many of the men whom he interviewed had been led to a sense of Christian vocation through their wartime experiences and the consequent conviction that in the Christian faith lay the only conceivable hope for the world. He was always at pains to impress upon these young men what Ordination involved. "The scandal of the Christian ministry," he told them, "is that it should never ever have seemed to many people to offer an easy life and a secure profession. Nothing could be further from the minds of those who are truly called of God and who know just how much they must be prepared to give. But there are two sides to the equipment of a Christian for his task – his own efforts against overwhelming odds and the strength which he receives from God to see it through."

The two Secretaries worked closely with their Chairman, Bishop Owen. He had a flat in Sloane Square and once a week they would go to Holy Communion in the small Chapel which he had made in the flat, then breakfast with the Bishop and his wife, before holding a staff meeting to discuss current problems. Life at Abingdon Court with Ken Carey was a happy partnership, though Ken used to say that two of Launcelot's habits at times nearly drove him up the wall. The first was Launcelot's virtual inability not to like everyone he met. 'Launcelot! if you say again that you like anyone *enormously* I shall brain you!' The other habit of Launcelot, familiar to all who know him and which he has never lost, is to give the impression that he is listening when really his thoughts are far away. Ken loved to tell how he and Launcelot came back to the flat tired after a long day's work. Ken picked up a postcard which had come for him, glanced at it and then said to Launcelot, 'Isn't it splendid? My niece has just passed her School Certificate.' There was no reply. Ken repeated the good news twice with no reaction from Launcelot, who went off to his bedroom. Later he reappeared, penitent for not having at once shared his friend's pleasure and asking forgiveness for his mind being on one of the men whom he had just been interviewing. 'I'm so glad for you. It's wonderful news that your aunt has had a baby.'

The pressure of work was very heavy but there was always Friday to which to look forward. Coming away from the office or a Selection Conference, accompanied by the unflagging Joan Hopkins, Launcelot would book seats in a first class carriage in the hope of getting it to themselves, and then would dictate remorselessly until the train reached Cambridge. After Hall on summer evenings he would go down to the river to coach the Rugger Boat, "generally doing this on foot to compensate for the immobility of work in a London office". He remained in Cambridge until he caught the early train to London on Monday morning. In this way not only did he get much needed breaks in the routine but he kept up his contacts with the College and thus was fully ready by July 1946 once again to give himself to the Hall and all its members. Indirectly the Hall benefited greatly from his eighteen months as Director of Service Ordinands, for although he struggled hard to be completely impartial, a surprising number of the best candidates found themselves in due course members of the College.

Chapter 9

DEAN AND CHAPLAIN (ii)

1946 – 1949

Launcelot had kept as closely in touch as possible with Trinity Hall during the war years. Friends still in Cambridge sent him the latest news of the College and much of this he passed on to old Hall men in occasional letters. Joan Hopkins dealt loyally with his many requests. "I should be most grateful," a typical letter to her ran, "if you could order from Heffers to be sent to me C. A. Cotton's new book on landscape as developed in the processes of normal erosion; also C. H. Dodd's Commentary on the Epistle to the Romans and J. H. Oldham's *The Church Survey Their Task*. Would you also send me another copy of the Westcott House Book of Compline, which is published by Heffers? Then from my own bookshelves would you please send *Arctic and Antarctic* by Colin Bertram. If my own copy is not there please send a new one from Heffers. In addition I should be most grateful if you could order for me either from Almonds in Cambridge or from Whipples in Exeter four new celluloid dog collars, size 14½ and depth 1¼ inches. The laundry situation here is so bad that I shall have to revert to the celluloid kind which can be quickly washed." Three months later he wrote asking her to deal with the Inspector of Taxes on his behalf and with his bank. He also asked her in the same letter to discover the whereabouts of his radiogram and to "ask Pecks, the chemist, to send a bottle of B82277." Being his secretary was no sinecure. Once he had left the Navy and started working at C.A.C.T.M. it was easy to pick up the threads again when he stayed in College at weekends.

The Cambridge to which he returned to his work as Dean and Chaplain of Trinity Hall in the autumn of 1946 was very different from the Cambridge which he had left in 1940. Men back from the

war were in haste to get their degrees before settling down to earning
their living. Their experiences had made them more mature and
serious-minded than their pre-war predecessors and at Tripos times
they often became over anxious. Among them were a number of the
Ordinands whom Launcelot had carefully earmarked for the
College. The chief difference was that many were married and had
brought their wives to live in lodgings with them in Cambridge.
Launcelot found himself in the unusual position of giving tea parties
for these wives. There was a friendly rivalry between Trinity Hall
and Clare College over the number of baptisms which took place in
each College Chapel. The two Colleges shared the same baptismal
register, namely that of St. Edward's. Although the smaller College
of the two, the Hall won comfortably. With the ending of the war the
normal intake direct from schools or after National Service was
resumed, but for the first year or two older and younger men mixed
well together.

The immediate post-war years were a period when undergraduate
interest in spiritual things was at its summit. The work of the
Chaplain and all for which he stood was readily accepted and,
according to Launcelot, "attendance at Chapel was fantastic". The
election of the Rev. Owen Chadwick to a Fellowship at Trinity Hall
at this time was a wonderful support. Chadwick had expressly stated
that he did not wish to hold any College office so that he could
devote himself as fully as possible to his own research work. In fact
he did eventually agree to be appointed an Assistant Tutor and
ultimately succeeded Launcelot as Dean, with the Rev. Anthony
Tremlett, later Bishop of Dover, as Chaplain. "Owen's
companionship, spiritual insight and sheer goodness meant a
tremendous lot to me," Launcelot has gratefully acknowledged,
"and he had the merit of knowing some theology!" In three golden
years Launcelot's influence throughout the College was at its height.
All his work seemed suddenly to come to fruition. Men in residence
during these years were as well behaved as it was reasonable to
expect and the years of protest, which would have deeply distressed
him, were two decades away. Trinity Hall was preparing to
celebrate its sixth centenary in 1950 and Launcelot was deputed to

plan the arrangements for that great event – convincing proof of his remarkable hold over past and present members.

As in the pre-war years Launcelot threw himself into every College activity. Now with renewed zest and humble thankfulness for having come through the war unscathed he took up his former life with joy and with no thoughts of other work or of leaving Cambridge. What proved to be his final brief period of residence saw some of the Boat Club's greatest successes. He had been elected a member of Leander in 1946 and during the next three years he coached every Hall boat and had the delight of seeing the First Lent Boat in 1948 go Head of the River. This was a personal success for him and led to his being invited to coach the Blue Boat in 1949, having in 1946 coached a university Trial Eight. He had become a very skilled coach and his expertise and untiring energy were rewarded in the outstanding achievements of these years. Not only had he coached the 1948 Lent Boat, but in the previous year he had coached the Boat which came first in the Fairbairn Cup and the Third May Boat of 1948 which went up four places. Life seemed very good.

Outside immediate College activities he resumed the Secretaryship of Dons and Beaks and he was on the committee which planned a Mission to the University. He saw little point in formal meetings between Deans and Chaplains of the various Colleges: each of them had, or ought to have, too much to do to spend time on meetings. This did not preclude a close friendship with Eric Heaton, Dean of Caius, and Charles Moule, Dean of Clare. The three friends felt that they had been so much helped in their work by the support given to them by the Masters of their Colleges that, despite the problems of post-war feeding, a dinner was given in their honour and held in Trinity Hall. Launcelot was also chairman of the Church of England Council in Cambridge, a body with which he was not greatly in sympathy, believing it wrong to have a special organisation designed to run meetings in a university on behalf of one particular denomination. His chief success as its chairman was to get it abolished. Far more valuable for him were the monthly dinners with Charles Raven and two lay Science dons, when after the meal they talked the night through on issues of belief and especially on the problems posed by Science for the Christian. Throughout his entire ministry Launcelot's scientific training and his keen interest in scientific discoveries have informed his theological thinking.

In other ways Cambridge life followed the pattern of the earlier years, but with one important additional activity. Historically Cambridge has been the natural seat of polar learning and it was in Cambridge in 1920 that Frank Debenham set up the Scott Polar Research Institute. The money to build the Institute came from the unexpended portion of the fund raised by the then Lord Mayor of London to ensure that the dependants of Captain Scott and the companions who died with him were not left destitute. Since a substantial sum remained it was decided to build the Institute as a permanent memorial to Scott and his polar expedition. Professor Debenham was its first Director but when he retired in 1946 Launcelot took his place. The work entailed could be covered in the mornings, which left the afternoons free for the river and the evenings available to all who poured into his rooms.

It was a good time to become Director as there was a growing interest in polar exploration after the war and a realisation of its value. Whether or not polar regions have valuable mineral deposits which can be extracted, these areas exercise a great influence on weather conditions, thus affecting agriculture and all trades ultimately dependent upon the climate. As Director Launcelot went over to Paris to discuss the Expéditions Polaires Françaises with Paul Emile Victor and he was closely in touch with Professor Hans Ahlmann, a remarkable man who had started life as an artist but had become a glaciologist and geographer, as well as being Swedish ambassador to Norway at the end of the war. Ahlmann was beginning to plan the first truly international expedition to the Antarctic and he tried to persuade Launcelot to go south once again. However tempted he may have been it was quite impossible to accept as the expedition left soon after Launcelot moved to Portsmouth.

30   Trinity Hall Chapel

31   Trinity Hall.
The Senior Combination Room

32   H.M.S. *Queen Elizabeth*

33   Launcelot emerging from the gun turret, September 1942

34   Launcelot with the Third
      May Boat, 1947

35   Launcelot and Charles Raven

36   Portsmouth Cathedral

37   Bishopswood

38   Running late

"What on earth does the
Bishop of Portsmouth mean
telling people not to judge
youth by appearances?"

39   Launcelot's interest
in Youth

opposite

40   Enthronement in
Norwich Cathedral

over

41   Bishop's House
at Norwich

The three years during which Launcelot directed the affairs of the Scott Polar Research Institute were years of considerable expansion in its activities. This meant the appointment of additional staff and Brian Roberts, who had been on the Graham Land Expedition, was able to work part time at the Institute as well as working in London in the Polar Regions Section of the Foreign Office. He undertook much of the executive work. Dr. Terence Armstrong, the first full-time Research Fellow, and Doris Johnson, the first full-time librarian, were both appointed at this period. To make the work of the Institute more widely known the "Friends of the Polar Institute" was inaugurated and regular lectures on polar exploration, primarily to interest and attract undergraduates, were also established as a regular feature of the Institute's activities. To have the keen support of Sir James Wordie, Professor Debenham and Sir Raymond Priestley ensured that modern research and exploration were not unmindful of the men who had gone to the Arctic and Antarctic in the "heroic" days.

After his own experiences it was natural that Launcelot should serve on the Council of the Royal Geographical Society and on the Falkland Islands Dependencies Scientific Committee. It has been said that once the excitement of polar adventure takes hold of a man it never lets him go. This has been abundantly true of Launcelot's life.

The peace and beauty of Innerhadden and the surrounding hills meant even more to Launcelot after the strain and danger of the war years. His Reading Parties were at once resumed. The aim was to read in the mornings and sometimes in the evenings, and to be out in the afternoon for "longish walks and climbs". It was the perfect way of getting to know well the men who came to the cottage, though when one party had six of its seven members embryo doctors "it takes quite a constitution to survive their shop". What his Scottish home meant to Launcelot was charmingly expressed in a poem written for him in 1945 by his friend Pat Rodger.

I will arise and gang the noo and gang tae Innerhadden,
Aye, I'll gang there as I've often done afore,
For the peace of yon wee howff is like Sheol and Abaddon,
And a muckle burnie whammles past the door.

I will arise and gang the noo and gang tae Kinloch Rannoch
And tak' some doited Sassenachs forbye,
And we'll a' live on Usquebaugh, on haggis and on bannock
And watch the fushes ettlin' for the fly.

When the logs are burnin' brightly we'll ha' crack
          and whigmaleerie
And gang to bed in surplices o' lawn,
And we'll scuttle off to Kirk when we've waxit ower cheery
Wi' the Piscies in the sober Sabbath dawn.

And I will have some peace there frae the battle and the clavers
O' dominies and dons around the port,
And lads that should be skelpit saying "a' releegeon's havers"
When they brawly ken 'tis naethin' o' the sort.

I will arise and gang noo tae the butt of auld Schiehallion,
For it's there amang the heather I'm at hame,
They can keep their Cambridge Colleges and palaces Italian
And I'll gang to Perthshire, thank ye, just the same.

However, it was unlikely that Launcelot would be left to enjoy life in Cambridge for an unlimited length of time. Once out of the Navy he became a possible candidate for a great number of posts. He himself had no wish to look for other work and no man has ever been less of a careerist. His work in the College and at the Polar Institute, together with many outside activities, gave him a sense of complete fulfilment, but several attempts were made to entice him away from Cambridge, most of which caused him great heart-searchings.

It has never been easy for him to make the big decisions, especially in his own career. His mother and his closest friends were always carefully consulted and their usually conflicting advice weighed and pondered. The desire to remain in Cambridge if possible was not due to a selfish wish to prolong an intensely happy existence. This is clear from a letter which he wrote in the autumn of 1947 to Joan Hopkins, in whose judgement he had great faith. "There are tremendously strong claims which bind me to my present work – trying to present the claims of Christianity to the young fellows who come up to Cambridge before launching out into all manner of work in professional and business life – and I believe I can be of much, and sometimes I think perhaps more, help to them as to Ordinands alone. [The reference here is to an invitation to become Principal of Westcott House.] And it seems to me that the future lies in the hands of the educated laymen as much as in those of the clergy, especially at a time when we are a largely non-churchgoing nation. And without I hope taking myself too seriously I do attach peculiar importance from being able to identify myself at this particular period in my present work with young men of scientific training."

Four of his friends had urged him to become Principal of Westcott House and four others had urged him to refuse the offer. The final decision, as always, had to be his. "I have found thinking this matter through," his letter to Joan Hopkins continued, "an extremely humbling experience – the more so for being thought of in connection with a job which, as in my present work, I feel dreadfully inadequate – but it is immeasurably encouraging to realise that God can and evidently does provide gifts of grace – however improbable that should seem in one's own case and I feel enormously grateful and indebted." He eventually refused.

Other offers were made which Launcelot had no difficulty in declining. The Chairman of Glenalmond, whom he had never met, sent him a telegram inviting him to become Warden of the school. He had also earlier been invited to apply for the headmastership of Loretto, with which school he had family connections. Despite his close association with public schools he was probably wise not to

consider a headmastership. Much of the work he would have
enjoyed and there is little doubt that masters and boys would have
responded to his lead. He would, however, have found the quick
decisions, which headmasters have frequently to make, difficult and
it is probable that he would have disliked having to take swift and
firm action with serious misdemeanours. Two other invitations
could be declined on grounds of health. Robert Stopford, later to
become Bishop of London, came to his rooms to try to persuade him
to be his successor as Principal of Achimota College on the Gold
Coast. Whatever he may have felt about this post his inability to live
in a very hot climate ruled this out. Much the same reason made
acceptance of the post of Principal of Fort Hare, the college in South
Africa for black students, impossible. "These things are a little
upsetting," he wrote to his mother in November 1946, "and I am so
terrified of getting swollen headed through being offered jobs
beyond my capacities."

A letter written home a month earlier shows that he had been
offered the Bishopric of Edinburgh. This was a far harder matter on
which to reach the right decision. He would have enjoyed being in
Edinburgh again, but he was sure that as he had been back in
Cambridge for such a comparatively short time it would be wrong to
leave so soon. None of the posts so far offered seemed so compelling
that he must give up the work he loved and for the next two and a
half years, despite suggestions that he should move to other work, he
remained tied to Trinity Hall.

On the 9th of July 1949 Launcelot wrote to his mother: "I have
had a letter this morning from the Prime Minister saying that he
wants to submit my name to the King for the vacant Bishopric of
Portsmouth and already the pros and cons are crowding in. It will be
such a help to me to be able to talk this over with you." He had
found Attlee's letter on his desk when he returned from Henley and
his first reaction was to refuse. Then for the next six weeks he tried
to make up his mind. He went up to Innerhadden to consult his
mother, who for some months had been a widow, and he sought
advice from his closest friends in Cambridge and elsewhere. There is
some evidence that Archbishop Garbett played a big part in the

original offer as he had been staying in Trinity Hall with the Master, who had encouraged the Archbishop to press Launcelot's candidature, although the loss to the College would be great. This time the advice of friends, including "two specially selected undergraduates at the Hall", was all in favour of acceptance. Slowly Launcelot came to believe that here was an offer which he must not refuse. It was a time when many appointments to important offices were being made and it was clear that he would continue to be pressed to fill one of them. The naval connections at Portsmouth were attractive and he realised that his work at Cambridge could not go on unchanged for ever. There must come a time when even he would have to retire from coaching boats. At the same time he was naturally worried that his lack of any parochial experience or knowledge of how a diocese worked were serious handicaps. He feared that the burden of administration would prevent the personal dealings with people which had hitherto always been his way of doing his job.

If the offer had to be made Launcelot must have wished that it could have come a few months later. The Arctic Institute of North America and the Defence Research Board of Canada had invited him as Director of the Polar Institute to visit the places in Arctic Canada where polar research was being carried out. His fare across the Atlantic had been promised by the English Speaking Union and on arrival in Canada he was to be flown to each research centre, also taking Services as circumstances allowed.

Before finally replying to the Prime Minister Launcelot went to see Archbishop Fisher to make certain of his approval. Fisher was able to reassure him on this point and the conversation turned to fixing a date for his Consecration. Launcelot had a faint hope that this might be delayed until after his return from Canada. 'I am afraid that Portsmouth needs a bishop,' was Fisher's firm reply and St. Luke's Day, the 18th of October, was the agreed date. The Canadian invitation had to be declined and Brian Roberts went there in his stead. So on the 18th of July he wrote to Owen Chadwick: "Just a short note to say that I have written to the Prime Minister this morning accepting, very much aware of my deficiencies and of the frightful wrench of leaving here. But in my bones I have felt it to be right."

When the news was eventually announced letters of congratulation and good wishes poured in. Those closest to him realised what loneliness lay immediately ahead. "As I try to pray for you," wrote Brother Denis Marsh from Cerne Abbas, "I feel that you may be called upon to suffer a kind of loneliness which will be new and terribly costly: you will lose much that is infinitely precious in going from Cambridge but I known that it will mean new opportunities for a more generous giving of love and sympathy." His friends also shared his fears that administration would destroy the man they admired. "*Dear* Launcelot," wrote one of them, "*do not* let 'them' turn you aside from the primary function of a Bishop. *Anyone* can administer and there is no need to have episcopacy just for administration." His godfather, William Holland, had no doubt what a Bishop's priority must be. "My regular prayer for Bishops is that, amid all the heavy pressure of business and administration, they may live so deeply and constantly in the sense of God's presence that they may instantly suggest Him to everyone who comes to them – particularly the clergy whose chief need so constantly is spiritual inspiration. Often dry as dust, they are hungry for that – and from whom as from their Bishop? But how deep that Bishop then must dwell."

Two recent Trinity Hall men who were Ordinands at Cuddesdon wrote in rather different vein:

"Dear Launcelot,
   Just two points:
   (1) The Morning Run.
   At what hour and in what vestments are Diocesan Clergy to assemble for this Daily Office? Rendez-vous, Bishop's Palace?

   (2) Diocesan Eight.
   When and where are Diocesan Clergy to assemble for Trial Eights? Rendez-vous Fort Blockhouse? Celibate Clergy for 1950 Ladies Plate? Also please name contractors for Diocesan Polar Research Institute."

A month later Launcelot wrote a circular letter to all past and present members of Trinity Hall. "I knew I should find it a very big wrench to leave the Hall, but I find I am an even more sentimental being than I realised, for it is no exaggeration to say that I have been blissfully happy here . . . I do not believe one could have found, at any College at any time, such a remarkable atmosphere, or such good people as the dons and undergraduates of Trinity Hall. I know I am prejudiced but I don't mind confiding my prejudices to you! . . . I can now say to myself, as I have often said to undergraduates whenever they have felt most nostalgic on going down, that the past is something you always take along with you and you need never lose your friends."

PORTSMOUTH

1949 – 1959

(i) Learning the Job

Towards the end of August 1949 Launcelot, very wisely, went off on a month's walking holiday in the Dolomites. The weather was glorious and for the moment anxieties about what lay ahead could be forgotten. On his return he sent an urgent message to his mother and sister: "Have either of you got a spare button-hook that you could let me have to do up my gaiters?" – a form of ecclesiastical dress which he always disliked and which he used to call his rompers.

On the 13th of October he went to stay at Rogate Rectory near Petersfield with an old friend, Ken Mathews, a very distinguished wartime naval padre, who was to become Launcelot's Honorary Chaplain. Here he made his retreat in preparation for his Consecration. This ceremony took place in Southwark Cathedral on the 18th of October, St. Luke's Day, a very appropriate day for the son of a much beloved physician. Canon Charles Raven in his sermon reminded Launcelot and the two other Bishops who were consecrated at the same time that although the task ahead of them was in human terms impossible, the resources available to help them were infinite. A senior Bishop, who had taken part in the Service, commented afterwards that he had never seen a new Bishop supported by so many or so wide a range of friends.

Launcelot now had a bare three weeks to get his domestic affairs settled before his Enthronement. He needed every moment. On the 1st of November he went to Buckingham Palace in order to do homage to King George VI.

To become a Bishop was then very costly. There were legal fees to be met and a Bishop was then expected to accept – and pay for – an

honorary Lambeth Doctorate of Divinity bestowed by the reigning
Archbishop of Canterbury. For Launcelot this meant an Oxford
hood, which he liked to say slightly rankled. In addition a Bishop's
formal wardrobe is expensive and Launcelot had never been one to
hanker after purple and fine linen. When forced to wear his full
evening dress he said that he felt like a conjuror about to produce a
rabbit from the tail pocket of his coat. A generous cheque from his
mother had gone towards his pectoral cross and ring. His crosier was
a genuine shepherd's crook from Scotland, made for him by Roddy
MacLean's father-in-law. He also had to face the cost and burden of
furnishing a large official house after being accustomed to living in a
set of College rooms. Fortunately he was not devoid of private
means, but his bank balance was not inexhaustible and in his early
years at Portsmouth it was by no means easy to manage on the
modest stipend which a Bishop then received.

Bishopswood, Launcelot's new home at Fareham, is a very
attractive long, two-storeyed building with a thatched roof. It had
once belonged to one of Nelson's captains but had been
considerably enlarged since then. On the ground floor is the fine
drawing-room, admirable for parties but not a room in which two or
three people could sit cosily on a winter's evening. The study,
though facing north and east, is much more comfortable, and close
by there is a charming small oval dining-room. Upstairs are eight
bedrooms, sufficient for a pre-Ordination retreat if the number of
candidates was small. Two much later additions were a very large
and rather gaunt dining hall and the singularly hideous chapel. "It
really is awful," Launcelot told his mother, "but apparently it was
given by someone and although I have heard that the man who
designed it is dead I am not sure about the donor. I am writing to
Bishop Anderson [his predecessor] and have asked him about the
position for I know that he and his family loathed it and it is just a
question of whether I could with impunity redecorate it. I have
already got a scheme for this with the help of Stanley Bate." This in
due course he was able to do. Bishopswood stands in about ten acres
of ground, part garden, part woodland, and is an oasis in the middle
of a heavily built-up area some eight miles from Portsmouth.

Not only had Bishopswood to be furnished but it had to be staffed. This was a totally new experience for a bachelor who had long enjoyed the comforts of College life, where the ordering of meals presented no difficulty and where personal servants were readily available. He inherited a cook and a gardener from the Andersons, but he had to appoint a housekeeper and other domestic help as well as his own personal staff. "I may tell you, Mrs. Fleming," he wrote home, "that all the housekeepers in London, Scotland, Ireland and Wales are clamouring to look after me and I have a good mind to fill all my bedrooms with housekeepers instead of Ordinands! It would be quite a party!"

After a few difficult weeks he appointed a Mr. and Mrs. Adamson, who had been working as butler/valet and housekeeper for the headmaster of Ardingly College. The faithful Joan Hopkins agreed to continue as his secretary for a few months but she did not wish to leave Cambridge permanently. Early in January 1950 Ernle Drax, an admiral's daughter, took over from her and remained with him for all his time in Portsmouth. Launcelot believed that with the growing shortage of clergy it would be better at first not to appoint an ordained man as his Chaplain but to have a lay Personal Assistant. This post was filled by Alastair Gold, who had served for two and a half years as A.D.C. to the Governor of Tasmania and had spent a year at a Theological College after the war, in which he had been badly wounded.

The diocese of Portsmouth had been separated from that of Winchester in 1927 and its population of half a million was spread among 135 parishes served, when Launcelot arrived, by 128 beneficed clergy and some 65 curates. When the diocese was formed it was decided that the ancient parish church of St. Thomas of Canterbury rather than St. Mary's Church, Portsea, a famous training ground for clergy in the centre of the city, should become the Cathedral and be suitably enlarged. This decision was highly controversial but was right. St. Mary's, rather a barn of a building, no longer attracted crowded congregations as in the days when Cyril Garbett was vicar. For people coming from the Isle of Wight or from

Gosport St. Thomas's was more easily reached. Above all the area around St. Thomas's was steeped in history. Down the ancient High Street many English sovereigns had passed on their way to the fleet. At one end of the street was Buckingham House in which Charles I's favourite had been murdered; at the other end was the Sally Port, the gateway in the still standing city walls, through which Catherine of Braganza had arrived for her marriage to Charles II in the nearby Domus Dei Church, a ceremony to which the bridegroom had preferred to send a proxy in his stead. Across the road from the Church was the George Inn in which Nelson had spent his last hours before going on board the *Victory*. High on the cupola surmounting the tower was the golden barque weathercock, a well loved landmark for returning sailors. Although much of Old Portsmouth was destroyed by bombing in the Second World War, the Cathedral had miraculously escaped serious damage.

There was, however, one disadvantage in the choice of St. Thomas's Church as the Cathedral. A small mediaeval parish church with eighteenth century additions and a mock-Norman nave of which only three bays had as yet been built made an awkward building for great occasions. Numbers had always to be rigorously limited and those who found places could often see very little of what was taking place.

The Enthronement Service on the 9th of November was a magnificent occasion. One advantage of Portsmouth being the smallest diocese was that in the packed Cathedral there was an unmistakable feeling of a family worshipping together in welcome to their new Father in God. The fifteen members of the Bishop's Company, supporting Launcelot in the procession, represented clergy and laity in the diocese and also reflected the various stages of his career. Among the latter were the Head Master of Rugby, the Master of Trinity Hall, the former Captain of the *Queen Elizabeth*, Vice-Admiral Sir Claude Barry, Petty Officer Percy Seden, who had previously served in the ship with Launcelot and, proudest of all to be there, Roddy MacLean. In his sermon Launcelot said that hitherto his life had been largely lived among young men in recognisable communities had he reflected on what had given these communities their vitality and zest. It was a spirit which 'was displayed where people were bound together by a purpose or aim which they shared in common and where they were so gripped and held by that aim that they had no time for petty, selfish desires or for the needless anxieties which might otherwise assail them'. Such a spirit should bind the diocese together.

When the Service and the subsequent official tea party were over, Launcelot returned to Bishopswood to relax over beer and buns with a body of Cambridge friends, mostly undergraduates, who had come to support their former Dean and Chaplain.

Early next morning Launcelot rang up Ted Roberts, then Archdeacon of the Isle of Wight: 'Ted, I have been hearing a lot about parochial councils. What exactly are they?' Given his previous experience it was not surprising that Launcelot's ignorance of diocesan and parochial affairs was virtually flawless. No Bishop can ever have begun his episcopal task with less idea of what was expected of him. This ignorance he made no attempt to disguise and would often refer to his early years in the Portsmouth diocese as the time when he was 'an L-plates Bishop'. Characteristically he was humble and wise enough to learn from anyone ready to help him. Three men were especially helpful: Ted Roberts, as one of the two Archdeacons, to a large extent taught him his job and was invaluable with his administrative and financial ability; Bishop Leonard Kitching, formerly Bishop of the Sudan and now Archdeacon of Portsmouth, was an unassuming and kindly man who could offer quiet and unobtrusive advice; and Canon John Beloe, a Portsmouth incumbent of a High Church parish, whose lively mind and quickly won affection for his new Bishop were greatly appreciated by Launcelot.

The diocese which Launcelot inherited was in good running order. Bishop Anderson had been much loved in Portsmouth, and apart from early experience as Bishop of Croydon had had the unique experience of having served at various times in his career in all three of the Armed Services. Moveover, even if Launcelot knew little about the actual duties of a Bishop, he was quite clear about what he hoped to achieve. His three main aims were to sustain the

family atmosphere of the diocese; to tackle the problems of the new
housing areas which the City Council had not located very cleverly;
and to develop parishes in which recently ordained men could be
well trained.

Inevitably the first year as a Bishop was a great strain. When
Launcelot's appointment was announced some long faces were
pulled among the parochial clergy. They wondered why they were
about to be saddled by a man who had such an unusual
background. It was not surprising that there were considerable
doubts and anxieties about how this young don, scientist, explorer
and naval Chaplain, without any parochial experience whatsoever,
would be able to handle the affairs of parish priests many years his
senior. Some of the more elderly clergy were a little taken aback at
being addressed by their Christian names on first meeting, a habit
much rarer then than it has become now. A few of the older men
grumbled that their new Bishop seemed more at home with curates
than with them. Others said somewhat acidly that it looked as if the
diocese was going to be treated as if it were a pale reflection of
Trinity Hall. It took the more staid men time to accustom
themselves to Launcelot's slightly unorthodox methods of
conducting diocesan business by means of somewhat incoherent
telephone calls or letters with innumerable alterations.

However, early snide remarks and honest doubts were replaced
very quickly by mutual friendship and trust. Launcelot's initial
ignorance of his new work was soon forgiven. He came through the
ordeal of his first Rural Deans' meeting with triumph, as with
transparent honesty and sincerity he showed how eager he was to
work with them – even if at the start he had only the vaguest idea of
what a Rural Dean actually did. It was clear how determined he was
to learn his job and as a senior Rural Dean wrote: "His amazing
knowledge of, and sympathy for, human weaknesses and his
'approachability' very quickly set our minds at rest". Long before he
left the diocese he had gained the full confidence, respect and
affection of all his clergy.

There was a great deal to learn. When he took his first

Confirmation Launcelot confessed to the vicar, John Beloe, that it was only the second such Service which he had ever attended. He did not reveal whether the previous occasion had been his own Confirmation at Rugby. He stayed the night with the Beloes and long after his host and hostess had retired to bed he discussed with Ted Roberts, also a guest, ways in which the Service could have been better conducted. He then proceeded to rehearse the institution of a new incumbent, which was the next hurdle ahead of him.

B. K. Cunningham once affectionately commented to Launcelot: "You know you are rather a liturgical rabbit", which was true if it implied that he could not regard the varying forms of worship followed by parishes to be a matter of the deepest importance. He was very ready to conform to the traditions of each parish when he visited it and he found no difficulty in obeying the warning sent to him by an irreverent Cambridge friend:

"For instance, when going to the Church of St. Ninian,

Whose customs, they say, are distinctly Arminian,

It's well to fulfil the popular hope

That 'rig of the day' will be mitre and cope;

For if one appeared in bands and Chimere

Such loss of prestige would be hard to repair."

Launcelot was temperamentally averse from following any party line within the Church. This led one extremely High Church incumbent to complain to one of Launcelot's Chaplains that the Bishop was 'sexless', meaning that he could not pin Launcelot down to taking sides on the issue of the place of women in the Church's work. On another occasion an Archdeacon criticised an incumbent for not knowing the names of all the accessories at Holy Communion. Launcelot refrained from comment but later confessed to his Chaplain that 'I am not sure that I known them all myself'.

The stress of learning such a many-sided job was aggravated by early tensions within Bishopswood. All save the cook and the gardener were new to the house and with little information to guide

them the staff had to feel their way. Launcelot believed that he was
in firm control of his household, but the genuinely devoted loyalty
of those who worked for him could at times be unconsciously
strained to near breaking point. Alastair Gold was a Personal
Assistant whose critical advice Launcelot valued, but after the
military precision of a Governor's office he found Launcelot's
hand-to-mouth improvisation difficult to accept. Fortunately he
could play squash and tennis and thus ensure that Launcelot had
much-needed exercise and relaxation. Joan Hopkins, who in
Cambridge days had been very much of an informal personal
assistant, now found herself less an adviser and more of a typist. She
did not find the new routine easy. "It is difficult to get any time to
oneself and one is kept on the go . . . The daily post is large and as
the Bishop and I are both new to the job we are perhaps slower than
would usually be the case. For example, unless he has to go to a
meeting he seldom finishes dictating before twelve noon, whereas in
Cambridge he finished by 10.30 or 11.0 at latest." If Launcelot had
to go away "the odds are that before the day is out he will ring up
and dictate letters over the telephone." As Christmas approached
the sending out of a thousand Christmas cards, a great many
addressed incorrectly by volunteers from the Fareham Youth
Centre, tried her patience sorely. When Ernle Drax arrived to take
over at the end of January 1950 she wisely insisted on not living in
the house, knowing that if she were at hand she would never be able
to resist Launcelot's calls for help at any hour.

In 1949 food rationing was still in force and Mrs. Nex, the cook,
and Mrs. Adamson had to use all their blandishments on local
shopkeepers to feed the never ending stream of guests – often young
men with hearty appetites who stayed to supper after working in the
garden. Life in College had made Launcelot quite oblivious of
catering difficulties or that guests meant additional work for his
staff. Yet in early days at Portsmouth his guests ministered to a very
real need, for he missed Cambridge badly and at times was very
lonely. The same irreverent friend at Trinity College, who had given
Launcelot advice about his robes, sensed this inevitable loneliness
when he wrote:

"At first when one joins the Episcopal Bench
It generally comes as a bit of a wrench,
For Fareham with Cambridge one cannot compare,
The ethos is – well, quite different there.
For mornings of Polar research are exchanged
Long sessions with curates from vicars estranged;
And outings to Clayhithe with promising Eights
Give place to attendance at missionary fêtes.
And problems which never appeared very great
Have somewhat increased in importance of late.
. . . .
It's easy to see that there's little affinity
'Twixt this and a life at Corpus or Trinity
                    BUT
Pompey's new Bishop is lucky in this,
For his was a College which no one would miss,
Problems and hardships and slummy conditions,
Difficult people and awkward positions –
Pompey's new Bishop is used to them all
For he was a member of Trinity Hall."

However therapeutic their visits, the guests had to be fed and looked after. It was not easy for the staff when at the very last moment Launcelot would invite two additional guests to a carefully planned dinner party. In due course reserves of food were built up to meet this kind of emergency and from time to time a haunch of venison arrived from Innerhadden to be put into cold storage. Food problems never worried Launcelot for another reason: he has always been a very spare feeder, largely unaware – unless venison or ice cream are put before him – of what he is eating. Furthermore, as Mrs. Adamson said, she could forgive a man anything who brought his guests into the kitchen to thank her and Mrs. Nex personally before they left the house. Despite the difficulties which Launcelot unwittingly caused, a bachelor's household is ideal for a domestic staff. To a very great extent he was in their power. That happy state was to be short lived.

After the death of her husband in 1948, it was clear that Eleanor

Fleming would not be able to remain alone at Innerhadden indefinitely. Now that Launcelot had a home of his own it became possible for him to invite her to share it with him. His sister and her husband lived near at hand and this was an added reason for his mother to pull up her roots and to leave Scotland. With much of her furniture and personal possessions she moved into Bishopswood in February 1950.

In a great many ways his mother's presence in the house was a help to Launcelot. Her health was beginning to fail and it was much easier for him to ensure that she was properly cared for under his own roof than far away in Scotland. She was helpful to him as a hostess and visitors to Bishopswood, greeted by her when Launcelot was engaged, found her gracious and charming. She was a voluble talker and there was no danger of awkward pauses in the conversation. She delighted in the garden in which she worked with her customary skill, and in her Budd, the gardener, met his match. As she grew older her life was more and more centred on Launcelot, whose patience and devotion to her were admired by all who sensed the close ties which bound mother and son together. Her deep love for Launcelot did not, however, prevent forthright expression of her views. She never hesitated to state her disapproval of his actions or words, even in the presence of his diocesan staff. When last thing at night Launcelot would go to her room and, sitting on the edge of her bed, read his latest sermon to her, her comments could be trenchant but always with the intent of being helpful.

If Launcelot was happy to have his mother at Bishopswood his personal and domestic staff were not. Although she made no claim to take charge of the household it was impossible for a woman with as strong a personality as hers, who had ordered her own home with great competence for over half a century, not to point out deficiencies. This increasingly irritated Mrs. Adamson, an equally strong-willed woman. She demanded much personal attention from the staff, not always fully realising that Bishopswood in 1950 could not be run on the same lines as Chester Street or Innerhaddenn. In due course the Adamsons left for another post. What his mother could not tolerate was any suggestion that those serving Launcelot did not come up to her exacting standards of what was his due as Lord Bishop of Portsmouth. Successive Chaplains would for this reason find her formidable until they had proved their worth in untiring devotion to Launcelot. When she was satisfied she gave them her affection and support.

Launcelot was aware of these tensions within his household but they tended to become greater at times when he was away from the diocese. He knew that it was unreasonable to expect his mother with increasing age not to become difficult to live with, and never for a moment did his filial love for his 'dear Mamma' falter.

At the start of his episcopate Launcelot may have had much to learn about some sides of his work, but when it came to the one thing needful – pastoral care for those committed to his charge and for all who came his way – advice was seldom necessary. Concern for others had always mattered to him as it had mattered to his father. To speak of Launcelot's "gift" of friendship might imply that friendship came easily to him. In one sense this was true for he was a naturally friendly person; but his exceptional power of friendship was controlled and disciplined to serve his purposes as a priest. He set himself to see and bring out the good which he believed was in everyone until this became second nature to him. There are very few people whom he has personally disliked even though he might disapprove strongly of their behaviour. Being totally devoid of self-importance he was immediately at ease with all walks of life.

His first concern was for his clergy. He never had any doubt that as their Bishop they had the first claim to his care. On arrival in Portsmouth he was appalled to discover the size of the stipends on which many married clergy had to exist. In his first Presidential Address to the Diocesan Conference in May 1950 – the first such Conference he had ever attended – he spoke of the urgent need to supplement many of the stipends, and thereafter he constantly reminded the laity of their responsibilities towards the clergy in their parish. Almost at once he set up a Special Commission "to advise on the minimum stipend and allowances needed to enable a parson to do his job effectively".

Much of the time at his Staff Meetings was spent on making appointments. He realised that with a parson's freehold once a mistaken appointment had been made it could not easily be put right. He learned through experience that a small parish should not be saddled with a tired incumbent who had been moved in order to bring life to his too demanding larger parish. He took endless trouble to ensure as far as possible that the right man for a parish could afford to accept the post. Fortunately he held the patronage of about two-thirds of the livings and he was grateful to find that private patrons nearly always consulted him.

The initiative for appointing curates lay with the parish priest, but Launcelot with his Cambridge connections and his experience of selecting Ordinands was able to draw a large number of keen young men into the diocese. He strongly urged his incumbents to look for their curates outside the diocese rather than to recruit locally when the diocese was so small. He also encouraged Ordinands who lived in the diocese to seek curacies further afield and not to be ordained on the doorstep of their homes. He was particularly concerned to see that incumbents were not only good parish priests themselves but were also sympathetic and forward-looking trainers of young curates. In addition he arranged that each man serving his first title had an experienced priest outside his parish, chosen by Launcelot himself, to whom he could turn on occasion for further advice and at times when it might have been awkward to consult his own vicar.

Some of the new housing estates presented special problems and Launcelot took immense trouble to find the right man for the parish. Occasionally when the appointment was announced there was muted criticism, but nearly always time proved him right in his choice. There was, however, one habit which he had when making an appointment, which was apt to put the man concerned in an unfairly difficult position. He often used to sound out a man with the question: 'Do you feel drawn towards a new parish?' but without revealing what was in his mind. This approach resulted from his insistence that complete confidentiality was essential until a formal announcement was made. Yet it was a question which was almost impossible and certainly unwise to answer without fuller information or without permission to talk things over with a friend.

Despite his lack of parochial experience Launcelot knew that his clergy would look to him for help and direction. So from time to time a "Bishop's Letter", a confidential document, was sent to each of the clergy suggesting the procedure that should be adopted when dealing with the kind of difficulty a parish priest faced with such things as the re-marriage of divorced persons or the burial of a suicide. On the thorny subject of divorced persons Launcelot had every sympathy with those concerned but he was quite forthright in his defence of the Church's discipline on marriage. As he said to one Diocesan Conference, it might well be that the Church would soon decide to change the rules but meanwhile these were the rules and they should be loyally obeyed.

He also knew how easily an incumbent could become disheartened and stale and how important it was for his clergy to have opportunities of thinking afresh about their work and of renewing their sense of vocation. The Retreat House at Catherington, a few miles north of Portsmouth, provided an ideal setting for post-Ordination courses and courses for older clergy, as well as being a place where a priest could make his retreat. Every year a conference was held for the Isle of Wight clergy, who often felt isolated from the main stream of diocesan life. As time went on courses were arranged at Catherington for small groups of clergy who had similar kinds of tasks. This proved valuable and was an early example of in-service training.

Launcelot greatly enjoyed visiting his clergy in their homes, whether for a sermon or a Confirmation or just a chance call as he was passing. Illness or some domestic or parochial crisis would bring him quickly to see what help he could give. A home, it was said, was somehow a better place after he had visited it. He soon became a friend of the family and was grateful for total lack of formality at a nursery tea. On entering a vicarage garden through a side gate he was once set upon by two small children of the house, dressed as Red Indians, and was only released from captivity in the wigwam on satisfying his captors that he had adequately memorised their war cries. On another occasion he surrendered his recently cleaned shoes to a young Wolf Club anxious to earn his "bob" by cleaning them again. The card was signed, the "bob" paid, and Launcelot was told that he could now go to 'Daddy's Service'. On the occasion of the Oxford and Cambridge Boat Race the line between Bishopswood and certain vicarages would hum with partisan comments on the result.

He was also insistent that his younger clergy should have time for proper recreation and he formed "The Bishop of Portsmouth's Hockey Eleven". The title was carefully chosen, he explained, to enable him to play for the team, whereas he might not have qualified for a "Diocesan Hockey Eleven". He played a vigorous game on the right wing of the forward line, to which side of the field, he said, it was less likely that hard hit balls would be passed to him. Woe betide the incumbent who was not prepared to release his curate from parochial duties on a winter Wednesday or Saturday afternoon! For a curate to score goals was said to be a sure step towards a benefice, even if he had somehow failed to have been a member of Trinity Hall. Furthermore, clergy who had once been oarsmen were encouraged to get back into training to row against Canford School and other opponents.

Squash Launcelot played with cunning, and an un-Christian reliance at moments on his need for a shower because of his inability since Rugby days to perspire freely. Opponents claim that this genuine affliction somehow became serious just as they were in sight of victory. Launcelot would leave the court for a short while, and return refreshed to snatch victory from the opponent whose concentration had been broken. One man remembers being hit violently in the back by a ball struck by Launcelot. 'Oh, I do hope I didn't hurt you? Are you all right? My point, I think'. In the summer tennis was his game. Memories of fielding for hours at longstop when at Rugby left him with no interest whatever in cricket.

Through his unremitting care for their welfare, his sharing in their joys and anxieties, Launcelot bound his clergy together as a family. One man remembers what a wonderful encouragement it was in his early days as a parish priest to receive postcards "from all sorts of unlikely places, and full of blots and corrections, telling you how much he had enjoyed your magazine letter, or your speech, or your sermon, or something else". Launcelot knew that 'to treat men as if they were better than they are is the surest way to make them better than they are'. A large family of clergy inevitably contained men of widely differing character and ability but he was able to respect and to draw out the potential worth of each man from the cleverest scholar to the occasional harmless "dotty", like the Canon who addressed the annual Service of the Portsmouth branch of the British Medical Association with the memorable opening words: "Ah! What a wonderful calling is yours! I was myself for a time a hospital chaplain. How well I recall the many happy hours I spent with the night sisters!'

It was at the request of his clergy in 1951 that Launcelot agreed, with some initial hesitation, to there being a Mission to the City of Portsmouth in 1952. He was never very certain that this kind of evangelism produced lasting results. However, the year after he had given his assent was spent in careful preparation. Cuthbert Bardsley, then Bishop of Croydon, was to be the Chief Missioner, but each parish was also to have its own missioner, sympathetic to the liturgical traditions of the parish and approved before appointment by Launcelot. This decision removed many of Launcelot's anxieties. John Beloe, who was secretary to the Mission, recalled the importance of Launcelot's influence during the year of preparation. 'I arranged a meeting in the Dockyard for all the missioners some months before the event. We started without Launcelot and with the Chief Missioner outlining the approach the missioners should take. Chaos ensued. They all disagreed and talked at once. The door opened and in walked a little man who came and sat beside me. He said very little and most of it without a single main verb. Almost at once order was restored by his presence among us and it became a very useful meeting.' It is never possible to measure the degree of success achieved by such a Mission but most of those involved were grateful that it had taken place and it strengthened the corporate life of the diocese.

That his clergy must have the first claim in their Bishop's care and attention did not mean that the laity were ignored. Nor was it only those who were active in parish life who knew Launcelot. He made a point of paying a half-day visit to all the major factories in the diocese. The sail makers and lifeboat builders in the Isle of Wight, the important corset industry and the local potato crisps factory, family firms like Brickwoods the brewers, all welcomed him warmly and he was surprised and encouraged to find how often those to whom he spoke mentioned their parish priest. He regularly visited the big hospitals and, accompanied by the Prison Chaplain, he met the prisoners at Parkhurst and in other gaols. Never was a Bishop less of a prelate and his total lack of pomposity endeared him to high and low alike. The pursers of the Isle of Wight ferries, seeing him running to catch the boat, took him into their cabins so that he could do some work on the journey but only after he had learned the latest news about their families. The Lord Mayor of Portsmouth's chauffeur has never forgotten driving a Lord Mayor to a Bishopswood garden party and being sought out in the car park by Launcelot, carrying a cup of tea and a plate of sandwiches.

A diocese cannot function solely on pleasant personal relationships, valuable though they are. The administrative machinery must be kept running smoothly and efficiently. Committee work was never Launcelot's first love and he realised the danger of becoming too involved in it. He knew that his Lord had always worked through people, never through committees. So as far as possible he avoided being an attending member of a committee even though, as Bishop, he was a member *ex officio*. This task he preferred to delegate to others who had more time to spare, but he insisted on being kept fully informed of all that was being decided. A valued lay adviser, who fully respected Launcelot's fear that excessive preoccupation with administration would be to the detriment of his pastoral work, pointed out to him that good administration meant a contented body of clergy and the removal of potential causes of friction before they could become serious: 'So it seemed to me that it had pastoral implications!' Ted Roberts insisted that Launcelot must attend meetings of the Diocesan Board of Finance even though he might pretend to 'come over all queer' at the sight of a balance sheet. In fact Launcelot was a much better administrator than he cared to admit or the chaos of papers on his desk might lead one to believe. Yet he was quite clear that for the kind of Bishop which he intended to be administration must never be an end in itself. With his priorities right, he was never afraid to delegate.

An important example of this delegation was his decision in 1952 to appoint two unbeneficed Archdeacons. Hitherto the Archdeacons of Portsmouth and of the Isle of Wight had held some additional office from which their stipend came. There had been talk of creating a suffragan bishopric within the diocese (probably for the Isle of Wight) but Launcelot felt that diocesan administration would be better served by two men, free from all parochial duties, who could act as his principal staff officers. It was not surprising that this decision met with some anxious criticism within the Board of Finance, whose members saw their very slender financial resources being called upon to meet two new appointments. At this difficult moment a stroke of good fortune enabled Launcelot to achieve his aim. The bequest of a very substantial sum of money "to the Bishop of Portsmouth for the time being for the advancement of the Kingdom of Heaven" fell into his lap, the lawyers having decided that such an extraordinarily wide remit did not create a legal trust.

Launcelot used the money to buy a house at Binstead for the Archdeacon of the Island. More money was then needed to buy a house in Fareham for Ted Roberts, who had become Archdeacon of Portsmouth. One evening Launcelot set out to visit the more affluent men in the diocese to raise the cash. He drove a considerable distance, returning home late at night exhausted but triumphant. The Diocesan Board of Finance gradually became able to take responsibility for both Archdeacons' stipends and expenses. As the years went by the purchase of the two houses, which seemed a heavy expense at the time, proved one of the best investments of the money which could have been made.

PORTSMOUTH

1949 – 1959

(ii) On the Job

Early in 1951 Alastair Gold had told Launcelot that the time had
come for him to have a resident Chaplain rather than a lay Personal
Assistant and that he would leave Bishopswood in six months time.
This change had been envisaged from the start. So from the autumn
of 1951 until he left Norwich Launcelot was served by a series of
ordained men, who greatly eased his burden and with whom he
could discuss diocesan affairs and personalities with complete freedom. They became during the three or four years as his Chaplain
close personal friends with whom he shared every aspect of his life
except his private finances. 'I really did have the most superb
succession of Chaplains. They were very different in gifts and
temperament but each in his own way contributed enormously to
my work and to the diocese'.

The daily routine was clearly established. At 7.30 a.m. Launcelot
and the Chaplain would say Matins together and their own prayers.
On Sundays or Saints' Days Holy Communion was celebrated. Over
breakfast the Chaplain opened all letters not marked "Personal",
passed them to Launcelot, who usually returned them with a
comment about the reply to be drafted. After breakfast the ringing of
a ship's bell summoned the household and any guests to the
drawing-room for family prayers. With a home of his own
Launcelot upheld the tradition in which he had grown up in
Scotland. A quick walk round the garden gave him some fresh air
before settling down to work in his study.

As soon as he had finished the Chaplain brought in his draft
replies to the morning's letters. These were considered at great
length by Launcelot with what could appear to be a maddening lack

of decision – at least to Chaplains with wartime experience of swift action over administrative matters. However they usually admitted that the long process of argument and counter argument and reference back to a Staff Meeting ensured the avoidance of serious mistakes. Evensong was said with the Chaplain and any staff or guests who wished to attend, provided that Launcelot was not due that evening to take a Confirmation or to institute an incumbent. On these occasions Launcelot made clear that his Chaplain was not in attendance merely to hold his crosier or to hand him whatever was needed, but his task was 'to pray like mad' throughout the Service. To have insisted on saying Evensong at Bishopswood in addition was wisely regarded by Launcelot as excessive.

Hours of work were long, for most Chaplains felt that they must remain at hand while Launcelot himself continued working. He had a tremendous capacity for sustained work and great powers of concentration. However hard he worked his Chaplains he worked himself much harder. At least they could always protect him from the telephone, 'which I am more and more convinced is a diabolical instrument.' They were able, by diplomatic avoidance of the complete truth, to suggest that Launcelot could not be found to answer the call personally, especially when the caller was known by experience to be a shrewder and less openly direct operator than his Bishop. All his life Launcelot has driven himself too hard and his engagement diaries give a picture of incessant Confirmations, Institutions, Dedications and special occasions, all of which involved a speech or an address of some kind. He reckoned that even in a small diocese like Portsmouth he travelled about 14,000 miles a year by car. Then there were the demands for a sermon from all over the country. His diary shows that in 1953, for instance, he accepted invitations to preach at Sedbergh, Winchester, Canford, Bryanston, Christ's Hospital, Loughborough, Sherborne Girls School and Liverpool Cathedral. On the 7th of June he preached the University sermon at Cambridge, as well as having in April given the Dons and Beaks addresses and a sermon at Trinity Hall.

There is no doubt that Launcelot greatly enjoyed a weekend spent in a school. Apart from the sermon, he challenged the Captain of

Squash to a game or requested a place in the School boat. There was often an invitation to give his Graham Land lecture and time was always found for meetings with prefects, members of staff or any individual who wanted his help. One of the secrets of his successful dealing with boys was that he never talked down to them but always treated them as equals.

Valuable though his visits were for the schools, they involved long journeys and a continuous process of giving out, which could become exhausting when added to the daily demands of the diocese. It was necessary for his Chaplains to watch out for the danger signals. When a man is overtired his sermons and speeches get longer rather than shorter, and there is a natural tendency to go on using the same address without realising that it has become thread-bare. Only his Chaplains could tell him that it was time to write a new Confirmation address, or that his sermons were becoming too wordy, or that the excellent Graham Land lantern lecture was lasting too long. Bachelors with no wife to keep things in perspective often have secret worries about their health and at one time Launcelot feared that he might be developing lung trouble. A Chaplain, with a sharp look out for overstrain, could insist on calling in a doctor to give needed reassurance and to prescribe a course of Vitamin B to revive his flagging energy.

Launcelot's compulsive need to use every unforgiving second often resulted, as one of his Chaplains recalls, in "a tremendous and nerve-wracking last minute rush" when leaving for an engagement. "Yet the nerve-wracking, though it affected me, did not appear to worry Launcelot. He would dash upstairs, two at a time, likely enough shave with a dry safety razor, change, pick up bits and pieces, and off with less time to get there than any ordinary person would recognize. Yet he (usually) got there to time and always seemed to be unhurried and unruffled when he arrived and able to say the right things to the wide spectrum of those he might see. This capacity to make full use of time stands as one of his characteristics."

Driving with Launcelot, even when he was not pressed for time, could be a nerve-wracking experience in itself. He enjoyed driving fast, scoring plus one for every car which he passed and minus one for every car which overtook him. He drove well unless preoccupied with what he had been doing, and so the emergence from the Bishopswood drive on to the main Southampton road was a daily hazard. It was generally believed that the Portsmouth police were indulgent, though a group of young men about to be ordained in the Cathedral were asked to keep a sharp look-out for any police cars. One friend has never forgotten being driven along Piccadilly straight through some red lights. 'But, Launcelot, the lights were *red*!' 'Surely not for very long.' Another friend was driving with him in the country when the car hit a sheep. The friend felt that Launcelot showed singular lack of episcopal concern for a lost sheep and was merely concerned that his car bore no scars from the encounter. Ever since that day Launcelot has received Christmas cards, postcards from various parts of the world, even a wrought iron weather vane for his Dorset home, all showing sheep, as a reminder of a Highland holiday incident.

Launcelot's inability to be for long on his own meant that the steady stream of visitors to Bishopswood did not dry up. To be Launcelot's domestic Chaplain involved being prepared to greet and to help his mother to entertain a quite remarkable range of guests with very little preliminary briefing. It was difficult to know whether the letter which ended ". . . much looking forward to my visit. Love, John" came from an ecclesiastical dignitary, a polar explorer, a Cambridge undergraduate or a man who had once served on the lower deck of the *Queen Elizabeth*. Nor were these guests only friends of long standing. He had an endearing habit of bringing back to Bishopswood for a meal or for the night Service men whom he had picked up on the road or had met in the train. One young sailor on National Service found himself at the end of a long railway journey agreeing to go up to Trinity Hall on his release. The Governing Body of the College grew accustomed to being urged to admit totally unknown candidates, who became nicknamed 'Launcelot's lambs'.

Another young man, who came from a very humble London home and who had hopes of Ordination, has told of the warmth of his welcome at Bishopswood. At first it was a somewhat overwhelming experience. Never before had he found himself making conversation with an elderly lady who poured out his tea from a silver teapot. Far more unnerving was the arrival of Adamson, the butler, next morning to call him. He dared not move from under the sheets for fear of disclosing his lack of pyjamas, a garment unknown to young sailors. Having only a jacket and pair of trousers it was difficult to answer Adamson's enquiry as to what suit he would like put out. When he told Launcelot of this dilemma he was at once put at ease by Launcelot's story of his own embarrassment with an inadequate number of shirts in Coleman Jennings' house in Washington. He was quickly made to feel completely at home and gratefully accepted the loan of one of Alastair Gold's suits. Some years later he served a highly successful term as a somewhat unconventional curate in the Portsmouth diocese. Launcelot was unerring in his ability to recognise true worth.

Launcelot did not confine friendship and hospitality to human beings. The Vicar of Liss's mongrel had been condemned to die for biting the local butcher but was saved by being brought to Bishopswood where the staff carried the burden of caring for "Bob", an animal which, in Alastair Gold's opinion, "had no redeeming features whatsoever." A year or so later Launcelot took pity on a thin, quarter-grown husky pup. Launcelot loved him dearly and to the alarm of many incumbents took Dusky with him on his visits to parishes. Eric Staples, Launcelot's first Chaplain, was expected to give the rapidly growing animal exercise by taking him for walks, from which he staggered back to Bishopswood in a state of complete exhaustion.

A cousin, staying at Bishopswood, was pleased to be invited to accompany Launcelot to a Confirmation. "As we loaded ourselves into the little car, Launcelot, his case of robes, his Crook, the husky and an enormous chain, a water bowl and a huge bone, it began to dawn on me that I was to be the husky's keeper more than Launcelot's companion." Inevitably they were late in starting off and, because Launcelot had promised his cousin that he would not drive too fast, they were late in arriving for supper at the Rectory.

The Rector was slightly perturbed when an animal the size of a wolf leapt towards him from the car. He was even more surprised to be greeted by his Bishop carrying a bone and a bowl of water. The husky was then chained to the car's bumper and as they entered the Rectory Launcelot hissed in his cousin's ear that when it came to the Confirmation would she please sit at the back of the church, prepared to leave instantly if Dusky began to howl. Luckily on this occasion Dusky behaved well but later on, when for safe keeping he had been locked into Launcelot's bedroom, he vented his annoyance by tearing open a feather pillow. He proceeded to tear the sheets, to make papier mâché of the underfelt of the carpet and ended by disembowelling the kapok stuffing of the mattress. In the interest of domestic economy rather than the feelings of the less dog-loving among his clergy and his sorely tried staff, Launcelot and Dusky had reluctantly to part company.

To be in close touch with the Navy once again was an important as well as a very enjoyable part of Launcelot's work. In days when formal calls were still paid admirals and captains came as a matter of courtesy to Bishopswood to pay their respects. To have returned each call separately would have been an unjustifiable waste of Launcelot's time, and so he used to invite his naval callers and their wives to lunch, which was far more enjoyable for both sides. Scottish dancing, at which he was delightfully skilled, was then very popular in naval establishments and Bishopswood's drawing-room was large enough to accommodate at least eight "eightsomes". The Commander-in-Chief, early in Launcelot's time in Portsmouth, gave a dance at Admiralty House for Princess Elizabeth, as she then was. At one point the floor was cleared to enable three sets to dance an Eightsome Reel. The Princess, who commented that she had never reeled with a Bishop before, was Launcelot's partner on the floor which was dangerously slippery. Those watching discussed the likely penalty were Launcelot to cause the literal downfall of the Heir Apparent.

There were about twenty Naval Chaplains in the Portsmouth Command at this time and Launcelot saw much of them. He was frequently invited to preach or to confirm at shore establishments and to dedicate the many war memorials which were then being designed. At the Coronation Review in 1953 he was an honoured guest.

To be back in Portsmouth gave Launcelot the opportunity of renewing wartime friendships, not only with naval padres but with officers and men. With the help of the national and local Press he made it known as widely as possible that all who had at any time served in the *Queen Elizabeth* were invited to a reunion party at Bishopswood. In discussing arrangements for the party with Ted Roberts one of those elusive conversations, treasured by all Launcelot's close friends, took place.

'What was the size of the ship's complement, Launcelot?'

(After a long silence) 'Yes . . . there must have been about that number . . .'

'What number, Launcelot?'

'About 500 . . . no, perhaps 1000 . . . probably 1300. We must have been . . .'

'Would there have been a regular turnover?'

'Oh, yes. Perhaps three a year.'

'So in your time in the ship there might have been 5000?'

(After an even longer silence) 'I don't suppose they will all come.'

The party was a triumphant success and another took place at a later date. Of the first occasion a guest wrote: "It was a grand party and I have never seen so much booze in a parson's house before or since."

In his years in Portsmouth Launcelot was not called upon to accept any very onerous work with the central organisation of the Church of England. As a diocesan Bishop he was a member of the Upper House of Convocation of Canterbury, which necessitated attendance at Bishops' Meetings and, with the feeling that his time could be much better spent in his diocese, at meetings of the Church Assembly. He was not by nature a good debater and at first his contribution to polemic discussion was minimal. His inability to speak cogently without long preparation was a disadvantage but less important than his distaste for heated arguments about the Church's ministry. Every friend of Launcelot affectionately knows how seldom in conversation his sentences come to a main verb or a clear finish. This surprising difficulty of clear utterance when contrasted with the lucidity of his prepared speeches only reinforced his dislike of formal meetings and open debate. On his first attendance at the Church Assembly it never occurred to him to wear gaiters, and he found that even if he would not become a great orator he had won unintentional popularity by breaking this tradition.

He did, however, undertake the chairmanship of the Church of England Youth Council and this interested him. The Council was the central organisation for the Church's dealings with young people and was especially concerned with the training of Youth Chaplains. Princess Margaret was President of the Council and in this way Launcelot's increasingly close connection with the Royal Family began. It was probably she who was behind Launcelot's first invitation to preach at Sandringham in January 1954. A naturally nervous Launcelot was ushered into a room where the Queen Mother was playing Hunt the Thimble with Prince Charles and his sister. On this occasion the "thimble" was a gold pen. 'You can't feel shy for long,' Launcelot later reported, 'when the thimble is hidden in your gaiters.' He just found time to write back to his mother: "This really is being a most perfect weekend, which I am enjoying quite enormously – and I want to get this off by today's mail which goes very soon. I would have started it earlier but for the non-stop activities of Prince Charles, who has now gone up to change for tea so as to leave the rest of us a few moments stand easy! He and Princess Anne are really a wonderful couple and of quite inexhaustible energy."

It was in the course of this weekend that Princess Margaret played the record of "You can't chop your poppa up in Massachusetts", which so delighted Launcelot that she gave him the record. 'I shall play this to my Rural Deans,' he promised. This he did and the Bishopswood drawing-room has probably never witnessed a stranger scene than this gathering of dignified clerics, with slightly bemused faces, listening to the record and not knowing quite what comments to make at the end. It was a form of episcopal behaviour to which they were unaccustomed. However they were saved by one of their number, an erudite canon, who was able to deliver an enlightening discourse to his colleagues on Lizzie Bordon.

Chairmanship of the Church of England Youth Council brought the chance of two visits to Germany. He was taken there by Kurt Hahn, former headmaster of Schloss Salem and then of Gordonstoun. Hahn and many others were deeply worried about the problems facing German boys and young men in the post-war world. In the course of the visit he was introduced by Hahn to President Heuss of the West German Republic and had the chance of discussing ways of rehabilitating German youth. He went to the schools which Hahn had initiated – Salem, Hermannsburg, the mountain school at Baad, with a sea-school in Schleswig-Holstein. Further discussions took place with Bishop Dibelius and with an outstanding Judge of the Juvenile Court, Judge Holzchuh at Darmstadt. There was also time to fit in a visit to both West and East Berlin.

In August 1954 Launcelot paid an official visit to the British Army of the Rhine. The main purpose of the fortnight's tour, 'which was as near to perpetual motion as anything I have yet experienced,' was to look into the whole question of Army Chaplains, their recruitment, their problems and their influence, especially on young soldiers, and to make recommendations for the future. In addition he was asked to comment on the use which the Army was making of its National Servicemen and to meet as many of them individually as circumstances allowed.

The report which he wrote on his return throws an interesting light on his views about the work of a priest. Shortage of Army Chaplains had led occasionally to bad appointments, more often to a Chaplain having to look after too many units. A good Chaplain (he wrote) can only do "a really effective job if he is essentially Padre of one regiment and is with that regiment long enough to get on personal and pastoral terms with them." His naval experience made him feel strongly that the work of Army Chaplains was being made more difficult by their bearing badges of rank. His report came near to achieving this abolition of rank, which most

Chaplains would have welcomed, but tradition proved too strong.

When commenting on the National Servicemen he stressed his dislike of intending Ordinands among them being publicly labelled as such. "A man who is thinking of offering himself later on for Holy Orders should make it his first concern to do his job as a normal soldier to the best of his ability, to prove himself among his contemporaries who are a cross-section of those to whom he hopes to minister later on . . . The cause of the ministry is not assisted by those young men who are labelled "Ordinands" and who after their National Service are not recommended for training for the ministry. Some of these young men are terribly "wet" and only tend to foster the notion that a fellow thinks of Ordination when he cannot hold down any other job."

It was not only German youth who caused their more thoughtful elders anxiety about their future. What would ultimately replace National Service for British young men and give them further discipline and a sense of purpose was a question to which many people were giving serious attention. In 1954 Launcelot was invited to join the Dulverton Trust in order to advise the Trust about its Youth work on which the Trustees planned to spend a considerable proportion of their resources and became chairman of the Trust's Youth Committee.

The most imaginative of the plans for helping young men and women to help themselves was the Duke of Edinburgh's Award Scheme. Launcelot was invited to take part in the early deliberations which resulted in the Scheme being launched on the 28th of February 1956 with Sir John (now Lord) Hunt as its first Director. He and all connected with planning the Award Scheme found Launcelot's particular qualities – personal experience of testing adventure, his appeal to young people and his insistence that the moral and spiritual side of a young person's development must not be neglected – of great value. He became a member of the Advisory Committee which controlled the Scheme and he served on it until his term of office ended in 1968.

In the idea of Voluntary Service Overseas (V.S.O.) Launcelot played a leading part. Alec Dickson, its first Director, had come to

Portsmouth to talk to senior pupils in a school and had stayed the night at Bishopswood. During the evening they talked together about how best young people might fill what became known as "The Year Between" – that is the year which many young men and women in increasing numbers found that they would have to fill between leaving school and going on to university or other form of further education. They decided that an organisation should quickly be set up for sending some of these young people to work for a year in the under-developed territories of the Commonwealth. Dickson said that the best way of launching the scheme would be for Launcelot to write a letter to the papers as Chairman of the Church of England Youth Council. "Alec drafted the letter. I amended it. *The Sunday Times* published it on 23 March 1958."

"The projects overseas that I have in mind – some governmental, some missionary, some the responsibility of social service councils – do not postulate specialist skills so much as a readiness to work alongside the local people; their need is urgent, just because of the new problems arising in this period of transition to self-government. Equally urgent is the need for the best of our young people – in their difficult period of transition before university or career – to have the opportunity of doing something worthwhile when it is most genuinely needed, of seeing a bit of the world into the bargain." The proposal was enthusiastically taken up and was an outstanding success. Launcelot had the pleasure of seeing off the first group of a dozen boys who went to Sarawak and two more who left for Ghana. Hundreds of young people since the start of the scheme have gained much from their year overseas and have given much in return. Many have been involved in exciting projects which, with the absolute confidence of an eighteen year old, they successfully completed. As the emergent countries gained independence so the need for young volunteers came gradually to an end. However, there is still room within the V.S.O. organisation for graduates to work in the same spirit as the earlier school leavers.

Launcelot's interest in young people meant not only constant demands on his time for a weekend visit to boarding schools but

many invitations to serve on their Governing Bodies. Outside the
diocese he served on the Councils or Governing Bodies of
Marlborough, Wellington, Bryanston, Canford and Atlantic
College. He was also a governor of Chichester Theological College.
He could not possibly attend every meeting but his interest and
advice were always available. Within the diocese he played a
valuable part in the affairs of Portsmouth Grammar School and he
became Chairman of the Governors. He came at a moment when
the School had largely recovered physically from the effects of the
air raids on the city, but needed his infectious enthusiasm in the
work of rebuilding all sides of school life after five years of evacuation to Bournemouth. He brought to the school men of distinction
to give away prizes, to lay the foundation stone of a new laboratory
or to preach at a Cathedral Service. Members of staff and their wives
joined senior boys and their girl friends at Bishopswood for Scottish
dancing, and prefects, labouring in his garden, came under his spell.
Sometimes this could be awkward. A mother telephoned the Head
Master to say that after a marvellous supper party her son had found
himself half-agreeing to be ordained, but in the cold light of morning
he felt less certain about the suggestion.

Inevitably Launcelot had to give away prizes at schools throughout the diocese and, as ever, the burden of composing a suitable
speech was heavy on him. When due to address a big girls' school in
Portsmouth he sought advice from a friend.

'What are you going to talk about, Launcelot?'

'I thought of striking out on a new line. I'm going to talk about
Glamour.'

'Splendid! How far have you got?'

'Well, really not very far . . . only the opening . . . "Now, girls . . ."'

One prizegiving is very much like every other one but one at
Portsmouth Grammar School over which Launcelot presided
remained long in the memory. The ceremony took place in the local
theatre with Governors and Staff on the stage. On this occasion it
was discovered that instead of the usual harmless scenery the stage
had been converted into an ice rink. To enable the speeches to be
heard the motor which kept the ice frozen was switched off. Not

only was every person on the stage extremely cold but with unconcealed delight the audience of parents and boys watched the water from the melting ice slowly rising over the Governors' feet.

One of the most successful of Launcelot's innovations was the Canford Summer School. For a week in the summer a conference was held at Canford School in Dorset to which members of Youth Clubs throughout the diocese came. The programme consisted of lectures and discussions, social activities, games and swimming, and daily worship. There was always one distinguished theologian, such as Canon Charles Raven, as the main speaker and, for less demanding listening, a polar explorer or similar speaker to excite the conference. The week was very stimulating and much enjoyed, and was continued by Launcelot's successor when Launcelot left Portsmouth.

A Portsmouth organisation which gained greatly from Launcelot's personal interest was the local branch of the Geographical Association. As President he lured a number of interesting and learned speeakers to address meetings and there was a marked increase in membership. The officers of the branch all remember with gratitude the convivial meals which followed an Association meeting, at which Launcelot was host, in the famous Monk's Oyster Bar in Old Portsmouth.

At one period the chairman of the branch was a member of a Roman Catholic religious Order teaching in Portsmouth. The ecumenical movement was not then as strong as it has become and "the idea of working with an Anglican bishop seemed very daunting. However, Brother Michael and I decided to go to see him. On the bus we decided to keep right off the subject of religion and stick to geography. We were warmly received by the Bishop and his mother and we spent the evening in animated and very friendly conversation mainly on religious topics. Geography was occasionally mentioned!"

In the course of the evening's talk Launcelot told the two Brothers of his experience with Irish Catholic labourers, who were working on the road outside Bishopswood. As the weather was very hot he arranged for a small barrel of beer to be sent out to them on a wheelbarrow during their lunch break. The labourers were delighted until they discovered that the donor was a Protestant bishop and they refused to touch a drop. Launcelot commented that he had never treated Roman Catholicism really seriously until that moment.

Despite the unending claims upon his time Launcelot managed to keep in touch with two of his great interests in Cambridge days. Any engagement in Cambridge was welcomed both as a break from an intensely strenuous life and as providing an opportunity to go down to the river and help in coaching a Trinity Hall boat. Having coached the Cambridge boat in 1949 he was rewarded in 1950 by being invited to watch the Boat Race from the Cambridge launch. As each June came round his clergy became happily accustomed to having the diocese run from Henley, where he often stayed with the Trinity Hall crew.

During the summer of 1951 Professor Hans Ahlmann came to Bishopswood to tell Launcelot about the progress of the Norwegian-British-Swedish-Antarctic Expedition which he had invited Launcelot to join before he left Cambridge. Shortly afterwards Commander Simpson, the designated leader of the proposed British North Greenland Expedition, also came to see Launcelot, who had agreed to become Vice-Chairman of the planning committee. Two years later in 1953 he had the great joy of once again seeing something at first hand of polar exploration. On the 12th of August he flew in a Sunderland from Pembroke Dock to Reykjavik and thence to Greenland, where he joined the expedition at Brittania Lake. He lived with the members of the expedition for eleven days, thereby providing through lengthy consultations a valuable link with the Committee in England. In the course of this visit he celebrated Holy Communion and conducted another Service. At Christmas time each of the twenty-five members received a personal letter of greetings and good wishes from him.

A new opportunity for speaking with authority on subjects nearest his heart opened on the 24th of October 1956 when Launcelot took his seat in the House of Lords. His maiden speech on cruelty to whales marked the start of his public and influential concern for everything to do with Conservation. This interest was the natural outcome both of his Christian beliefs and of his earlier scientific work. To those who did not know him whales seemed an odd subject for an episcopal maiden speech. The slightly apocryphal story gained currency that the letter "h" had accidentally been inserted and that Launcelot had received a message of gratitude on behalf of the Principality from the Secretary of State for Wales. Launcelot, who had found debates in the Church Assembly and elsewhere uninspiring, had no doubt that it was right for him to spare the time to make his informed contribution when the Lords turned their attention not only to Conservation but to the Youth Service, University education, the problems of leisure and Family Law. Although the laborious task of composing his speeches took many hours he increasingly found his work in the Upper House both fascinating and worthwhile. In this he was strongly encouraged to play an active part by Bishop George Bell of Chichester.

Faced with a challenging task a man either grows in stature or shrinks. After ten years in Portsmouth Launcelot had grown from the rather shy man who was only completely at home with Cambridge dons and undergraduates or among the Scottish hills, into a man who spoke with authority, however incapable he remained of realising his true stature. Fortunately for the Church others realised his worth and only Launcelot was surprised when the Prime Minister, Harold Macmillan, wrote to him on the 8th of September 1959 saying that he wished to submit his name to the Queen as the new Bishop of Norwich. It had been clear to those who knew him well that he was unlikely to remain in Portsmouth much longer.

Once again he was thrown into an agony of indecision and he sought advice from his closest friends. There were personal and private difficulties in the way of a move. "Do you think," he wrote to Ken Carey, "that considering this last year [when he had been unwell] (and the fact that I'm incapable of taking a regular day off!) I ought to accept a job which for two years anyhow is going to mean *very* hard work? Or would I be wise to put off moving until I've got over this recent trouble?" He would certainly need reassurance from his doctors after ten years of constant overwork. Then there was his mother. She was becoming more frail and at her age would find it difficult to make the move though, as Ken Carey reminded him, "Home to her is where Launcelot is." Furthermore, Dan de Pass had made it clear that 'Mamma' and Jean could not easily live together permanently in the same house, and in any case his home was too small to accommodate her. If Launcelot moved she must go with him.

Most of his friends had no doubt that Launcelot should accept the Norwich offer. Bishop Montgomery-Campbell with characteristic directness told him, "Of course you have got to go to Norwich . . . Since Pompey has been relegated to the second division you can hardly be expected to remain there. Seriously, these things are a perfect nightmare but when a call of this kind comes at you I think you are bound to look upon it as the guidance of the Holy Spirit and follow. There are, of course, great difficulties in Norfolk, parishes you can't fill, etc.; but it has its compensations – a glorious cathedral, a new house we are just going to build for you, and some very nice people, Gurneys in large quantities, a very godly Lord Lieutenant and some nice people who spend a bit of time at a place called Sandringham." His former Trinity Hall colleague and old friend, Owen Wansbrough-Jones, who was a Norfolk man himself, knew what the diocese needed and believed that Launcelot should move before he became too deeply embedded in Portsmouth. He stressed the need which the clergy felt for a pastoral bishop, who would also uphold the dignity of the see. He told Launcelot that at Norwich he would speak with greater authority than at Portsmouth on subjects of importance like the nuclear dilemma or the relations of Christianity and Science and he would greatly help the new University of East Anglia. He would be lonelier than in Portsmouth but "does that matter so much as you get older?" and anyhow Launcelot was unlikely not to go on drawing people to himself.

There was also some plain speaking. Dan de Pass urged him to move "while you are at the height of your powers" but just wondered if Launcelot was personally suited to this particular work. "You are not an intellectual nor have you a forceful personality. On the other hand you have above average powers of leadership. You can make decisions when circumstances compel you to do so and you have plenty of moral courage." A brother-in-law is not necessarily right in all his judgements. His Chaplain was more outspoken in a private note weighing up the pros and cons. "You simply must make up your mind in the next two days. That has nothing to do with the Archbishop or the Prime Minister . . . but because you won't be good for anything unless you do." He then put three direct questions to him. "Are you tough enough to take it? Is it basically a right job to take on, or is the whole set-up irrelevant in the twentieth century? Have you the ability to do the necessary planning, make decisions, delegate the administration wisely and well with a fairly elderly staff?" He summed up his exercise in speaking the truth in love by saying that "because you see the real issues and aims and also the snags so clearly you are both the best man potentially for the job and also more likely to be got down by it."

On the 4th of October 1959 Launcelot told the Prime Minister that he was ready to allow his name to be submitted to the Queen. Next day Archbishop Fisher wrote warmly approving Launcelot's decision. The Queen's formal approval was given on October the 8th but the announcement was delayed for a week in view of the impending General Election. Two letters after his decision was made known must have cheered Launcelot and moved him greatly. Ken Mathews wrote: "It *will* mean husbanding your resources a bit more cleverly, won't it? However, now it seems to me you have a priceless opportunity to re-plan all this side of things now you start with a clear diary. I hope you will print in large type: Rule 1. Bishops must have a day off. Rule 2. Up with SLOTH!" From his outspoken but devoted brother-in-law came another letter: "It occurs to Jean and me that considerable expenses lie ahead of you, so we ask you to be good enough to accept the enclosed and devote it *exclusively* to the replenishment of your wardrobe – an item which we think would otherwise find itself low in your priorities. We both feel that with help from above you have decided to do what you did ought."

NORWICH

1959 – 1971

(i) The Main Task

It would be difficult to imagine a greater contrast than that between the dioceses of Portsmouth and Norwich. Launcelot had moved from the smallest English diocese to the second largest. His new see covered over a million acres and consisted of the greater part of Norfolk and one Deanery in Suffolk. Each Archdeaconry was larger in area than the entire Portsmouth diocese. There was a population of around 600,000, of which nearly 40 per cent was concentrated in the city of Norwich and the surrounding area. Officially there were 477 benefices, though in 1959 over sixty were without an incumbent.

The Prime Minister's patronage secretary had told Launcelot that if he accepted the see his main problem would be the pastoral care of the country clergy and the appointment of men prepared to work in a remote country benefice. Ted Roberts had made the same point when describing the need at Norwich for 'someone to breathe life and encourage hope in some 400 rustic clergy.' The then Archdeacon of Norwich, when invited by the patronage secretary to outline the needs of the diocese, expressed the hope that the new Bishop would set great store by pastoral work, 'especially with an eye to evangelism in our many country parishes.' An eminent scholar or a bishop of 'statesman-like gifts' was not the primary need, but a 'man of sheer goodness of heart, friendly, easily approached, with a genuine love of simple country folk and a wise understanding of their particular ways.' Superficially it appeared as if the job was tailor-made for Launcelot.

At the same time the patronage secretary warned him that 'Norfolk has very much a life of its own and the leaders of that life are the families like the Buxtons, Gurneys, Barclays and Hoares, who have lived there for generations. Norfolk is conservative in outlook, radical in politics and prides itself on going its own way. It used to be a stronghold of non-conformity and the puritan tradition dies hard.' The City of Norwich might return two Labour Members to parliament but resistance to change throughout the thinly populated countryside was very strong. When in 1940 local units of the Home Guard kept watch along the coasts for Hitler's threatened invasion the traditional Norfolk spirit was well expressed in the comment: 'We'll beat 'em again, as we did last time.' By 'the last time' the speaker was cheerfully referring to the Danish invasions in the ninth century.

Between the 23rd and 26th of January 1960 Launcelot once again chose the home of Ken Matthews – now the Deanery at St. Albans – as the place in which to make his retreat. Two days later on the 28th of January he was enthroned in Norwich Cathedral in the presence of Princess Margaret, his clergy and the representatives of all sides of Norfolk life. Among the Bishop's company was the Master of Trinity Hall, chosen not only because of Launcelot's long association with the College but because the College had been founded by Bishop Bateman of Norwich. Once again Roddy MacLean proudly walked in the procession. Launcelot had readily agreed to the Dean's request that the Service should be televised, only stipulating that the cameras should not be intrusive. He was assured by the engineers that, as for bird photography, they would be 'up a pillar in a hide'.

As the text for his sermon Launcelot chose St. John's words: "In Him was life and the life was the light of men." He had come to what was widely known as the Dead See, and he knew that his prime task must be to bring new life to his clergy and the diocese. At the end of the Service a Te Deum was sung with the whole congregation facing the High Altar, above which, resplendent in a cope and mitre originally brought from Russia, he sat somewhat precariously on what remains of an 11th century episcopal stone chair. Some Bishops might have revelled in this moment of glory: Launcelot felt shy and 'distinctly embarrassed'.

Launcelot had no doubt that the care of his clergy must be his first and overriding task. Such pastoral care was, in his opinion, the prime duty of a Bishop, and he knew that it was even more urgently needed in a large diocese like Norwich than in Portsmouth. His predecessor, Bishop Percy Mark Herbert, was a saintly and kindly man, who had made the diocese respected in the county after the long and deadening reign of Bishop Pollock. He was very tall, with beetling eyebrows, a huge voice and a sepulchral cough; a magnificent figure in mitre and cope. As heir to an earldom he moved easily among the powerful Norfolk squirearchy, staying in their homes rather than in the vicarage when visiting parishes and shooting regularly with them throughout the season. He was probably the last Bishop who could be described as a Prince of the Church, autocratic and somewhat remote, almost a relic of the eighteenth century. To the humble country parson, who never had a chance to get to know him as a friend, he was a respected but rather daunting figure. By contrast Launcelot was a Bishop of whom nobody could be frightened.

Before he moved from Portsmouth Launcelot had told the Norfolk Archdeacons that instead of sitting on innumerable committees he intended to meet every parson in his home, thereby also meeting his wife and family. They were asked to make a plan for these visits in consultation with the Rural Deans. All weekends not irrevocably allocated to the major Festivals, Ordinations, Diocesan Conferences or other traditional special commitments – like the journey by wherry to the site of St. Benet's Abbey on August Bank Holiday weekend – were to be devoted to the parishes. In this way he got round to all twenty-nine Deaneries in the first sixteen months.

Once this plan got under way Launcelot used to leave Bishop's House at lunch time on a Friday and stay in the pre-arranged part of the diocese until Monday morning. At least an hour would be spent with each family and he always stayed with the parish priest rather than with the local squire. It was one of his Chaplain's tasks to make sure that the invitation to stay in the vicarage was forthcoming so that the kindly invitation to stay with the squire could be truthfully declined. The thought that the Bishop would actually be staying in her home at first worried many a vicar's wife and it is said that, until the word got round how enjoyable these visits were, lots were drawn to decide on whom the fearful responsibility would fall. Launcelot made plain that the hospitality shown him should be simple and not too great a financial burden on his host. On one occasion, however, he found his bed so damp that he had to get out of it and dress completely before being able to sleep. It was a night which, he said, outdid any polar experience.

Apart from the time spent in the parson's home, getting to know him and his family, hearing their problems and guessing at secret worries, Launcelot celebrated Holy Communion and attended Matins and Evensong in different neighbouring churches, insisting that he only preached once. On the Sunday afternoon he met the lay representatives of the parishes and on Monday morning, before returning to Norwich, he took part in a meeting of the local Chapter. It had been an exhausting but very rewarding experience by the time that the visits ended in May 1961. Something of the isolation of his country clergy came home to him when one parson said as he left the vicarage, 'Well, Bishop, it has been very nice having you in our home. I don't suppose it will ever happen again.'

Launcelot might have many of the qualities which his new diocese needed but he had no illusions about the tremendous task ahead of him. How could the 400,000 people who would look to him as their Father in God become more of a real family and also be encouraged to meet the changing needs of the modern world? What should be the policy of the diocese towards its six hundred mediaeval churches, architecturally beautiful but often in need of urgent and costly repairs? By his visits to their homes he had seen at first hand the desperate loneliness and financial straits of so many of his clergy. How could he ever persuade keen young men to come to Norfolk under existing conditions? The root of the problem was the inadequate stipends on which so many clergy were struggling to exist. The nearest incumbent might be six miles away, a world apart if you could not afford to run a car. Local gentry were warm-hearted and friendly people, but if you could not afford to stand them an occasional drink it was difficult to accept their hospitality and not repay it. How could a man with a wife and family retain his original enthusiasm and not become totally dispirited while ministering to a handful of people in a large mediaeval church and living in an often beautiful but hopelessly inconvenient and decaying rectory? Partly because of the conditions in which many clergy had to work, Launcelot, on arrival, had had to deal with five tragic cases of serious misdemeanour.

Despite modern transport villagers could occasionally still remain as isolated from neighbouring villagers as were their parsons. Launcelot was amazed to learn the reason for the marked lack of co-operation between two villages. 'You see, Bishop, they were on opposite sides in the war.' Launcelot became even more perplexed. 'The Civil War, Bishop.' It transpired that one village had been passionately royalist and the other had ardently supported the cause of parliament. It still was not easy for a boy from the one village to walk out with a girl from the other village.

When he met his first Diocesan Conference in the Spring of 1960 Launcelot in his Presidential Address made it clear that he was going to be primarily concerned with the needs of the Norfolk clergy. He realised that the ministry of a country parson 'where it is rightly exercised is one of the most exacting, most difficult and most rewarding to which any clergyman can be called.' But he insisted that a man cannot do his job without a 'decent house, manageable in size and in reasonable repair for the parson and his family, and sufficient money so that he can do his work without a constant weight of financial anxiety hanging over his head.' So, as in Portsmouth, he appointed a Commission to report to him on what the minimum income of a parson should be.

A year later he spoke to the Diocesan Conference about the isola-tion of so many parish priests, which his visits to their homes had amply confirmed. He admitted that isolation may have certain virtues. It 'stimulates independence of mind because you are not one of a herd . . . It allows a man time to think, because you are spared some of the rush of modern life.' But the virtues are quickly outweighed by the evils. Isolation makes people depressed by feeling cut off from their fellows, and this was a particular problem for clergy and their wives 'since by definition the parson is the only one of his kind in the parish.' Furthermore, isolation has 'the other bad effect of making you too self satisfied. You have no yardstick by which to measure your standards or your effectivenss. You lack the spur and inspiration which come from seeing how other people are tackling the same work as yourself.' Isolation, he had found, could lead to eccentric forms of worship, to opposition if it were feared that the Bishop was intruding and even to resentment at any offers of help.

Launcelot could not personally cure the ills of isolation and loneliness to which many country clergy are prone, but he could help them to help each other. His method was always to help people to help themselves by doing all in his power to create the right conditions, and then to leave it to those concerned to make best use of them.

As far as clergy stipends were concerned the Commission reported in 1961 that only eighteen men had an income which the members recommended should be the minimum for effective discharge of duties. Money was not immediately available to implement the Commission's Report, but Launcelot lost no opportunity of impressing on lay people their responsibility towards their parish priest and steadily the situation improved.

Meanwhile Launcelot sought to draw his clergy closer to each other by making each Deanery more of a unit. He wished Chapter meetings to be held nine or ten times a year and not to be devoted solely to routine business. These meetings, in his view, should become a means of strengthening and refreshing the clergy by mutual study 'and prepared discussion of definite theological, pastoral and practical topics,' and he expected them to 'regard it as a matter of obligation to attend these meetings.' He drew up a list of able and experienced men, including several Cambridge dons, who were prepared to address Chapter meetings, and the Rural Deans were told to report to him the names of those who failed to attend without a valid excuse.

This was a side of Launcelot which many of the older clergy had not expected to encounter. A man who at first meeting might appear as rather hesitant and indecisive turned out to be very determined once he had settled on a course of action. It might take him time to make up his mind on a particular issue, but having made a decision it was extremely difficult to make him change his mind, as all his Chaplains discovered. One described the way in which Launcelot would listen with courteous inattention, his mind far away. 'You old devil,' the Chaplain thought, 'you have no intention of changing your mind. You aren't even listening to my arguments.' Chaplains, like everyone else, always forgave him for his decisions were only reached after much agonizing and usually turned out to be right.

Not all of the clergy welcomed these plans; some regarded them as an encroachment on their independence. Hitherto they had pursued their studies, or had neglected them, as they wished. Voluntary clerical societies had long been a feature of the diocese but virtually compulsory attendance at Chapter meetings was something new. It was unkindly said that the clergy loved Launcelot for trying to raise their stipends but that the love of some of them for him cooled rapidly when he expected them to justify a better standard of living by greater devotion and efficiency.

Although he had never been a parish priest, Launcelot knew that unlike other professions there was no ordered timetable, no clocking in, with a parson's job. It was all too easy to become lazy. To counter this danger every new incumbent was asked to write a report which would be confidential to Bishop and Archdeacons. The report should contain a description of what the incumbent found on arrival, what he was attempting to do and what at the end of a year he felt he had achieved, together with plans for the future. He was also expected to state what holidays he had taken and what were his responsibilities towards his family. At the end of his first three years in the parish he was to report again. Regular stock taking of this kind gave Launcelot valuable information and also helped to keep a man up to the mark.

This was only the first step in Launcelot's struggle to bring new life to the parishes. Summer schools, post-Ordination training for junior clergy and refresher courses for senior clergy were instituted.

Whenever possible Launcelot was present on the first evening of a
course to welcome its members. A Calendar of Intercessions was
drawn up and the diocese was asked to join with him in prayer for a
particular priest each day. The man concerned would have received
a personal letter from Launcelot that morning, assuring him of his
Bishop's prayers for himself, his family and his parish.

Effective pastoral care for over four hundred clergy was a bigger
task than one man could discharge, despite the great help and
support given him by his old friend Pat Leonard, Suffragan Bishop
of Thetford. That Pat Leonard would be there to help him from the
start was a powerful factor in deciding to leave Portsmouth for
Norwich. Launcelot planned to re-organise the diocese so that,
apart from the Dean of the Cathedral, there would be three senior
appointments. He wanted each of the three men to be in episcopal
Orders as Suffragan Bishops and also to act as Archdeacons. It was a
way of avoiding too many dignitaries and each man would combine
the necessary administrative work with pastoral care. Unfortunately
Archbishop Ramsey, while sympathetic, could not agree that the
population of Norfolk demanded four Bishops and he was only
willing to allow Launcelot to appoint one additional Suffragan.

Pastoral care, however essential, did not fill empty benefices. It
became increasingly clear to Launcelot that he must face a clear
choice. He could take the line of least resistance and keep the old
feudal system going. This meant that somehow he must find enough
men to give each parish its incumbent and enough money to keep
all the churches in good repair. Alternatively he must have the
vision and the courage to accept that the old ways with all their
virtues could no longer be completely maintained and that new
forms of ministry must be devised. He chose the infinitely harder
course.

The diocese of Norwich has 700 church buildings; most are
mediaeval and a great number are set in sparsely populated areas.
The traditional structure of the rural Church of England – a resident
parson in each parish – evolved from the great variety of functions
which a parish priest had to perform in the Middle Ages and for

centuries later. Today many clergy find that much of their work has
been taken over by the State and they are left bewildered and feeling
very much outsiders, irrelevant to an industrial and secular society.

The changes which modern developments have brought to urban
life are all too obvious; but change in the countryside, though
outwardly less dramatic, has been almost as profound. Mobility has
virtually destroyed the old village community. Increasing
mechanization of agriculture has meant fewer jobs on the land and
has forced young men to leave their homes to seek work in the
towns. Villages have become dormitory areas. At the same time
both wealthy and retired people now seek to escape from the noise
and ugliness of the modern town and are building their homes in the
countryside. The number of people who have moved from the town
to the country in the past thirty years has more than made up for
those who have migrated to the towns, but the newcomers often
have no real stake in, or understanding of, country ways. Thus the
country parson all too often finds that there is no community to
which the Church can relate. Much of the unhappiness of many
Norfolk clergy sprang from not having a man-sized job to do.

The idea of what became known as a Group Ministry originated
in Lincolnshire in 1949 and an account of the first ten years of the
experiment was published in 1960. It was at this moment that
Launcelot had nine parishes with no incumbent in the northern part
of the Breckland area of West Norfolk. He decided that he had no
alternative but to try out the Lincolnshire scheme. Not only would
it save manpower and money but – and this was what mattered most
to him – it would provide a challenging and worthwhile task for
clergy ready to work at full stretch.

The setting up of a Group Ministry involved hours of very hard
work. Launcelot and his Chaplain had to write more than a hundred
letters before a Group was finally accepted by those affected.
Preliminary background work was essential to ensure that the
parishes to be grouped into a single benefice formed some kind of
social and geographical entity. Endless consultation with all who
might be concerned was a slow but very necessary process. Then
came the vital choice of the man who was to become Rector and

leader of the Group. He must be welcomed and approved by those
who once had had their own parson. He must be a man of sufficient
calibre to attract able men with specialised and complementary gifts
to work with him. For Rector of what became known as the
Hillborough Group, which was established in 1961, Launcelot
made the admirable choice of Hugh Blackburne, Vicar of Ranworth
on the Broads and, later, Suffragan Bishop of Thetford. The
Hillborough Group consisted of a union of ten parishes, ministered
to by the Rector, with an assistant priest and a deacon. It covered an
area of 40 square miles and had a population of about 1800. Within
two years it had proved an undoubted success.

It would be idle to pretend that in spite of hours of careful
planning and consultation the idea of Group Ministries was
immediately popular. Indeed, he had to face powerful opposition
from many quarters but Launcelot was completely convinced that
for part of the diocese there was no valid alternative, and he
proceeded with his plans. He was not a canny Scot for nothing, and
he made sure of support in high places. When the Queen agreed that
Sandringham should become part of a Group and Sir Edmund
Bacon, then Lord-lieutenant, gladly supported the idea for his own
village of Raveningham, it became harder for reluctant squires and
hankerers after old ways to hold out indefinitely.

Opposition there may have been but in the words of Canon Peter
Bradshaw, one of the Group leaders, 'those of us who were engaged
in the marvellously exhilarating early days of the creation of rural
teams and groups look back upon those times as the highlight of our
ministry.' From first hand experience they knew that they were the
instruments through whom new life was being brought to moribund
parishes, and those who threw themselves into these new forms of
ministry found their very hard work both exciting and richly
rewarding.

Nobody could claim that the Group Ministry was the sovereign
remedy for all the ills of the rural Church but it did enable the
Church to become, as has been said, 'people centred' instead of
'building centred'. At any rate by the time that Launcelot left
Norwich for Windsor a quarter of the parishes had been grouped

together and about eighteen per cent of the clergy worked in them –
hardly the revolution which some had feared but a transformation
of the life of many a country parson and country parish.

Although agriculture was of great importance throughout Norfolk,
Launcelot did not forget that there were large industrial areas in the
county – not only Norwich but also Lowestoft, Yarmouth, Kings
Lynn and Dereham. There were also other interests to be served in
hospitals, schools, the new University of East Anglia and in Youth
work. Launcelot believed that this called for the appointment of
special Chaplains with responsibility for sections of the community
largely untouched by parish life; something of a novelty for the
diocese. Canon Michael Mann, later to succeed Launcelot at
Windsor, did brilliant work as the first industrial Chaplain. He
hoped to see an industrial Chaplain, who if possible would also be
the vicar of the parish, in each centre of industry.

Perhaps the most forward looking of Launcelot's innovations was
to appoint Canon Peter Freeman to combine a City parish with
being Chaplain for television. He realised the importance of
television as a medium for reaching people who would never enter a
Church and he was determined that what professionals called 'the
God Slot' must be of high quality. He himself was never a
sufficiently impromptu speaker to become a television star, and his
innocence of the medium was revealed when he arrived for his first
interview armed with the written questions which he expected the
interviewer to use and also the written answers which he intended to
deliver. He quickly came to understand the importance of mastering
the techniques and he urged those clergy likely to be televised to
attend a training course first. He believed that parsons should not
only be godly men but also professionally competent.

The result of all this activity was that the news began to spread
that exciting things were happening in Norfolk. Experienced men
from other dioceses were ready to leave possibly more prestigious
posts to work with Launcelot, and Ordination candidates grew in
numbers. His fellow Bishops came to regard him as the most
scandalous poacher in the business. If a man whom he had

approached were not able to leave his present work for another year
or two a note was made of the date when a further letter should go to
him with a reminder that he could now be free to move to Norwich.
He was always ready to listen to pleas from men who had failed or
were unhappy in their present diocese. His natural compassion
made him anxious to help a man in trouble by giving him a new
start, but he knew the danger of Norwich becoming a rehabilitation
refuge for too many misfits. He was also very much aware of which
Bishops could be trusted not to recommend a man whom they were
only too anxious to lose.

Given his early career, it was inevitable that Launcelot found it
easy to enjoy the company of young and able men and their
families. "Launcelot's Lads" was the nickname jealously bestowed
on those whom he had lured into the diocese. No man of any
strength of purpose, with a clear view of what he hoped to achieve,
will be liked by all who work under him, and there is no doubt that
some of the older and more entrenched clergy were highly critical of
the Bishop. A small minority disliked him. They complained that
he was not really interested in parish life and that his sole qualification, brought from the Antarctic, was an ability to endure the cold of
north Norfolk. The truth was that Launcelot always felt that his lack
of any parish experience made him appear inadequate when con-
fronted by powerful and slightly hostile elderly clerics. The
minutiae of parish life probably did not interest him deeply and it is
perhaps significant that on retirement from Windsor he did not seek
a small parish.

But nobody could ever fairly accuse him of not being interested in
the people who ran the parish. Nothing was more encouraging for his
clergy than Launceot's remarkable availability when they needed
his help. To be able to ring up Bishop's House, make an appointment
for an early meeting and then to pour out your troubles to a man
who really cared for you was a new and heartening experience. It is
true that when one of his young men wanted him he was rather more
ready to drop everything than when an older man, perhaps unsym-
pathetic to his Bishop's policy, wished to see him. This apparent
favouring of the young came from his knowledge of how much a man

in the early years of his ministry needed help and encouragement.

Furthermore, Launcelot had an uncanny gift of somehow knowing what was the right job for each man – laymen as well as parsons. In the days of his predecessor all moves from one benefice to another were described as "preferment". At his second staff meeting he forbade the use of the word in future: the sole purpose of all discussion about where a man should serve must always be on the basis of fitting the right man to the right job.

It was his intellectual openness which appealed, especially to young men, for Launcelot was the least dogmatic of Bishops. In the opinion of one young priest he made the whole business of the Church seem credible, and that to be a parson was not only a worthwhile but a possible job to do. The physical well-being and happiness of his men mattered. On the birth of a child five pounds and a bunch of grapes would arrive. As in Portsmouth he insisted on the importance of keeping fit for what should be a very demanding life. He encouraged his clergy to follow his example of making regular entries for games in his diary. As he grew older he was fully aware of the dangers of playing squash. If for some reason he had not played for a while he would choose an easy opponent so as to get back into form and run no risk of straining his heart. In fact he believed that he was a better squash player in his sixties than in his twenties. The Bishop's Hockey XI was a feature of Norwich as it had been of Portsmouth. Only once did it lead to trouble. The Press took some photographs of Launcelot in action, which were widely published, on a day when he should have been at an important engagement which he had forgotten.

Launcelot's care for his clergy endeared the great majority of them to him. They might disagree with some of his plans for the diocese; they might not all be ardent believers in Group Ministries. This did not matter. They had a Father in God whose genuine affection for them and glorious sense of fun made them his friends for life. This is why he could so easily be hurt when anyone whom he had tried to befriend turned against him. Being extremely sensitive he was terribly vulnerable to personal attack. When a man suddenly resigned from some office without warning, or when a senior cleric,

without giving any notice of his intention, openly attacked a Report
with which he had been closely associated at a Diocesan
Conference, Launcelot was bewildered, angry and deeply hurt.
'What have I done wrong?' he asked his Chaplain in dismay. For he
instinctively laid down the failure to have established a Christian
relationship at his own door.

Before Launcelot came to Norwich it had been decided that the
next Bishop would not live in the old Palace but that a new house
should be built. In spite of being a new building Bishop's House was
not as attractive nor as convenient as Bishopswood. Friends had
helped with the burden of moving house and one of them, Denny
Brock, took over the arranging of Launcelot's books in his study,
firmly placing the records of the Trinity Hall Boat Club on the
shelves reserved for fiction. Domestic help was becoming harder to
obtain and increasingly expensive. Nor could he any longer turn for
help to his mother, who was now too frail. She had travelled from
Fareham to Norwich by ambulance with Launcelot accompanying
her on the long journey. For a short while she lived in Bishop's
House, but soon she moved to a nearby nursing home where
Launcelot could visit her easily. It was clear that her life was
drawing to a close and she died peacefully on the 20th of October
1960. Launcelot had lost someone utterly devoted to him. Although
reconciled to her eldest son before she died, it was always Launcelot
who had mattered and who was her pride and joy. Her influence
over him had been far greater than he realised, though it had been
to her that for over half a century he had always turned for help and
encouragement. He was now very much on his own.
    Although the claims of his clergy always came first, Launcelot
quickly became popular with lay people throughout Norfolk. His
polar and naval background appealed to them, and once they had
got over their initial surprise at the difference between him and his
predecessor they welcomed him warmly. In a very traditionally
minded county it took time to get used to a man who took his office
as Bishop of Norwich very seriously but himself not at all.
    It was not beneath his dignity to go to London by train, travelling

on the footplate in order to make friends with the engine driver. The train only arrived six minutes late. Soon after coming to the city he gladly drank the first pint of beer in the restored Dolphin Inn in Norwich after performing the opening ceremony. It was said that the highest point in his episcopate was reached on the day that, accompanied by the Vice-Chancellor of the University and the Cathedral architect, he climbed the scaffolding to the top of the spire of Norwich Cathedral. Relaxing in a friend's garden at teatime he said that what he really wanted to do was to try to ride her penny-farthing bicycle. He quickly mastered the machine and was delighted when he was allowed to take it to Bishop's House on loan for a month. Here he and his Chaplain raced against each other by seeing who could ride fastest from the top of the grass slope, across the lawn to the summer house.

All of this was great fun and valuable relaxation, but what Launcelot really wanted to do was to involve lay people in his plans for the diocese. He believed that among the younger men there existed an untapped source of tremendous goodwill. He asked parish priests to suggest names of lively men whom he could approach, irrespective of whether or not they were churchgoers. In due course each man received a personal letter of invitation to a meeting at Bishop's House where plans were made for getting hold of interested people all over the diocese. Groups for discussion on matters of faith and Christian living were to be held informally in private houses, and through them Launcelot hoped to learn at first hand the needs of the man in the pew or, more often, the man who did not go to Church.

It was a brave idea, which deserved a better fate. It began well but ultimately foundered on the innate shyness of English people, who so often regard religion as a private concern and not as something to be discussed in a drawing-room by people with little in common and who at the start were often strangers. A magistrate, who greatly admired Launcelot and wanted to support him, found himself to their mutual embarrassment discussing beliefs with a young man whom he had recently had to sentence for a serious offence. Nor was the plan always helped by the local vicar, who was sometimes known to protest at meetings of this kind, from which he was excluded, being held in his parish.

However there were other ways of winning the hearts and helping hands of lay people. 'Confirmation tonight', Launcelot would call out to his Chaplain. 'Just time for a game of tennis first.' In the middle of the game he would break off to sign a batch of letters brought on to the court by his secretary. Then back to the game where his knowledge of the pits in the court was invaluable. After a quick bath he and his Chaplain set off, driven by the devoted chauffeur, Mr. Brothers. In the back seat Launcelot scratched out and amended his sermon to the point of invisibility. After the Service he met parents and godparents and parishioners. He had an enviable gift of moving quickly round the room before setting off for home, but able to make all feel that they had met him personally and that they mattered to him. Once after a Sunday Service at Wymondham the congregation left the church in pouring rain and ran to their cars. To their surprise Launcelot stood in the rain and shook hands with the occupants of each car through the hastily lowered window. As in Portsmouth, so in Norwich. In quite simple and unpremeditated ways he endeared himself to all who met him. After his lordly predecessor at Norwich he delighted people by being what they called 'perfectly normal'. 'Ey, who's that nice man that came in to talk to us just now?' asked a woman working in the kitchen where she was serving tea after an Induction. Her friend replied, 'Don't be silly. That's not a man. That's the new Bishop.'

In 1965 Launcelot decided that the time had come to pay a second round of visits to each parson and parish in the diocese. This time he set out with a different purpose. He intended to use these visits as a means of consultation in preparation for a proposed "Visitation Charge". It was very necessary to prepare the diocese for the inevitable changes which would have to be faced in the 1970s. Fewer clergy would be available; fewer would be employed in agriculture; there would be more industrial development in Norfolk; everyone would become more mobile. In the past Bishops had frequently used their legal right to require the attendance of clergy and churchwardens to receive their instructions. Modern methods of communication had made the regular use of a Visitation less necessary. On this occasion Launcelot decided to turn the Visitation into a way by which he received advice from the diocese.

To this end a series of sixteen questions were devised dealing with five main topics: the Church's teaching; the pattern of Church worship; the care and maintenance of Church buildings; pastoral reorganisation, and relations with other Christian Bodies. A year would be spent in Deaneries and parishes discussing the questions and the conclusions reached were to be sent to Bishop's House. At the Visitation, planned for April 1967, Launcelot intended to announce his decisions on the advice tendered to him. It was to explain what was in his mind and to strengthen the ties between Bishop, Clergy and people – in itself a typical and total reversal of traditional episcopal methods – that Launcelot started off on this second round of visits.

Before he had completed his journeys an event of the utmost importance to his own happiness, and thus to the well-being of the whole diocese, occurred. It was an event totally unexpected by anyone, perhaps unexpected even to himself. During 1964 Launcelot fell in love.

Launcelot's close friends had hitherto always been men. He liked women, especially the wives of his friends, though he was seldom quite as relaxed when alone with them as he was with men. His mother had maintained that she hoped to see him married before she died, but it is doubtful if she truly wanted to be supplanted in Launcelot's affections. Her daughter, Jean, believed that her mother kept a list of those whom she would be prepared to accept as a daughter-in-law, but nobody ever saw the list and the story is probably apocryphal. Had Launcelot married during her lifetime his wife would have had a very powerful mother-in-law. As for Launcelot, the possibility of marriage had presented itself once or twice in his earlier life but he always said that the happiness which came from his various jobs left him fulfilled and contented.

Several years before this time Ken Mathews had introduced Launcelot to his very able and charming sister, Dame Barbara

Brooke, whose husband, Henry Brooke, became Home Secretary. Both of these fine people have later been rewarded with life peerages. Launcelot became very much one of the family and joined them on holidays in Scotland, Wales and on the Continent. In 1962, and again in 1964, there was another friend of the family in the holiday party, Jane Agutter, a widow with a son and daughter.

Jane had grown up in the small Gloucestershire village of English Bicknor on the edge of the Forest of Dean where her father, Henry Machen, was the squire and owned a small estate which had been in the hands of the family since 1615. Over the years the estate had very much diminished in size but it still extended to Symonds Yat on the river Wye. Before the First World War Henry Machen had married a girl from Germany whose devotion to her new country ensured the continuing affection and respect of the local inhabitants in days when anti-German feelings ran high. Jane's only brother, James, an officer in the Royal Navy, could seldom be at home for long and she found herself greatly involved in helping her parents with estate work and village activities.

In July 1939 Jane married Anthony Agutter, who was then working for the Shell Company. When war came in September Anthony, already an R.N.V.R. officer, was called up and it seemed sensible for Jane to move back from Blackheath, where she and Anthony were living, to English Bicknor and it was here that their two children, Richard and Margaret, were born. When the war ended the family moved to Sussex, but in 1956 Anthony became seriously ill and could no longer continue to work in the City of London as a Shipping Broker. So in 1958 Anthony and Jane bought Church Farm at West Littleton in Gloucestershire, a lovely Cotswold house with about twelve acres of land. In March 1960 Anthony suffered a severe stroke and Jane had the agonising experience of watching over him while he lay unconscious for nine months. He died on New Year's Eve. Two years earlier her father had died and a year later her mother died. It had been a terrible three years for her.

Jane continued to live at Church Farm, though aware that it was too large a house on her own with the children away for much of the time. She had started working again for the Women's Royal

Voluntary Service, as she had done during the war years, and Lady Reading asked her to help at Headquarters in the work of housing elderly women of limited means. This involved travelling round the countryside for three days a week and it soon became clear to Lady Reading that in Jane she might have found someone who could one day succeed her. When Jane broke the news of her engagement to Launcelot Lady Reading replied: 'I'm only prepared to let you go as it's Launcelot you are marrying.' As Jane later commented: 'She apparently had a very high regard for him.'

Very early in the war Anthony Agutter was at *H.M.S. King Alfred* when Launcelot was Chaplain there. Jane has no recollection of meeting Launcelot then but distinctly remembers sitting on the terrace with her husband one Sunday after Church and saying what a marvellous sermon they had just heard. Little could she know how often she would hear his sermons in years to come.

The Brookes felt that Jane should not remain a widow for the rest of her life and that it was high time that Launcelot married. To put it for the moment no higher, Launcelot badly needed someone to look after him. His sister Jean used to come to Norwich from time to time in a vain attempt to solve the latest household crisis. Launcelot was far too busy to deal properly with his domestic staff. He never really learned that cooks find it difficult to provide a meal at the last moment for a number of unexpected guests. Nor was he always sufficiently aware that salaries and wages were rising. When with the invaluable aid of Mrs. Leonard, the Bishop of Thetford's widow, Christmas presents were bought for the staff, the housekeeper at the time said, somewhat acidly, to the Chaplain, 'What the staff would prefer is cash.' All too often Launcelot was not properly fed, and Jean worried about him coming home tired and too late to feel that he ought to bother anyone to give him supper.

Formal entertaining without his mother's help as hostess was less easy than in Portsmouth days, and Norfolk people are notoriously much harder to get to know quickly. Sherry parties were easier, and for these and other special occasions additional help in the person of a Miss Salmon was engaged. She had been trained as a parlour maid in some of the great Norfolk houses and was delighted to come to

Bishop's House in return for a small wage and a bath, not having one in her own house. She instructed the Chaplain to usher the ladies upstairs where they could leave their coats and where, on a wet evening, she awaited them, towel in hand, to clean any spots of mud from the backs of their stockings. This was entertaining in the grand style. Yet in spite of willing helpers Launcelot was leading a lonely life and even his most devoted Chaplain could not make Bishop's House a home.

Jane's first sight of Launcelot is a vivid memory. She had been invited to stay at the Brookes' house in Hampstead where Launcelot was also to be a guest for the night. Late in the evening there was a tremendous noise in the hall signifying the return to the house of the host, Launcelot and Gerald Ellison, from a dinner of "Nobody's Friends". Gerald Ellison was a very old friend, an Oxford rowing Blue and wartime naval padre, who was an incumbent in Portsmouth on Launcelot's arrival as Bishop and was himself to become Bishop of Chester and then of London. In the hall Launcelot had found a motor cyclist's helmet, and Jane's first sight of her future husband was of a helmeted figure capering about the room and proclaiming loudly, 'I'm a Space Bishop.' She was not quite sure that she was going to like him as much as her hostess hoped.

However, Scottish holidays gave her a more attractive picture and the Brooke family, to their delight, began to notice Launcelot's anxiety that Jane should travel to a picnic in his car. They gradually came to know each other well and Jane came to stay at Bishop's House when Jean was on one of her periodic visits. On the day that Jane left to go home Launcelot, coming back late from a meeting, seemed unusually anxious to learn what his sister had thought of Jane Agutter. Jean was slightly surprised at his repetition of the question, and replied that she had liked her very much indeed, but why was Launcelot so interested in her opinion. 'Well,' replied her brother rather shyly, 'I rather think that I would like to marry her but I don't think that I've got the time.' Fortunately Launcelot has always been able to find time for the things that really matter.

'Walking out and being a Bishop are difficult to combine,'

Launcelot recalled. It was not easy to do his courting without the whole diocese becoming aware that something was afoot. He must have felt that Sydney Smith had not been too far wide of the mark when he wrote: "How can a bishop marry? How can he flirt? The most he can say is 'I will see you in the vestry after Service.'" The Leander Club at Henley seemed a good meeting place and he once arranged to lunch there with Jane. It being the end of November they would be undisturbed. He had forgotten that it was St. Andrew's Day, a holiday for Eton boys, and the Club was crowded with parents, including Gerald Ellison, who were taking out their sons. Gerald Ellison on a later occasion was again an unwitting stumbling block. Jane had come to the House of Lords and had been told that when Launcelot left the Chamber she should come and meet him outside the Bishops' Room. As ill luck would have it Gerald Ellison left at the same moment as Launcelot in order to discuss some business with him in the Bishops' Room. Fortunately Jane realised in time what was happening and did not appear until the coast was clear. Despite these minor difficulties, Launcelot and Jane became engaged; a moment celebrated, as Launcelot said, with a lunch 'crowned with a banana split'.

On 6 January 1965 *The Times* carried the official announcement of the engagement. Congratulations poured in from high and low. "So delighted to hear your news. The Queen joins with me in wishing you both every possible happiness. Elizabeth R, Queen Mother" was the message in one telegram. Princess Margaret sent a letter of congratulations and good wishes, and Archbishop Ramsey wrote "Well, this is a surprise! and a very lovely one." A telegram from George Reindorp, then Bishop of Guildford, read, "Strongly approve this magnificent example of mutual interdependence." One of the more entertaining messages came from Mervyn Stockwood, then Bishop of Southwark, one of the three other bachelor diocesan Bishops. It was in the form of a mourning card with the widest possible black edging. On one side he had written "Launcelot – you cad!" and on the other side a very warm message of congratulation. All their friends were overjoyed at the new happiness which each had found.

Both Launcelot and Jane had wanted their engagement to be announced formally in the usual way but both hoped that the date and place of their wedding would be kept a secret among their families until after the event. Were the marriage to take place in Norwich Cathedral Launcelot would have found it impossible not to invite most of the diocese. Had they been married in Jane's country church it would still have been difficult to ensure reasonable privacy. The problem was solved when the Dean of Westminster, Eric Abbott, offered the beautiful St. Faith's Chapel in the Abbey. This was entirely private and could only accommodate a small number of relations and very close friends. Moreover the Chapel was familiar to Launcelot, for he had at times spoken to boys from Westminster School there on the evening before their Confirmation and had occasionally celebrated Holy Communion there on a weekday for boys from the school.

So on the afternoon of the 27th of April Dean Abbott escorted Jane from the Deanery into the Abbey, suggesting that to avoid undue attention she might try to look as if she were a sightseer. Ken Mathews performed the marriage ceremony and the Dean celebrated Holy Communion; Owen Wansbrough-Jones was the best man. Following the Service the Brookes held a party at their Hampstead home where Jane had been staying prior to the wedding. There was just time in Launcelot's overcrowded diary to snatch a week's honeymoon at Kinloch Rannoch before returning to Norwich for his second round of parochial visits. These had been planned before he envisaged matrimony, and although Jane often joined him on the Sunday it was not possible for her to accompany him throughout the weekend. So from the start Jane experienced the demands and pace of Launcelot's life.

It would be impossible to exaggerate the change which marriage brought to Launcelot in happiness and well-being. Jane is a very striking woman, most attractive to look at and charming to meet. As a Bishop's wife she was no Mrs. Proudie but she played her part as an equal partner in Launcelot's work, winning the affection and respect of Norfolk people as a personality in her own right and not as someone living in Launcelot's reflected glory.

All who have experienced deep happiness in marriage know that a great deal of mutual understanding and tolerance of each other's foibles and shortcomings are needed. Launcelot at the age of nearly fifty-nine had to adapt himself to the ways of one who had been happily married once and who had two grown-up children. To become a grandfather after four years of marriage was, he claimed, something of a record, and it took some getting used to. Jane was marrying a man with all a bachelor's habits and one who, except for the war years and his polar experience, had really lived a very sheltered life. With an adoring mother and surrounded always by devoted friends and helpers, a lesser man than Launcelot would have been horribly spoiled. Both had come from very different worlds, and since Launcelot's work would continue along familiar lines it was inevitably Jane who had to adjust the more.

All this is part of marriage. What mattered to Launcelot is that marriage came for him at a very important moment. He had always driven himself too hard and he could be too strict with himself. In anything involving self-discipline he has an iron will, always believing that with yet greater effort he could do his job better. Driven on by a sense of guilt, his determination to fill the unforgiving minute came less from his Presbyterian ancestry than from his deep humility. One of Jane's gifts to Launcelot was to bring out his gentleness which was in danger of being lost, and she saved him from the isolation which might have come from overwork and an inability to relax.

In countless other ways Jane helped Launcelot. She at once brought sanity to the domestic set-up and the standard of cooking improved markedly. Launcelot was alarmed when she appointed a cordon bleu cook, fearing that her salary would be beyond his means. Miss Elizabeth Taylor quickly proved to him that a good cook can actually save money by avoiding waste and she became a friend of the family. She discovered and ministered to his love of sticky, sweet puddings, especially if liberally covered with chocolate. Of greater importance was Jane's deeper understanding of what by then had become known as "the permissive age". With children of her own she knew at first hand more of the attitudes of young people towards sex and marriage than Launcelot, despite his magnetic hold over the young, could readily appreciate. She made it easier for him, with no sacrifice of his basic principles and beliefs which she shared, to keep abreast of rapidly changing values.

Not only did Jane bring happiness to Launcelot, she brought it to many clergy wives as well. If Launcelot had to be away on a Sunday she would ring up the wife of a parish priest, tell her that as she would be on her own she would much like to come to the morning Service and, if it were not too much trouble, to have lunch in the vicarage. In this way she not only came to know the wife as a personal friend but she could see and later tell Launcelot about the kind of difficulties which an overlarge vicarage presented to a woman. She also entertained them with unexpected informality. To be invited to a party for clergy wives at Bishop's House turned out to be a very different affair from what her guests had at first feared. To watch Wimbledon tennis on television, to wander at will round the garden or just to gossip happily over a good drink ensured a very successful party and not an irksome social duty.

This very happy partnership led Launcelot to say from time to time to a boy or a young man, 'Do you mind if I give you a piece of personal advice? Get married by the time you are fifty-eight.'

On the 19th of April 1967 Launcelot delivered his Visitation Charge to his clergy and their churchwardens. Writing about it afterwards in *The Norwich Churchman* – a lively paper which he had been instrumental in starting – he described the Visitation as "a Stock Taking with a view to taking action." Its main purpose was "to consider how the teaching, worship, the structure and organisation of the Church may be better related to the circumstances and needs of individuals and society today in a world which has passed and is passing so swiftly through radical and revolutionary changes." Of the need for the diocese to adapt to meet these changes he was acutely aware. "We have become so used to seeing the evidence of God's presence in the world in a certain former order of society, a certain former order of the Church, a certain set pattern of behaviour, that when these alter – as they must in a society in flux such as ours – we feel God is absent; that we are fighting a losing battle – a battle seen in terms of trying to recover the old forms in which we think God can be present."

The Charge was a lengthy document and there was a break in the proceedings, which had begun at 7.30 p.m., to enable the congregation to adjourn for refreshments. In the opening section dealing with Church teaching Launcelot announced developments along lines already laid down: systematic and supervised courses for clergy under a Director of Training, and advanced courses of study for certain laymen. He hoped that a study centre, with its own library and with provision for residential courses, might be established. This in fact began in Centre 71 shortly before Launcelot left Norwich. In every way the clergy were encouraged to equip themselves to defend their beliefs intelligently.

There were two related topics which were likely to cause much disagreement: the problem presented by the mediaeval churches and the whole question of pastoral reorganisation.

There were two diametrically opposed views about the future of a number of beautiful Norfolk churches, often in a bad state of repair and with tiny congregations. The traditionally minded held that where only two or three are gathered together it was wrong to deprive them of their much loved place of worship. Some went further and argued that even if no congregation existed these churches by their very beauty and atmosphere spoke to casual visitors and passers-by about things of the spirit. To them the suggestion that a single church could be labelled "redundant" was abhorrent.

Launcelot sympathised with this point of view but could not endorse it. He knew that it was 'difficult to estimate the "value" of a church' but he had come to the reluctant conclusion that the retention of so many virtually unused churches demanded the payment of too great a price. 'Clergy and faithful laity often find themselves so preoccupied with the immense task of preservation that it does appear to usurp a disproportionate amount of time, effort and money and also does affect their whole outlook to the Church.' He therefore required the Archdeacons to work out, in the light of modern requirements, proposals for the use of the country parish churches. They were to consider which should remain unaltered, which should be preserved as shrines, and which declared redundant.

He ended this part of the Charge with an earnest appeal. "Some of us feel that to close any church – particularly our own church – is a betrayal. If you feel like that, consider whether your feelings about what the Church exists for are the feelings of the New Testament. The Church is Christ's Body. The Church's members – clergy and laity – are in the world to continue Christ's work of healing, teaching, forgiving, reconciling men to God; and we must be careful to give this first place and not to put buildings before people."

Pastoral reorganisation had already gone ahead for the past few years. In his Charge he announced that there would be full discussion on the merits of extending Group Ministries and, in particular, whether they should be established in market towns. The City of Norwich presented a peculiarly difficult problem of its own with the large number of churches within its boundaries. Launcelot said that he had invited Henry Brooke (who had by then become Lord Brooke of Cumnor) to chair a special commission and that there might be another commission for Lowestoft. The Brooke Report was issued early in 1970, proposing a considerable reduction in the number of inner City parishes and churches, the establishment of a lay training centre, a separate Archdeaconry for Norwich, and the use of specialist ministries to supplement the work of the parishes.

Looking back it is now clear that everything in Launcelot's first eight years as Bishop of Norwich led up to the Visitation and that his remaining four years in the diocese were largely devoted to implementing his Charge. Centuries ago the prophet Ezekiel in a vision had been asked 'Can these bones live?' and he had been allowed to see that 'the breath came into them and they lived and stood up upon their feet, an exceeding great army.' Launcelot had been granted the same kind of vision. There are many who maintain that, taking into account all that Launcelot did in his years as a diocesan Bishop of two sees, the reorganisation of the diocese of Norwich and the new life which came to it through his vision of what the Church should be marked the crown of his episcopate.

NORWICH

1959 – 1971

(ii) Other Concerns

One of the most forceful reasons which made Launcelot feel that he would be justified in leaving Portsmouth for Norwich was the recent decision to found the University of East Anglia. Planning for the new University was only in the very early stages when he reached Norwich and he readily agreed to become a member of the Promotion Committee. Once the University had opened in October 1963 he served on both the Council and the Executive Committee.

A majority of the Promotion Committee and of the dons believed that any new university should not aim at copying Oxford and Cambridge but should reflect the twentieth century and not the Middle Ages. It should therefore be a secular institution with no Theological Faculty and no formal provision for organised religion. The first Vice-Chancellor, Frank Thistlethwaite, had been a Fellow of St. John's College, Cambridge, and his College had been closely associated with the newly founded Churchill College. He had therefore known much of the bitter hostility with which some of the Churchill dons had opposed the building of a College chapel. As Vice-Chancellor of U.E.A. he had to steer a difficult course between the opposition of most of his professional colleagues to any kind of religious presence on the campus and the wish of the influential Norfolk figures, generous contributors to the University, who disliked the total exclusion of religious activities.

It was at this point that Launcelot arrived. He was in a strong position to influence the character of the University, for even the most atheistic dons respected him as a former don himself, and as a man with a scientific approach to problems rather than a traditionally minded Arts man. He could have no sympathy with

the idea of a wholly secular university for he profoundly believed
that personal relationships throughout the campus must be 'loving'
and this implied the recognition of a spiritual dimension. At the
same time his freedom from any kind of rigid churchmanship and
his instinctive understanding of the changing needs of students made
him an invaluable and powerful member of the Promotion
Committee.

With the ready agreement of the Vice-Chancellor, who did not
share the views of his more extreme colleagues, Launcelot set up a
"Churches Committee for the University" to act as an informal
advisory body. He invited the heads of all the principal Christian
denominations and also a Jewish Rabbi to serve on this committee
and he was delighted when all of them agreed. For quite apart from
its primary purpose of helping the University, the Committee led to
greatly improved relations on other religious matters within the
diocese.

Launcelot knew that nothing could really be achieved until there
was a recognised place for Chaplains on the campus. The original
suggestion was that students and dons would be able to satisfy any
wish they might have to worship by going to a City church or
chapel. A proposal was made by one of the Archdeacons that the
University might take over one of the "redundant" Norwich
churches. Neither suggestion in Launcelot's opinion met the
University's needs.

So the first step was to gain the agreement of the University to the
appointment by each religious denomination of a "delegated
representative" to minister to the spiritual needs of any who might
consult them. This hideous title was scarcely encouraging. He had
no official position in the University and he was not a member of
the Senior Common Room; he was not even given dining rights.
The appointment of the Church of England representative caused
Launcelot some embarrassment. He was convinced that the task
required very distinctive qualities and experience and that such a
post could not automatically be entrusted to the vicar of the parish
in which the University campus lay. Launcelot's "representative"
must be a man appointed to one of the special ministries which he

was forming in the diocese, and in John Giles he found the right man. Giles has said that it was only the knowledge of Launcelot's support from his position on the University Council and his determination to improve the impossible conditions under which all the "representatives" had to work that made his life tolerable and gave him hope.

As U.E.A. grew in numbers from the original 113 students to nearly 3,000 during Launcelot's years in Norwich, the students themselves began to press for some way of holding meetings for worship and religious discussion. A Carol Service had been held in 1963, attended by about two-thirds of the student body. A year later at this service Launcelot preached a very moving sermon on the text "How shall we sing the Lord's song in a strange land?" By August 1965 the University Council recognised that the time had come when the original idea of a wholly secular university was no longer tenable. They relieved the "delegated representatives" of their unhappy title, allowing them to be known officially as Chaplains and recognising their position in the University.

The Council also recognised the need for an appropriate place on the campus where religious activities could take place. Here Launcelot's influence was again of prime importance. He pressed for the building of a "Chaplaincy Centre" at the heart of the University buildings, to be shared between all religious faiths, Christian and non-Christian alike. The Vice-Chancellor was very sympathetic to this idea and agreed that the Chaplaincy should at one and the same time be both central and accessible to students but also 'not too conspicuous'. This was bound to be a costly undertaking and Launcelot took a leading part in the Appeal for funds which was launched early in 1970.

In his speech supporting the Appeal Launcelot made his own position very clear by answering two of the questions raised by those doubtful of the rightness of such a project. First, he replied to the comment that to ask for and to spend money on a Chaplaincy Centre was wrong when the demands on Christian compassion to bring relief to the starving were so strong. 'To divert all our resources to meeting the needs of the world outside is like eating

your seed corn. Today's and tomorrow's students are the very
people who have the biggest contribution to make to the needs of
the world. Would anyone in their senses wish, for example, to cut
down on training doctors in order to provide funds for relief of
famine and disease?' He believed that university students must be
concerned with the things of the spirit. There would always be
discussions in students' rooms, in cafés and pubs, but what was also
needed was 'formal and informal discussion, debate, questioning –
yes, and worship – at some recognised centre within the University
itself which is set aside for this kind of thing'.

Secondly, he replied to the criticism that if the Chaplaincy were
really necessary then the University authorities or a government
grant should provide the money. He could not agree that public
funds, raised by taxation, should be spent on anything which was not
supported by all members of the University, recognising that many
dons and students denied the truth of any religion. More important
to him was his own belief 'that part of the essence of Christianity –
indeed of spiritual integrity of any kind – is that we should assent to
it of our own free will. Just as the concept of the Chaplaincy is non-
compulsory, so the support of it should be voluntary'. He ended his
speech: 'This age and this University do not call for a St. Peter Man-
croft [the lovely mediaeval church in Norwich] or for a Long Melford
church; but they do call for a centre in which members of the University can be helped to find the truth about God and themselves'.

To Launcelot's great delight the University Council, when the
Appeal was half way towards achieving its target, offered to make a
matching grant of £1 for £1 up to a total of £15,000. The sole
stipulation was that the building should contain no fixed
ecclesiastical furnishings. Each denomination would provide what
was necessary for its form of worship. The simple and dignified
building which the architect, Bernard Feilden, designed to be
erected at the heart of the University, close to the main Common
Rooms and the Restaurant, met with Launcelot's full approval. He
had however moved to Windsor by the time that Bishop Eric
Cordingley formally opened it and conducted a Service of
Dedication in January 1972.

Four years later Launcelot was back again to receive an honorary Doctorate of Civil Law, the highest honour which the University could bestow, in recognition of all that he did for it in the vital formative years, especially – in the words of the Public Orator – as 'one of the sanest, most sensible and dependable advisers in the long discussions about the place of organised religion in a twentieth century secular University'.

Launcelot was by no means solely concerned with the Chaplaincy at U.E.A.: the welfare of dons and students through the provision of adequate living and working conditions mattered greatly to him. Speaking in the House of Lords in May 1962, before U.E.A. had opened, he stressed the urgent need in the new universities for dons to have time both for teaching and for their research. Like their students they must live close to their work for 'the total environment of university life and of the university as a community go a very long way to make the standards of university education'.

In what was almost his last speech in the House of Lords in March 1971 Launcelot returned to the theme of what makes a good university and enables it to meet the needs of the nation. He defined the aim of a university as being 'to teach a man or a woman to distinguish the true from the false; the genuine from the spurious; the valuable from the meretricious; the significant from the insignificant whereby he may refine his sensibilities, order his thoughts and exercise his powers of judgement and of expression to the point where he is capable of intellectual maturity'. This could not be achieved unless the physical conditions of university life made it possible for students to associate easily with their contemporaries and with scholars and teachers in different faculties.

In 1962 Launcelot's plea had been for the expansion in the number of students, for 'it is a serious matter to bring young people to the point of readiness for higher education and then to submit them, after rigorous competition, to undeserved rejection'. Yet he became increasingly worried at U.E.A. where the academic and administrative departments had been built but where there was 'a near vacuum so far as social and recreational facilities were concerned'. He was particularly worried that no public money was available for student accommodation. He had orginally hoped that the University could be built within the City but this had proved too costly. However the site chosen at Earlham, some three or four miles from the City centre, proved admirable if only a community life could be developed.

The peculiar circumstances of U.E.A. highlighted the importance of personal relations between the Council, academic staff, students and the City. Launcelot did his utmost to get to know as many students as possible. He played squash with some, took a close interest in the cross-country athletes and came into easy contact with the geographers and environmental scientists. He was much involved in the Expeditions Society. Parties at Bishop's House enabled him to make friends with dons and students and he regarded it as a valuable contribution to the life of the University to help to build up a sense of being a community. He knew how important this was in lessening the dangers of isolation, and the frequent loneliness of students far away from home for the first time and compelled to live apart from each other in lodgings.

This interest in student welfare was repaid by the trust which many of them, by no means all religiously minded, placed in his judgement. Two incidents illustrate Launcelot's hold over young people.

A graduate scientist had been before the Courts and fined for pedalling heroin; he had subsequently been expelled from the University. This led to students occupying many of the University buildings in protest against what they claimed was the injustice of a double punishment. Late one evening six students arrived at the door of Bishop's House, asking to see Launcelot. He agreed to see them provided that they assured him that they were not an official deputation but a group of private individuals and on the understanding that total confidentiality about their talk was maintained.

After hearing why the students felt that pedalling heroin did not merit such drastic treatment by the University Launcelot put three questions to them. Did they believe that there should be murderers on the campus? Those pedalling hard drugs were, in effect, murderers. Did they believe in academic work? If so they were inhibiting this by their occupation of the buildings. Did they think it justifiable to damage University property as they had done? In civil life they would have been liable to terms of imprisonment. He ended by hoping that at least they would apologise to the Vice-Chancellor for the disruption to the life of the University. As far as he could discover no apology was offered but the trouble died down almost at once.

When Sir Humphrey Gibbs, the last Governor of Rhodesia before U.D.I., was given an honorary degree in 1969, a number of students disrupted the proceedings in protest against a man whom they failed to appreciate was resolutely opposed to apartheid and a far better friend to Black Africa than Ian Smith's government. Launcelot was unable to attend the ceremony and was very distressed when he learned what had happened. It was a sign of the students' belief in him that the editor of the main students' paper accepted an article which he wrote about Sir Humphrey in which he set the record straight.

Launcelot knew how gullible young students could be, how easily swayed emotionally to demonstrate for the half-understood cause and how quickly they could become frustrated when working for a degree which promised no subsequent employment. As one who had taught and lived alongside students in the kind of dedicated proximity which he hoped would one day be possible at U.E.A., he was able to explain to occasionally outraged members of the University Council that the unkempt and not always very clean young men and women, who were causing so much trouble and who expected to be consulted on University policy, were not barbarians clamouring at the gates of Rome but too easily led astray young people, immature and not always very intelligent but who responded to a sympathic approach.

The years of student revolt which began in 1968, and the continuing lack of government grants for students' amenities, led him in his 1971 speech to the House of Lords to conclude rather sadly that 'a young person will be much better off with no university education at all than with frustration, disillusionment and apathy, which can all too easily result from inadequate provision within our university life'. However, even if his high hopes for U.E.A. when he first encountered it had not been fully realised a decade later, his contribution to its early years was outstanding. Inevitably a few of his clergy failed to understand the long-term importance of setting the new University on a right course and constantly grumbled that their Bishop's time would be better spent on strictly diocesan business. They perhaps sensed that Launcelot was at his happiest in university life and they may have resented it. Yet Launcelot's broader conception of a Bishop's work and his belief that his particular gifts should be used to the best advantage ensured that at U.E.A. the things of the spirit were not denied.

Launcelot was convinced that the Youth work within his diocese needed a new approach. He was keen to appoint a Youth Chaplain for each Archdeaconry and one for the City of Norwich, who would act as a kind of chairman. What was right for U.E.A. and for work in industry and education would be right for Youth work. He was very much a believer in specialist, extra-parochial ministries, which he was convinced were more likely to make a stronger impact on secular society than the traditional parish organisation. Thus he was determined only to appoint men whom he felt would be first class at the particular job. These men were not greatly in evidence when he came to Norwich and he was prepared to move slowly. It took a long time to find the right men, to secure the appropriate appointments, stipends and facilities. As with the Group Ministries determination and courage were needed to change the accepted structure. Some parish priests, especially those with extreme High Church or Evangelical views, tended to resent any activities not under their control and which might take "their" young people away on a Sunday.

Gradually the team was completed, with the Reverend Ron Ingamells as Diocesan Youth Officer. A centre at which young people could meet was established under one of the Chaplains at Horstead Rectory and the planning of activities was organised and guided by Ingamells. The first Diocesan Youth Weekend was held in 1963 at Caistor-on-Sea Holiday Camp where those attending were generously given special terms. These weekends became a central feature of the Youth Work and during Ingamells' years in Norfolk about 1,500 young people attended them.

Launcelot always came for the whole weekend. He never interfered with the organisation and trusted the men whom he had chosen to use their expertise even if their experimental methods, which gradually replaced the usual talks and discussions, sometimes puzzled him. His full involvement in the activities included a very early morning swim in the icy North Sea on the Saturday morning and, before his illness, taking part in the game of soccer during the afternoon. Throughout the three days he was available to all who wanted him in his châlet, and the weekend finished with a celebration of Holy Communion at which he usually spoke in simple terms to a congregation which now knew him as a friend.

Like most other people in high office Launcelot found that being a Bishop tended to distance him from lay people as a whole and not least from young people. The barrier could only be broken down by sharing with them in some activity such as worship, discussion or, above all, sport. Once the barrier was removed he could discover for himself what young people were thinking about and what were their needs. In the difficult task of really getting to know and understand the young he was greatly helped by the County Director of Education, Sir Lincoln Ralphs. A Methodist himself, with a wife who was an Anglican, his leadership in education both in Norfolk and nationally, was explicitly Christian. At Ralphs' invitation Launcelot visited a number of maintained schools in the diocese and valued these opportunities greatly.

The Outward Bound Schools were obvious places for Launcelot to visit and after marriage Jane went with him. In about 1960 the Schools Hebridean Society had been founded and Launcelot became an official "Adviser" to the Society. Each summer he spent a long weekend with the expedition on one of the Hebridean Islands, living alongside schoolboys and taking part in their arduous and imaginative activities. Nothing could be less episcopal than

Launcelot in his kilt, playing touch rugger and joining in the day's programme. He was quite content to celebrate Holy Communion on one occasion on an altar made from two woolsacks covered with a rug. The Cross was made out of two sticks and a mug had to serve as a chalice.

One reason which had been put to Launcelot in favour of his move to Norwich was that as Bishop of an ancient see he would be able to speak with greater authority on matters of national concern. He was never the man to seek the limelight of a public platform or to become politically involved – save on one occasion. He believed that the race theories as propounded by Mr. Enoch Powell were a denial of human dignity and basically unchristian. With considerable courage he offered to meet the Press to explain and put forward views which at that time were seldom expressed by his fellow Bishops. Only Archbishop Ramsey had condemned Mr. Powell's speeches in forthright terms. However, if public meetings were usually uncongenial, he had been completely convinced by Bishop Bell that to take an active part in the House of Lords debates was an important part of a Bishop's responsibility. As Bishop of Portsmouth he had spoken from time to time but as Bishop of Norwich he intervened far more frequently in debates when he could speak with authority. He was sure that the hours spent in preparing his speeches were well worth the effort.

Because in his House of Lords speeches Launcelot's fundamental beliefs stand out so clearly it is worth spending time studying them.

All men are created by God and must therefore have a reverence for life. They do not possess the earth on which for a short while they live: they are trustees of God's gifts, which must be handed on to the next generation unimpaired. This implies responsibility – a word used again and again by Launcelot in his speeches. Responsibility must dictate man's attitude towards the animal creation, towards the environment and, above all, towards the whole of mankind.

Because being children of God demands responsible behaviour Launcelot deplored the steady decline in this vital sense of

responsibility. Speaking in March 1965 he gave what he saw to be
the reasons for this decline. The ending of national military service
had removed one form of responsible service to the community.
Because the threat of poverty had been largely banished no longer
have boys and girls 'to work long hours and hard to keep the family
from poverty. Temporarily, at least, it looks as if the economic
compulsion towards responsibility has been relaxed. Thrift makes
little appeal in an inflationary economy.' Society had become much
more mobile with the result that 'if your behaviour is not subject to
the eye and tongue of your neighbour, the influence of convention is
likely to be rather less'. Most important of all was the rapid progress
towards universal education which had accelerated the process by
which every generation questions the beliefs and behaviour of the
previous generation, so that everything, especially moral traditions,
was being questioned.

What worried him most was the misunderstood teaching of
psychiatry, which could be taken to imply that 'there is no real
distinction between right and wrong, that we need not and must not
ever feel guilty; that guilt is bad for us and that, anyway, we cannot
help what we are and what we do, for we are not responsible'. He
ended this speech by blaming 'our own adult responsibility for the
inadequate and confused pattern of ideas through which we have
been leaving young people to find their own way.'

Broadly speaking Launcelot took part in those debates which
dealt with four main topics: Youth – education, community service
and general welfare; the dangers to the environment; the issues
raised by nuclear, biological and chemical warfare; and, perhaps
nearest to his heart, the future of the Antarctic continent and the
need to prevent exploitation of the ocean seabed.

Launcelot had come to believe that schools were setting far too
great store on examination results, thus enhancing an unhealthy
competitive spirit leading to the evils of the "rat race". This side of
education had been stressed to the virtual exclusion of developing
the whole personality. 'There is an important sense in which every
child has to be educated for himself alone . . . and equipped to live as
a human being in a human society or, as I should prefer to say, a

child of God in a world which God has created and which is subject
to His sovereign rule.'

Furthermore most adults had become uncertain about what the
norm of conduct should be. 'We have become incredibly apologetic
about the moral values which we do possess and, in particular,
about our public witness to them.' People had come to act as if
'morals, so to speak, are a private affair and not society's business. I
believe that this is a confusion which brings great difficulty to those
who are engaged actively in education. This, together with our
reluctance to make dogmatic assertions, or to try to impose our
beliefs on anyone else, has meant that there has been a tendency to
profess a new virtue of ethical neutrality.'

While young people, in Launcelot's opinion, had a right to the
best which society could provide in school hours or in leisure
activities, they also needed to be trained in making a responsible
return to society in varying forms of community service. Again and
again he expressed his hope that 'during the last years at school . . .
the pupils should be encouraged to regard some contribution to the
life of the community as an essential ingredient of their own
education . . . It is the paradox of the Welfare State that the more it
expands its social facilities the less able does it become to man them
. . . There are fields in which the young can make a distinctive
contribution . . . and we shall show that we are taking them seriously
when we make it abundantly clear that we recognise this and give
them the opportunity.'

Like so many of his generation Launcelot was deeply disturbed by
the growing menace of youthful indiscipline, made worse by their
relative affluence. Somehow ways must be found 'to claim and
utilise the more generous and idealistic impulses which all young
people potentially possess.' Hence his continuing involvement in
the Outward Bound Movement, Voluntary Service Overseas, the
Duke of Edinburgh's Award Scheme or the Brathay Hall training
courses. He became a member of the Templer Committee, which
the Colonial Secretary had appointed to consider ways in which
young people could make a positive contribution towards a more
peaceful world by wider travel and increased chances of meeting

students from foreign lands. One of the recommendations of this Committee was the building of a large hostel in London to make easy contacts possible. Little came of this but in the work of Atlantic College he saw an excellent way of allowing young people in their formative years of sixteen to eighteen to grow up and be taught alongside those of different countries, cultures and faiths, and he became increasingly active as a Governor.

In all of this concern for Youth Launcelot was certain that the Church had a big part to play. 'The basis of a specifically Christian attitude of mind towards young people is a concern for them for their own sakes, all the deeper because they are recognised as persons who have an eternal destiny.' There was, however, a danger of too much talk about 'Christian values'. As he wrote: "You don't add anything to 'Christian values' by always feeling the need to use the adjective 'Christian' for the values concerned. To the average person this simply looks as if the concern of the Christian has more to do with propaganda than with the values themselves." Everything turned, he said, on whether those who talk in this way are seen by young people to speak with integrity, sincerity and conviction.

His belief that young people must be trusted was seen in his support of the proposed lowering of the age of attaining majority from twenty-one to eighteen. He rather hoped that this could be done in stages, especially in its application to early marriage. 'Every other decision they [young people] make is capable of being changed, cancelled or amended in the light of experience. But marriage, if it is to remain a meaningful institution, is a once-for-all decision of ultimate importance, both in its nature and its consequences, for the individual concerned and for society as a whole. In this area we should not be happy to allow young people to learn by their mistakes.' Earlier physical maturity made a lowering of the age of majority essential and such lowering would promote, in his view, a more rapid growth towards maturity and, he hoped, responsibility. He disliked any suggestion that the decision to marry should be dependent on the consent of anyone but those directly concerned and he voted in favour of reducing the necessity of parental consent to marriage before the age of eighteen.

'Since man does not live by bread alone, we must also consider
what man requires of his environment in non-economic terms. Man
himself is essentially part and parcel of nature and the quality of his
life depends in no small degree on his relationship to nature. That
he has authority and power over nature is indisputable, but just as
he makes demands upon nature, so nature makes demands upon
him. His authority over nature must, therefore, be tempered by
responsibility; his power over life by reverence for life.' In these
words Launcelot stated his position in the debate on the difficult
problem of balancing economic development against environmental needs.

Launcelot was not starry-eyed in his approach to this problem.
His Norfolk farmers had to earn a living and this often meant
intensifying their output by modern methods to the detriment of
natural resources. But it was essential to man's well-being to
maintain 'a fruitful relationship between man and nature, in
particular between man and animal life'. Hence his opposition to
the hideous methods employed in producing veal and to some forms
of "factory farming". 'It is not only a matter of whether animals are
treated cruelly but a matter of whether they are treated as things
rather than as animals . . . When an animal ceases to be itself and
becomes in the eyes of the operator a thing, a mere unit of factory
production, then I suggest that an attitude of inhumanity has
entered in which is incompatible with the responsibility of the
operator as a human being.'

As far as "factory farming" was concerned, he accepted the view
expressed in the Brambell Committee's Report on Codes of Practice
for animals reared in intensive units. Their criterion was that
animals should enjoy sufficient freedom to exercise certain basic
behaviour patterns, such as dust bathing and room to spread their
wings for hens. It was arguable that in some forms of intensive
farming the creatures might enjoy better conditions than otherwise:
they were warm and given a well balanced diet. Launcelot's
opposition was not to "factory farming" as such but to any form of
intensive farming in which the behaviour patterns were inhibited.
He did not blame the farmers. He insisted that it was the duty of a

government to remove from the farmer the economic pressure which leads him to increase his output by inhuman means.

Launcelot saw the increasing danger to the environment as coming primarily from the "population explosion". More and more land was being taken for housing and the provision of urban amenities. The coastline was being progressively despoiled; pylons marched across the landscape; there was steady pollution of air and water. In East Anglia he feared that the planners were so intent on creating new industrial centres where London's overspill could find work that they were forgetting that they must also make "human communities". Somehow, probably by overall government planning and a recognition of the dangers already affecting the environment, moral considerations must be acknowledged. 'The natural environment of man provides for basic needs which cannot be provided in any other way; needs which are aesthetic, emotional and spiritual'.

On the issue of nuclear warfare Launcelot had stated his view to the Lords in February 1959 while still Bishop of Portsmouth. He could not accept the extreme pacifist position as he believed that warfare could be morally justified 'in defence against blatant aggression or to remove some intolerable injustice, it being understood that the scale and degree of destruction must be the minimum required to secure the end in view'. He argued that the moral sanction against the use of nuclear weapons 'is a positive one – namely the absolute necessity under God of respecting the sanctity of human life. The evidence seems to be quite inescapable that the use of these nuclear weapons which cause vast indiscriminate destruction at the time of their use, and afterwards . . . is utterly repulsive to man's moral sense'.

In the same speech Launcelot made a plea for as much information as scientists can give commensurate with the guarding of defence secrets. 'The fall-out from misinformed opinion causes widespread contamination'. In all this the scientists must bear a heavy responsibility. While they cannot be held morally responsible for the way in which the knowledge, resources and power which they placed within men's reach are used, yet like the dispensing chemist they know when to label the bottle "poison – not for internal use" even if they cannot prevent anyone from swallowing the contents'.

Exactly ten years later he spoke again on the same subject. He had become increasingly worried at the secrecy surrounding defence plans because secrecy bred fear. Nor could he argue that one form of warfare is necessarily more cruel than another. 'All one could say is that sudden death is to be preferred to slow or painful dying and that whatever the method of slaughter any wholesale attack on a human population is repugnant and especially repugnant when it includes small children'. The nuclear bomb had given mankind a weapon of unprecedented barbarity and he denounced its use, particularly on the grounds of its long-term effects such as cancer, leukaemia and as yet unknown genetical results. Equally unjustifiable were all forms of biological and chemical warfare with the resulting devastation of herds and crops and of human beings in large numbers. He concluded that the likelihood of any general renunciation of such weapons was remote and that the only course was to work by every means for the banning of war itself.

'The Antarctic is the least spoiled continent in the world'. Launcelot had welcomed the Antarctic Treaty, which had been signed in Washington in December 1959, and his first speech in the House of Lords as Bishop of Norwich had been a plea to the British government to ratify the treaty. In May 1967 he undertook to pilot a conservation measure for the Antarctic through the Upper House aimed at promoting international co-operation in scientific discovery for peaceful purposes and the protection of wild life. It was a measure requiring endorsement by signatory nations of the Antarctic Treaty and it had the distinction of being probably the first occasion when conservation provisions had presented any real threat.

On this subject he could speak with the authority of first hand knowledge. Since the days when his Antarctic parish had consisted of at most sixteen men there were, thirty years later, over three thousand men working during the Antarctic summer and some seven hundred throughout the year. He feared both dangers from international rivalry and the risks to wild life. The value of Antarctica to mankind at that time lay not in the remote possibility of economic gain but in the scientific information which was being gained in the spheres of meteorology, geophysics, glaciology and in some branches of biology.

Speaking of the danger to seals, penguins and other forms of bird life, he told a charming story of penguin curiosity. One day, while geologising, 'I became aware that I was being observed. I looked up and there were sixty or seventy Adélie penguins peering over the ice-foot. I spent the day hammering the rocks and every time I looked up there were my "faithful flock". Their curiosity was constant but evidently unsatisfied.' He feared that there was a danger of indiscriminate killing of seals, which might not long be immune from commercial exploitation, and he believed that the sole justification for the killing of animals was 'if a completely scientific purpose is to be served'. No longer were Antarctic expeditions dependent upon seal meat as they had been in the nineteen-thirties.

Along with his intense personal interest in the fate of Antarctica was Launcelot's growing concern for the preservation of the ocean seabed. He first spoke to the House of Lords on the general subject of marine science and technology in July 1969 when he pointed to three dangers. He feared that the ocean seabed might provide a 'gratuitous bonus' for the developer as opposed to the under-developed countries. There was also the likelihood of marine pollution and military installations which would heighten international rivalry. Some form of control was essential before it was too late, not only to forestall disaster but because 'ocean space offers a remarkable opportunity for breaking through the system . . . whereby sectional interests continue to dominate over common good.'

A year earlier in August 1968 he called the attention of the Lambeth Conference to these dangers. When referring to the military dangers he quoted a Soviet scientist who had claimed, 'the nation which first learns to live under the seas will control the world'. Launcelot's Resolution, seconded by the Bishop of the Virgin Islands, urged that development of the ocean seabed should be conducted in a manner consistent with the principles of the Charter of the United Nations. It was carried without dissent.

Launcelot maintained that lack of public awareness was one reason for inaction by the British government, even though 'for the first time the sea is going to become something more than a highway'. He was quite certain that 'the exploration and exploitation of the ocean space is going to be a major concern for the twenty-first century'. Thus it was that just over a year later he moved a motion that 'the seabed, beyond the limits of national jurisdiction, should be administered as a common heritage of mankind, and a world ocean régime should be created to that end through an international convention'. He pointed out that the seabeds constituted some five-sevenths of the earth's surface and that there was no agreed form of jurisdiction over them. No adequate definition existed of where national sovereignty ended and it would be morally wrong for the expected benefits from exploiting the seabed to accrue solely to nations with a coastline.

He illustrated the danger from what had already been seen in the North Sea oil drilling. If the oceans were to be parcelled out between nations 'all over the world, the oceans will look like the North Sea but with every oil concession boundary turned into a frontier with a potential of international conflict'. It was, in his view, useless to look to national governments to control the coming dangers, for oceans constituted a unified global system and nothing less than 'a world government for the ocean deeps' would suffice. A new type of authority must be set up 'operated not on behalf of a proliferation of national governments but on behalf of the functional needs of those undertakings which are going to explore and exploit the oceans on behalf of mankind.' His plea based on his own scientific knowledge and his Christian conviction met with the support of his peers.

"I regard it as a minor disaster that he is leaving us," wrote Lord Shackleton in the *Norwich Churchman*, when by moving to

Windsor Launcelot could no longer be a member of the House of Lords, "To those of us who have worked together to raise and develop consideration of particular issues which are of great importance but are not initially of popular appeal, the presence of a man – himself an authority – like Launcelot is invaluable." So many peers regretted his having to leave their House that an attempt was made to get a Life Peerage for him but to no avail. It was probably felt that to ennoble one former diocesan Bishop in this way would create a precedent and raise the difficulty of special treatment for one man. There were many who saw no difficulty, for to them Launcelot was unlike other Bishops.

As can be seen from his speeches in the House of Lords the approach of a scientist to Christianity was Launcelot's constant theme. It is a theme which has run through his personal life ever since the early inner debate on where his work should lie – in continued scientific research or in the ordained ministry. This tension and its resolution was the subject chosen by him for the sermon which he preached in Norwich Cathedral in September 1961 on the occasion of the Norwich meeting of the British Association.

'The scientist for the purposes of his work must be detached and dispassionate, and his conclusions provisional. When it comes to his social relationships, however, the values and forms of truth which relate to this side of his life apply very differently. He cannot, must not, remain detached – he cannot, must not, remain dispassionate. He must be prepared to stand committed, for better or for worse. Integrity in relationships requires commitment. Integrity in the scientific sense forbids it.' The choice which every man must make is to decide whether his life is purposive, sustained by a power greater than himself or a chance arrangement. 'The way one lives requires an affirmation or a denial concerning the very nature of Creation.

'The Christian belief about Creation does not involve any necessary ground of contradiction between the scientist and the Christian in regard to the observable facts . . . the question which

remains is the interpretation which we set upon these facts . . . To
give precedence to caring – to maintain that other factors must be
subservient concerning the end and purpose of Creation . . . From
the image of God, as Creator, whose hands have made and fashioned
him, the believer moves into the relationsip of a son – a relationship
sustained by Love – a relationship of giving and receiving which
lasts as long as life itself . . . Caring involves and even demands an
openness of mind as well as of heart to the spirit of enquiry . . . Love
is also a unifying power within man – for once given its place, the
different sides of our personality at last fit purposively together. And
Love is a unifying power between men, enabling them to sacrifice
their personal interests for the good of others . . . The Christian
symbol is the Cross, because it was on the Cross that the power of
Love was, above all, displayed – a power which, in the very act of
sacrifice, sows the seed of new life, liberating such a Spirit as will
continually lead mankind into all truth.‘

No full understanding of Launcelot's personal faith and its
proclamation is possible without recognition of his integrity as a
scientist. As a young man on the brink of Ordination he felt bound
to confess to the Bishop that he could not accept the doctrine of the
Virgin Birth. As scientific knowledge grew he became less narrowly
orthodox for his theological thinking had always to embrace
scientific truth. This to some extent explains his hold over educated
people. Never from Launcelot would they receive conventional
answers to their searching questions. Like them he has always been
a seeker for truth into whatever difficult paths this might lead him.
But unlike some of his fellow scientists he has no doubt that, as he
said in his British Association sermon, 'there is such a thing as
ultimate truth – however limited my understanding of it may be – a
value outside myself to which every side of my personality must be
related . . . I am part of a Creation made and sustained by Love.'

Launcelot's work for the University of East Anglia and his share
in the House of Lords debates took place while he was actively
engaged in the re-organisation of the diocese and in the day to day
demands which being a Bishop made upon him. Archbishop

Ramsey invited him to become Chairman of a body known officially as the Archbishop's Advisers on Needs and Resources, more familiarly known as the Archbishop's Wise Men. Its purpose was, in effect, to try to keep the peace between the Church Commissioners and the Central Board of Finance. When Launcelot protested that finance and administration were not his greatest strengths Archbishop Ramsey said that he wanted him because of his knowledge and understanding of the conditions under which so many of the clergy had to work. So Launcelot added this to his other duties. Furthermore from 1970 he was Vice-Chairman of the Parliamentary Group on World Government and a member of the Royal Commission on Environmental Pollution.

Travelling all over a diocese as large as Norwich was a time consuming business but Launcelot, driven by the devoted Mr. Brothers, used the time profitably. In the words of his chauffeur, 'I was always amazed at the extraordinary ability as to how when travelling in the car he could do so much work. On journeys of any distance he would arrange himself with piles of letters, papers, etc. and a dictaphone in the back of the car and for the whole of the journey dictate into the machine letters to be typed by the secretaries on return. Even in London . . . he seemed able to shut out all outside movement and distractions and work just as well. This he would do at night just the same, there being special reading lights fitted in the rear of the car.'

Fortunately he could also find time for vigorous exercise – tennis and swimming in the summer, hockey in the winter and squash all the year round. His enjoyment of swimming could lead to problems. On his way to a Service Launcelot suggested to his Chaplain that there was just time for a swim. He had set out in old clothes, intending to change after his bathe. When it came to dressing he found that his case only contained his robes and was devoid of shirt or studs. He borrowed his Chaplain's back stud to fix his stock and covered his nakedness with his cassock. All went well until he started to remove his cassock in the vestry after the Service.

In the summer of 1967 Jane had noticed that Launcelot was

dragging his right foot slightly although he himself was scarcely conscious of this. Suddenly, when playing in a tennis four at Keswick, his leg ceased to work properly and he was forced to stop. For the moment his condition was not sufficiently hampering to prevent his going to Kenya with Jane.

The invitation to Kenya had come from the Principal of the University of East Africa as a result of the raising in Norfolk of some £50,000 for the Freedom from Hunger Campaign. The particular project to which this money was to be given was for a residential block and extension to the Veterinary College at Kabate, part of the University. Launcelot had been responsible for launching the Appeal which was generously supported by the leading men in the County and by the Churches. The farming community of Norfolk saw the scheme as a wise and realistic way of helping the peoples of East Africa. The main purpose of the visit was to hand over the cheque to the Principal at an official ceremony. Being Launcelot, he thought that only a weekend need be devoted to this engagement. until Jane very firmly pointed out that people did not go all the way to East Africa for a weekend but for a fortnight at the very least. She hoped that a rest and constant swimming in warm water would cure his leg.

In fact the visit lasted for three weeks. Once the official business was over he and Jane visited several young men working on V.S.O. projects, and they went to the Outward Bound School on the slopes of Mount Kilimanjaro. They stayed with the Assistant Warden of Tsavo National Park, went on safari in a wide circle round Mount Kenya and met Doctor Michael Woods, the Flying Doctor. One week was spent surfing at Malindi, a week of complete idleness.

Unfortunately the holiday did not produce the hoped-for result. On his return from Kenya his condition deteriorated rapidly and began to cause considerable anxiety. His doctor sent him to the London Hospital for Nervous Diseases in Queen Square for a series of tests and a thorough overhaul. Here he won over the Matron to understanding the necessity of having a supply of sherry available for his constant stream of visitors. Apart from what Jane brought in, a bottle arrived with the compliments of the hospital management to a popular patient. For Jane this was a particularly agonizing time. Her deep anxiety for Launcelot was made worse by the fact that he was in the room next to that in which her first husband had lain during his final illness.

Diagnosis of Launcelot's condition was not easy. Overwork was ruled out as a possible cause. To his relief he was pronounced organically very sound and it seemed that he was suffering from a very rare symptom – a tiny failure in the spinal column. There was a probability – no doctor could be certain – that this failure was traceable to the days of his illness as a boy at Rugby and his consequent inability to perspire normally. The days of hard games playing were suddenly over but on the credit side was the knowledge that in every other way he was fit and well and that his mobility should improve. Launcelot said many years later that the knowledge that he was not the victim of some incurable progressive disease enabled him to come to terms with a limitation of his activities more easily than he feared. He made no reference to the courage and determination needed to fight against his disability.

During 1968 he was fully back at work, first on two sticks and then only helped by one. The pages of his diary in 1969, for instance, show very little lessening of his activities, with the occasional note of a visit to the physiotherapist. His travels all over the diocese and to various parts of the country continued, while the number of visitors to Bishop's House did not grow less.

It was fortunate for Launcelot that retirement, even in the sense that he would later interpret that word, lay some years ahead. With all forms of vigorous exercise ruled out there was little beyond his work to satisfy his ferocious energy. He enjoyed reading books on polar research and, as far as time allowed, he tried to keep up his theological reading. But books have never really been an essential part of his life; he has never been what a Thomas Hardy character would call "a perusing man". Music he always enjoyed but it was almost impossible to persuade him to go to a concert. If Jane managed to achieve this he would return home full of enthusiasm for the music which he had heard but it would be a long time before

he went again. His interest in Art had never been much developed
and on a visit to the Chinese Exhibition at Burlington House the
exhibits interested him less than looking out for possible friends in
the crowd. Many years later in retirement he went with Jane to New
Zealand for a holiday. Jane suggested breaking their journey in India
as neither of them had ever visited that country. 'Why do you want
to go to India? We don't know anyone there' was his puzzled
response. In fairness to Launcelot to have included India in an
already costly holiday was more than he felt that he should afford
and would have meant cancelling engagements which he thought
should be kept.

During 1970 the Dean of Windsor, Robin Woods, was appointed
to the Bishopric of Worcester. The Queen, who had come to know
Launcelot well during his years at Norwich, asked Robin Woods to
sound him out about the possibility of his moving to Windsor. A
direct invitation from the Queen would have been impossible to
refuse. The suggestion forced Launcelot to think seriously about the
years ahead. Despite his illness he had not yet contemplated leaving
Norwich. He was not aware of the work proving too exhausting and
the reasonable hope of getting progressively better banished any
thought of retirement. However, he came to see that to be Dean of
Windsor would be less physically exacting than to remain at
Norwich and that were he to accept it would be likely to mean
extending his full time ministry longer than if he continued for a
year or two as Bishop of Norwich.

So on the eighteenth of December 1970 it was officially
announced that Launcelot would be leaving Norwich in some six
months time to become Dean of Windsor. Because of his health the
announcement did not come as a complete surprise, but the genuine
expressions of regret that poured in on him and Jane testified to the
love which their unremitting work had won for them. One issue of
the *Norwich Churchman* was largely devoted to accounts of all that
he had achieved in his twelve years in the diocese, but space was
found to print this limerick:

"My Lord, you must not be a martyr
To fashion, nor yet a non-starter.

Be pavilioned in splendour
Reject the suspender
And place all your faith in the Garter."

The farewell Service in Norwich Cathedral was a moving occasion. It took the form of an evening celebration of Holy Communion. After the Service a table and chairs were placed on the steps at the head of the nave and Bishop Eric Cordingley spoke simply and informally of the debt which the whole diocese owed to Launcelot, and he then made the parting presentation to him and Jane. His speech and Launcelot's reply were punctuated with bursts of laughter and prolonged applause from the large congregation – something which could never have happened in Norwich Cathedral before Launcelot's years as Bishop. One priest present saw this as symbolic of Launcelot's great achievement. He had shown by his vision and by the warmth of his personality that an ancient Cathedral and diocese could be given new life. Out of the treasures of the old he had brought forth in a great episcopate something new.

42   The highest point in the diocese

43   On the Broads with a group of young men from whose activities the
Endeavour Training organisation was later formed.

44   Launcelot with the Brooke family in Scotland. On the left, Ken Mathews

45   Second thoughts
      on a sermon

46   Jane Agutter, 1961

47   Launcelot and Jane 1965

48 The wedding reception. On the left, Launcelot's eldest brother.
On the right Margaret and Richard Agutter

49 Making another
friend for life

50   Sunday morning in the Lower Ward, Windsor Castle, by Joseph Nash – 1848

51   H.M. The Queen with Launcelot after his installation as Dean of Windsor.

52   The entry to the Deanery, Windsor.   (Photographed by
Derry Moore)

53 The Royal Family leaving St. George's Chapel after the Service of Thanksgiving
for the Quincentenary, 23rd April 1975

WINDSOR

1971 – 1976

On the 16th of July 1971 in the presence of the Queen, the Queen Mother, Princess Margaret and Prince William of Gloucester, together with the "Windsor Community" and as many personal friends as could be found places in St. George's Chapel, Launcelot was installed as Dean of Windsor.

By statute the duties of the Dean are not exacting. His main function is to preside over the meetings of the Chapter and thus to be ultimately responsible for the upkeep and well-being of St. George's Chapel, in which he is only required to preach on the great festivals of the Church. However, if the statutory duties are light the opportunities open to the Dean are considerable. As Domestic Chaplain to the Sovereign he is a member of the Royal Household and so is likely to be in close contact with all the Royal Family. By virtue of the fact that St. George's Chapel is the Chapel of the Knights of the Garter he is involved as Register of the Order in the pageantry and the Services which the Knights attend.

The Dean officially holds "the cure of souls" of all living within the Castle walls and in the Home Park. Launcelot inherited a situation in which the Dean delegated much of the day to day pastoral work to one or two of the many available clergy. A retired Canon looked after those living in the Home Park, such as the men employed in the Mews or the gardeners and their families. A Minor Canon had the care of those living inside the Castle walls, the Military Knights, the Lay Clerks, Virgers and their families. A specially appointed Domestic Chaplain was in charge of the Royal Chapel beside Royal Lodge and had the care of all living in the Great Park. So although the Dean still had a general pastoral oversight for those who lived in the Castle and the Home Park, in practice this was no great burden. Needless to say in Launcelot's case this did not mean that he ceased to be a pastor. His main pastoral activities were with individual clergy and laity, young and old, who came to Windsor to seek his help from far and wide.

The comparatively light burden of official duties laid on the Dean enables him to undertake work outside the Castle to the benefit of the Church at large. In recent years it has generally been assumed that the Dean would be a person anxious to continue his involvement in Christian activities and to have the freedom to use his experience and initiative where he felt that he could best help. This freedom, as will be seen later, Launcelot used to the full.

Despite the prominence of his position the office of the Dean of Windsor is not easy to fill. He has often to walk as delicately as Agag if he is not to offend too many susceptibilities. The rigid hierarchy of Windsor Castle, which no Dean can ignore, is symbolised by the order of the houses which visitors pass as they climb the hill from the main entrance gate. First come the houses of the Lay Clerks and then that of the organist of St. George's Chapel; next are the houses of the Minor Canons, followed by the grander houses of the Canons of Windsor. Further up the hill stands the Deanery, and beyond it the Windsor residence of the Queen's Private Secretary. At the entrance to the Quadrangle is the house of the Governor and Constable of Windsor Castle, and finally the State Apartments and the private home of the Sovereign. Surrounding the Castle are high walls which can appear to isolate the residents from the realities of the outside world and thus breed a suffocatingly conservative attitude, militating against change of any kind.

This isolation was much more pronounced in Victorian times than it is today. Then the Canons lived as though they existed by divine right and were accountable to nobody. Deans and Canons, safe in their ivory tower, could live out their days in agreeable and idle seclusion. This world has now largely vanished, thanks in no small measure to Launcelot's predecessor, Bishop Robin Woods, who did much to break through the rather cosy atmosphere which had for too long prevailed.

However, traces of it still remain, not least in the upholding of strict hierarchical protocol, which at times is almost ludicrous. In the Chapter Garden traditionally the Dean's wife had the right to order the gardeners to pick flowers and bring them to the Deanery. The Canons and their wives might pick flowers themselves; the Minor Canons might enjoy the garden but must not touch the flowers; all lower down the scale were rigidly excluded. Although this privilege still existed it was not invoked in Launcelot's time. Launcelot, always anxious to see the best in everyone, has suggested that the jealousies which occasionally developed within the hierarchy were usually no worse than will be found in a parish among the flower arrangers or between town councillors and wives on a civic occasion. It was probably inevitable, he admitted, that where privileges stemmed from the generous readiness of the Queen to share some of the Castle's resources with its inhabitants their propensities for pride and jealousy could raise the temperature unduly at times.

Launcelot had been known jokingly to remark that at Norwich his ambition was to bring the diocese out of the eighteenth into the nineteenth century. This he said when describing the very conservative views of Norfolk people, whom he came to hold in great affection. At Windsor he faced a far more subtle task. As a diocesan Bishop he had been at pains to consult his staff before decisions on matters affecting the diocese were made; but in the last resort his responsibility for the final decision was recognised.

As Dean, Launcelot, in common with the practice in many Cathedral Chapters, was merely *primus inter pares* among his Canons. Thus his aim must always be to reach a common mind in the Chapter, which often proved impossible. He believed that it was very undesirable to decide an important issue on a majority vote when only four or five men were concerned but such a vote was at times inescapable. If there were any matter directly affecting the known wishes of the Queen he could override any opposition but this was infrequent. Norwich certainly had its peculiar problems but the authority and responsibility of the Bishop were far more clearly defined that was the authority of the Dean. At Windsor Launcelot was in charge of a building of unique historical and architectural importance, the personal property of the Sovereign as the Chapel of a royal castle, and this task had to be shared with three, and later four, Canons whose views from time to time could differ markedly from his own and from each other's.

The immediate problem was the Deanery. It is a lovely house but acres of carpeting were needed for floors and staircase, and big windows with long curtains added to the heavy initial expenditure. Both Launcelot and Jane had to dig deep into their not unlimited private means to meet these costs. The Queen, who praised Jane for the way in which she had made the Deanery look so charming, became aware of the financial problems involved and arranged that the Privy Purse, which had hitherto only helped with the loan of furniture for the public rooms, should now become responsible for a share of the upkeep of the house. Launcelot greatly enjoyed living in such a house. On one wall of his panelled study are the Coats of Arms of all the Garter Knights since the Order was founded. This magnificent room also contains a long oak table from the Old Palace of Whitehall on which the body of Charles I had been laid after execution, so as to enable the head to be stitched to the trunk before burial. Before the house was fully furnished and while the stairs were still uncarpeted a friend who was staying in the Deanery remembers meeting Launcelot one Sunday morning coming back from an early Celebration in full robes, climbing the stairs with the aid of his Crook and singing at the top of his voice,

'Oh, what a beautiful morning! Oh, what a beautiful day!

'I've got a wonderful feeling everything's coming my way.'

Time was to prove him a little too optimistic but there is no doubt that he and Jane were to find life at Windsor very demanding but exciting.

In order to get to know the Windsor community as quickly as possible they decided to give a series of parties for everyone in any way connected with the Castle. By issuing invitations in alphabetical order Jane ensured that each party was a cross-section of the community. Throughout the five years entertaining was endless.

Launcelot recalls 'not only personal friends but all manner of
visitors from the eminent to the eccentric (and sometimes both).' It
was desperately hard work for Jane with comparatively little
domestic help but the extraordinary range of visitors was fascinating. Dr. Luns, the Secretary General of N.A.T.O. came to lecture
and was delayed for two or three days by a strike at Heathrow. He
more than repaid his hosts by his fund of hilarious stories. Sir Hugh
Casson, President of the Royal Academy, frequently came to give
advice on problems connected with St. George's Chapel. His letters
of thanks for lunch were always amusingly illustrated. Yehudi
Menuhin, joint Chairman with Launcelot at a St. George's House
"Consultation" for creative artists, played in the Chapel after Evensong and made his summing up of the discussion in the form of a
prayer. Then, to Launcelot's especial delight, came Trigve Gran, a
Norwegian who was the last surviving member of Captain Scott's
last expedition. He sat in the study for an hour talking about Scott
and Bowers and Edward Wilson as if he had been with them on the
previous day. Lord Cobham, at Windsor to discuss a "Consultation"
on sport, could not refrain from telling a stream of literary and
cricketing anecdotes to illustrate his points. Tommy Steele and his
wife, whom Launcelot and Jane had met at a Buckingham Palace
party, became close friends and were welcome visitors. The variety
of people coming to the Deanery was infinite and was by no means
restricted to those who were well known.

One of the great occasions for entertaining was Garter Day. Jane
invited a remarkable mixture of guests: some of the family, with a
children's party in the Long Gallery; a group of blind girls from a
nearby school; a couple of ambassadors and their wives; friends
from home and overseas; and, perhaps at Launcelot's suggestion, the
Trinity Hall crew then training at Henley.

From the point of view of the interest in meeting so many
different people, the Windsor years were an unforgettable
experience. By careful planning ahead Jane worked wonders in
providing meals and only occasionally protested, as when Launcelot
put his head round the door in mid-morning to say, 'I can't
remember if I told you that Prince Philip is coming for a quick

lunch. I don't suppose he wants more than cheese.'

In assessing Launcelot's five years as Dean of Windsor it is important to remember certain facts. For over twenty-two years he had worked unsparingly and devotedly as a Bishop of two sees. He had learned his task in a small and friendly diocese and had left it beloved by all who had known him. He had come to the vast diocese of Norwich where by his vision and his determination he had breathed new life into old bones. These years of unremitting work, however happy and successful, had inevitably taken some toll. His illness, though in no way caused by overwork, had made him less mobile and thus more easily tired physically by the effort of getting about. Shortly after his installation as Dean he celebrated his sixth-fifth birthday, and no man – not even Launcelot with all his energy – can be quite as resilient at that age as in younger days.

There is no doubt that new work with new challenges acts as a stimulus and can give a new lease of life. Certainly Launcelot had no thought that the Windsor Deanery would provide a comfortable base from which to undertake part-time work. Nor did he envisage an early retirement. Yet the varied demands upon an active Dean were exacting. Broadly speaking there were three main different, though related, sides to his work: the conduct of St. George's Chapel; the courses at St. George's House; and the relationship with the Royal Family. To these must be added the large number of out-side activities with which he was associated. In the work at St. George's House and in his duties with the Royal Family he was out-standingly successful and very happy. It was in managing the affairs of St. George's Chapel that he was less successful and where he met with a degree of frustration which he had never hitherto experienced and with which he was not by his nature equipped to deal.

It was in 1473 that Edward IV, secure on his throne after the final defeat of the Lancastrians and with ample revenue at his disposal, decided to replace the small royal Chapel with the present magnifi-cent building. He spent much of his time at Windsor, and in an age of increasing ostentation, reflected in his own love of gorgeous clothes, he wanted a Chapel worthy of the royal House and of the

Order of the Garter, able to stand comparison with the splendours of the Burgundian Court and its Order of the Golden Fleece. Moreover he lived at a time when men were obsessively concerned with death and were firmly convinced that the length of time that a soul remained in Purgatory before attaining the bliss of Paradise was largely dependent upon the prayers and pious works of those still alive. To this end between 1475 and 1522 in the reign of Henry VIII nine chantries were established with sufficient endowments to pay for priests whose duty it was to say Masses for the repose of royal souls, the souls of departed Garter Knights and of all who had lived and died in the Christian Faith. It is to the 1520s that the three most splendid examples of late perpendicular architecture, all royal foundations, belong: the Chapel of King's College in Cambridge, King Henry VII's Chapel in Westminster Abbey and St. George's Chapel at Windsor.

Launcelot did not come to Windsor anxious to make sweeping changes. Rather it had been suggested to him that after Bishop Woods' years as Dean a period of consolidation would be appropriate. However there were some changes which he believed to be necessary, but it quickly became apparent that they would be difficult to make. There were several reasons for this.

No man charged with the daily care of St. George's Chapel, its Services, its great musical traditions and the maintenance of the beautiful fabric, could fail to be moved by its splendour and its long history. What Launcelot described as the 'triumphal' character of the Chapel 'was liable to obscure the character of Christian life and worship', but he was sufficiently sensitive to the value of tradition to know that a radical break with the past was likely to be unsuitable.

Furthermore every Dean owes his position to royal invitation and he is the servant of the Sovereign. Although the Queen and her family, largely for reasons of security, only attend services in St. George's Chapel at Christmas and Easter and on special occasions associated with the Order of the Garter, her love of Windsor and her close interest in all that affects her Castle make it impossible for a Dean to introduce fundamental liturgical or other changes without her consent. However it should be added that she was always extraordinarily sympathetic to any suggestions which Launcelot might make.

By far the most important reason preventing change was the personalities of the Canons. The two senior Canons, Canon Bentley and Canon Fisher, were men of considerable intellectual powers but strongly opposed to any break with tradition in St. George's Chapel. In the affairs of St. George's House, however, Canon Fisher played a constructive part. Canon Verney on the other hand believed passionately that the Services in the Chapel were quite irrelevant to the needs of the age. Among other changes he wished to introduce popular Services with varying forms of modern musical accompaniment, and when a fourth Canon, sympathetic to his views, was appointed, he felt that Launcelot should have given him greater support so that the three of them could have outvoted the two traditionalists.

Launcelot was in a difficult position. He saw the need to make St. George's Chapel a living spiritual force and not a lovely relic of a glorious past; he sympathised with many of Canon Verney's ideas, not least his skill in arranging special Services such as that for the annual St. George's Day Scout Service. Yet he felt that too many of these ideas were over-dramatic and that Canon Verney, who had come from the new Cathedral at Coventry, was too impatient for speedier change than was possible at Windsor. On the issue of modern non-liturgical Services he tended to regard the views of the two senior men as wise in the circumstances. Given such a clash of personalities within the Chapter there was little hope of reaching a 'common mind' on any matter.

It was the general administration of St. George's Chapel which caused Launcelot most trouble. Here he was very much on the side of reform. He became convinced that the ancient statutes by which the Chapel was governed needed revision if they were to be appropriate to the present day and that to achieve this expert advice must be sought. With the consent of the Chapter he called in the services of a well known firm of business consultants, Messrs. McKinsey, who had generously offered to give their help free of charge. Their advice was especially needed on the finances of St. George's, for

Launcelot was sure that the problems facing the Chapter in an age of inflation were unlikely to be best solved by men with a theological training and insufficient business expertise.

Until the mid-nineteenth century St. George's Chapel had been richly endowed through ownership of land. When the revenues were handed over to the Ecclesiastical Commissioners in return for a fixed annual grant of money all continued to go well until the value of money fell. Although a new and increasingly valuable source of revenue came from the charge made to tourists for entering the Chapel, the financial problems could not be solved by tourism alone. Launcelot initially disliked the admission charge but became reconciled to it, realising its necessity. But what needed a thorough overhaul was the whole conduct of Chapter business.

The Report made a series of valuable recommendations, covering such matters as the management of Chapter housing and property. On the actual conduct of Chapter finances it was proposed that an experienced layman should take over much of the work traditionally performed by the Treasurer and the Steward, each of them being a Canon. To Launcelot's dismay all action on the Report was thwarted on the grounds that implementation would be an infringement of the ancient rights of the Canons and was thus unthinkable.

Chapter meetings were interminably long. Launcelot's suggestion that they might profitably be held in the less formal setting of his study met with no approval. Long hours were spent in discussion of highly controversial matters like the lighting of St. George's Chapel, an admittedly awkward problem. There was a monstrously expensive scheme proposed to enable tourists to leave the Chapel by a new exit and thus to guide them on a one-way route. This was a sensible aim but the solution involved constructing a lift and a new doorway beneath the steps leading to the main west entry. Fortunately this proved impracticable. On matters affecting the fabric of the building and its interior decoration Launcelot had no expert knowledge. Detailed care of Church architecture, though important, matters less to him than the care of those inside. Nor, to be honest, is his aesthetic sense very highly developed.

He was particularly frustrated by the failure to make good and profitable use of the Mews site by building housing units on it, some of which would have been allocated to masters at St. George's School and also to widows of the Military Knights. An approach was made to the Women's Royal Voluntary Service, an organisation which had an excellent reputation as good housing developers. The whole scheme came to nothing largely because of the support given by at least one Canon to a comparatively unknown American firm. Launcelot felt inhibited from giving more determined support to the W.R.V.S. proposals because of Jane's connection with the Service.

Many people would maintain that it is within Cathedral Chapters that Christian brotherly love can be in shortest supply. The life which Canons can lead, the heritage from the past which it is their duty to preserve and pass on, the comparatively little work which it is statutorily incumbent upon them to perform, the beauty of their houses in which they may spend half a lifetime – all these things can make it only too easy for them to remain sheltered from the outside world and to equate their Christian duty with their share in the Cathedral worship and the conduct of Cathedral business. Such a life can be liable to breed an uncharitable attitude towards anyone or anything which threatens to disturb the privileges and security of their office.

While St. George's Chapel is not a Cathedral, its royal status makes it dangerously easy for a Canon to believe that the guardian-ship of tradition is all important. At both Portsmouth and Norwich Launcelot had inevitably experienced differences of opinion but the remarkable unity of spirit which informed both dioceses had contri-buted greatly to his happiness. Windsor was different. Here he genuinely appreciated the qualities of the two Canons most in disagreement with him; nor was he ever conscious of personal hostility towards him. What at moments bewildered and increas-ingly distressed him was the lack of 'collegial' spirit. It was the attitudes which they adopted on matters of Chapter business, betraying a total lack of mutual support, which he found 'so maddening.' It is arguable that a man of Launcelot's temperament, with his patently sincere and gentle approach to people, was not ideally suited to this side of the Dean's work. Compared to his achievements in other spheres at Windsor little progress was made in the affairs of St. George's Chapel. The unenviable task of more determined action, much needed after an interregnum, fell to his successor, Bishop Michael Mann, who had done such good work in Norwich and who had behind him a training at the Harvard Business School.

Ever since about 1400 a school has existed to educate the young choristers who sing the daily Services in St. George's Chapel. Today St. George's School, Windsor Castle, is a boys' preparatory school in which some twenty choristers are scholars. Launcelot was *ex officio* Chairman of the Governing Body. This originally consisted solely of the Dean and Canons of Windsor but he managed to get it enlarged by the addition of a local solicitor, a public school headmaster and the wife of the then headmaster of Eton. Launcelot much enjoyed this side of his work, getting to know masters and boys and becoming involved in the life of the school. Choristers, who had to remain at school over Christmas, were entertained in various houses including the Deanery, a house superbly designed for playing "Murder" and "Sardines". On the wall of the narrow passage leading to the study was hung a row of six prints of Trinity Hall before which the choristers were expected to do obeisance. Launcelot frequently tried to get other guests visiting his study to acknowledge the superiority of his College. Refusal to pay this tribute was most marked in the case of the Prince of Wales, a loyal member of Trinity College.

Every term Launcelot lunched once or twice with the whole school and his visits were eagerly awaited as the boys were never quite sure what he would do next. Once he announced that he had written a special grace, which he intended to pronounce at his next visit and which he hoped that everyone would know enough Latin to understand. Expectant and slightly anxious heads were bowed over the tables when the day arrived. To general relief Launcelot used words long associated with his naval years and daily used by him: 'Thank God for all.'

Despite his lack of interest in cricket Launcelot used to raise an eleven to play against the school. He aimed at making his team, which was handicapped by being made to play with small bats, representative of the various groups within the Castle. He enlisted the services of the Governor of the Castle, a Military Knight, one of the Governing Body, the Headmaster, the Warden of St. George's House, a Canon, a Page, one of the Castle Police, a Lay Clerk and one of the sentries. The Dean's Virger, Mr. Read, was sure of his place as a great cricket enthusiast. A member of the School staff writes: "On his route from the Deanery to St. George's Chapel he was always preceded, in solemn state, by his Virger carrying his staff of office, who conducted him to his stall, bowed and then withdrew. When the time came for the Virger to bat the Bishop reversed the role and, rising to the occasion, marched majestically out to the wicket, preceding his Virger, carrying his cricket bat as a symbol of office, bowed to Mr. Read and retired to the pavilion."

The proximity of Eton to Windsor enabled Launcelot to get to know many of the masters and some of the boys, especially those whom he was asked to confirm. Bishop Woods had organised a scheme whereby several Etonians volunteered to act as stewards in St. George's Chapel on Sunday afternoons. They were rewarded with tea in the Deanery or with one of the Canons or a Military Knight. One such Etonian who came under Launcelot's spell said that his smile was unforgettable and reminded him always of a passage in Scott Fitzgerald's *The Great Gatsby* – not a book which immediately comes to mind when thinking of Launcelot: "It concentrated on you with an irresistible prejudice in your favour. It understood you just so far as you wanted to be understood, believed in you as you would like to believe in yourself, and assured you that it had precisely the impression of you that, at your best, you hoped to convey." A perceptive and interesting comment for a young man to make.

Additional stewards to help the Virgers became increasingly necessary to shepherd the crowds of tourists who streamed through the Henry VIII Gateway from mid-morning till early evening. A team of voluntary Sunday stewards, drawn from the Community and Windsor residents, was enlisted by Canon Verney. On some

days the crowds were so dense that it took time and patience to drive
a car the short distance from the Deanery to the Gateway. Launcelot
occasionally joined the tourists in St. George's Chapel, even though
the barriers of language often made it impossible to say much or
explain who he was.

If meetings of the Chapter of St. George's Chapel were at times
frustrating and unhappy for Launcelot, his involvement in the
running of St. George's House gave him great enjoyment.

In 1348 King Edward III had founded the Order of the Garter
with its twenty-six Knights at Windsor. In the same year and in the
same place he had founded the College of St. George with twenty-six
priests, devoted to prayer and worship – "a good way of
merchandise whereby with a happy bartering transitory things are
given up in exchange for things eternal," as the Letters Patent of
foundation unashamedly defined Edward's purpose. Since the
Knights of the Garter would not live permanently at Windsor provision was made for the maintenance of twenty-six poor Knights, the
predecessors of the Military Knights of today, whose duty was to
represent the Garter Knights at the Services in St. George's Chapel.
Quite apart from his bargain with God, Edward found that the joint
advice of secular Knights and spiritual clerks was often very helpful
in governing the Kingdom. Some two centuries later Queen
Elizabeth I required the College to add the advancement of learning
to its duties of prayer and worship. Thus, until the seventeenth
century when parliament became a force which no Sovereign could
ignore, an additional body of advisers was always available at
Windsor.

It was Bishop Robin Woods who put to Prince Philip the
imaginative idea of renewing and re-interpreting this ancient partnership. Together they evolved a scheme whereby two Queen Anne
houses close to St. George's Chapel were made into a residential
conference centre where leaders in widely differing walks of life –
politicians, Churchmen, employers and trade unionists, artists and
sportsmen – could meet to discuss important value judgements in
our society against the background of a Christian community. The

discussions, which took place in the fifteenth century Chapter library, were not confined to immediate problems but often took a longer view at the way the present might affect the twenty-first century.

On the 23rd of October 1966 St. George's House was officially opened by the Queen. In the first ten years of its existence nearly fifteen thousand lay people and clergy took part in its courses and Consultations. These have ranged over a very wide area including business ethics; problems facing Members of Parliament in the performance of their duties; differentials between employees within a single industry, trade or profession; the contribution which Sport can make to the quality of life; and regular discussions between scientists and theologians. This is one side of the work of the House.

There is another equally valuable service provided by St. George's House. It had been accepted, almost without question, that once a man had been trained at his theological college and ordained he would become an efficient priest through the mere exercise of his ministry. St. George's House became one of the leading places where this complacent attitude was challenged. Clergy, it was here maintained, needed in-service training as much as any profession if they were to keep abreast of theological and social developments. So two special courses were devised. Twice a year a Mid-Service Clergy course was held. The course lasted for a month and was preceded by a nine month research project. It was designed for men who had been ordained for some fifteen years. The purpose of a Senior Clergy course was to help men of between fifty and fifty-five, who at that age are likely to be undertaking their longest and most important period of sustained ministry in one place and so in much need of fresh vision and encouragement. From time to time there were other courses such as those for Rural Deans or lay Chairmen of Diocesan Synods.

Launcelot delighted in sharing in the work of St. George's House. His personal contribution enriched a going concern by bringing fresh ideas. Before his arrival scientific topics had rarely been discussed. He came at a moment when the ecological debate had become important and his interest in this was invaluable. Not only were his own interventions in the discussion the product of informed knowledge, but he knew from his personal contacts those scientists whom it would be helpful to invite to Windsor. As a Christian and a scientist he was able to show the theological implications in many ecological problems as he had done in the House of Lords. As in the past he never brought a simplistic approach to discussions for he understood all sides to these problems. He was never a starry-eyed debater and his experience in the Upper House had made him sufficient of a "politician" to realise what could actually be achieved. He found the Consultations fascinating and a welcome intellectual stimulus.

On the other side of the House's work he strongly supported the establishment of a Senior Church Leaders course, designed for Bishops and their equivalents in other denominations – Abbots, Mother Superiors, Moderators and Free Church leaders. The staff of St. George's hoped that such a course might encourage the idea that the House was the "Staff College" for actual and potential Church leaders. It was agreed that the course should be so planned that the four aspects of a Bishop's work – as Pastor, Prophet, Teacher and "Leader in Affairs" – were discussed. Launcelot took the chair for these meetings and here his instinctive wish that the members of the course should reach 'a common mind' came nearest to realisation. His attitude to the evils of denominational barriers is shown by his offer to the Abbot of Ampleforth, now Cardinal Hume, of his private Chapel in which to say Mass. It was perhaps inevitable at the start that a "Staff College" type of course should reflect the views of the Establishment. Certainly one or two attending the first of these courses had hoped for a much more radical approach to the work of the Church. At the same time nothing but good could come from these meetings of men of very different theological views.

Launcelot gave a great deal of his time to St. George's House. This was not merely because he enjoyed the intellectual challenge and the interesting men and women who were drawn to Windsor. The aims of the House reinforced his beliefs about effective pastoral work. 'The pastoral approach must be from the known to the unknown, the human to the divine. You don't start wading in about

God but start with Man.' Yet the existence of St. George's House
alongside St. George's Chapel symbolised the difficulty which
confronts a modern Dean of Windsor. St. George's House is
concerned with the future but it must also make use of a Chapel rich
in tradition. This influenced the appointment of a new Canon when
a Canonry fell vacant; for it was necessary to look for a man of
sufficient theological stature who would also be sympathetic to the
social, political and economic problems which loomed ahead.

When she invited Launcelot to become Dean of Windsor the
Queen was appointing someone whom she and her family had come
to know quite well. As Chairman of the Church of England Youth
Council, through his work for the Duke of Edinburgh's Award
Scheme and through regular visits to Sandringham when Bishop of
Norwich, he had been privileged to meet the Royal Family both on
formal occasions and in the relaxed atmosphere of their homes. In
making such a personal appointment to her Household it was
helpful both to the Queen and to Launcelot that they were not
strangers. At the same time to be Dean of Windsor was going to
mean closer contact with all members of the Royal Family than
Launcelot had hitherto enjoyed, and he was sensitive enough to
realise that while he had a great deal to learn about his new work the
Queen would also need time to get to know her new Dean well.

Before the official announcement of the appointment was made
the Queen invited Launcelot to lunch with her in private so that she
might describe the work which she believed lay ahead of him. Apart
from his habitual uncertainty of his worthiness to tackle any new
position, Launcelot was worried lest his lameness might prove a
handicap in the proper conduct of the ceremonial at Garter Services
or on other royal occasions. He was quickly reassured on this and in
fact became an adept at concealing his stick in the folds of his robes.

In discussion about the contents of this chapter Launcelot was
especially anxious that this close connection with the Royal Family
should 'not be played up too much, please.' At first he felt that it
would be prudent to make little or no reference to this side of a
Dean's work. Realising that total silence was impossible, he

conceded with some hesitation that there was one thing which might be permitted. 'I think that you *could* say that the Queen is rather nice – because she is.' This glorious understatement could only have been uttered by Launcelot. It was a far greater tribute to the Queen than any more elaborate compliment. In his anxiety not to betray any secrets his choice of words did not conceal his deep admiration. In his attitude to the Royal Family he was a complete contrast to his ebullient predecessor. He was at great pains not to be intrusive and there is good reason to believe that they appreciated his determination not to presume in any way upon their kindness to him.

As far as this chapter is concerned Launcelot was fearful of two possible consequences. First, he was afraid of appearing to have gossipped in any way about details of the domestic life of the Royal Family. There was of course no danger of his revealing anything about his work as Domestic Chaplain for the seal of the confessional is absolute for Queen or commoner. But he dreaded the inclusion of any material which might suggest that he had abused the friendship shown him. His other fear was equally typical and was for himself. 'I do hope that I don't get spoiled.' Both fears were groundless. No man served the Queen and her family with greater devotion and discretion. Nor was there ever any doubt that he was a man who could "walk with Kings – nor lose the common touch."

Even for a man as determined as Launcelot not to push himself forward the office of Dean of Windsor involves something of a tight-rope walk. In private the Royal Family treated him with friendly informality and showed him great kindness. Knowing that swimming would help to strengthen the muscles in his legs, the Queen invited him to use her swimming pool when she and her family did not want it and allowed him to take a friend with him if he wished. After the Christmas and Easter Services they would all come into the Deanery for sherry. From time to time he and Jane would be invited to dine with the Queen and her guests. These were occasions of fascinating interest and great fun, often ending long after midnight with party games or charades. They had to be ready at a moment's notice to help in any way. The Deanery telephone would ring and Launcelot would be asked by the Queen to look after

the Emperor Haile Selassie and his suite for a couple of hours by
showing them round St. George's Chapel. It was a wonderfully
privileged and exciting experience but it had its difficulties. Treated
at moments almost as members of the family, they had always to
remember that the Dean is the servant of the Sovereign and must
never for a moment presume upon royal friendship. The morning
after an enjoyably hilarious dinner party the demands of strict
protocol had to be observed. This probably troubled Launcelot less
than some Deans. What the Queen and her family are said to have
appreciated was his complete naturalness in their company.

As Senior Domestic Chaplain to the Queen Launcelot could offer
advice on a wide range of problems. Should he wish for the Queen's
advice and help about St. George's Chapel or on any other matter an
appointment would be made through the Queen's Page, and in spite
of the heavy burden of her work she was very generous in sparing
him time. On anything to do with St. George's House Prince Philip,
an active member of its Council, was a valuable ally.

Launcelot was responsible for the conduct of the Services in St.
George's Chapel on State occasions, such as the Garter Service each
year, preceded by the familiar procession from the Castle. It also
sadly fell to his lot in his comparatively short time at Windsor to be
ultimately responsible for several royal funerals. The ceremonial
details of these occasions are worked out many years in advance of
the actual death but even so the Dean has an important part to play.
On at least two such occasions Launcelot and Jane were on holiday
abroad and had of necessity to return home early. The first royal
funeral which Launcelot conducted was that of young Prince
William of Gloucester, who was tragically killed in a flying accident
in 1972. This had occurred long before any plans for his funeral had
been made. Then followed the death of Prince William's father, the
Duke of Gloucester. Most elaborate of all the funeral pageantry was
that for the Duke of Windsor, since the funeral Service was preceded
by a Lying in State. This was the first occasion that there had been a
Lying in State at Windsor rather than in Westminster Hall and it
proved a most moving setting with over 50,000 people slowly
passing the catafalque. The Duchess of Windsor had come from

Paris and the whole royal party assembled in the Deanery drawing-room before the Service. The funeral Services of Princess Patricia Ramsay and of her husband took place in St. George's Chapel in Launcelot's time there, as did that of Viscount Montgomery, a Knight of the Garter. Launcelot's simplicity, completely unawed by the grandeur of the occasions or by the royal personages present must have been helpful and comforting to those most closely concerned. The chief difficulty confronting Launcelot during the actual interment at Frogmore was to defeat the incessant noise of aircraft from Heathrow.

No member of the Royal Family has been more grateful to Launcelot than Princess Alice, Duchess of Gloucester. She has spoken of how much she valued his sympathy and encouragement at the time of the deaths of her elder son and her husband. Prince William had known Launcelot from the time that he was an undergraduate at Magdalene College, Cambridge, and a close friendship began then which lasted for his all too short life. Like many a young man of intelligence who thinks for himself, Prince William found it difficult to accept all the tenets of the Christian Faith. But he once said that if one day he came to be a fully committed Christian it would be entirely thanks to Launcelot's influence.

It was with Prince Richard, now Duke of Gloucester, and his wife and family that Launcelot and Jane have been most closely associated. Launcelot had officiated at Prince Richard's marriage, and after the difficult birth of the young Duchess's first child he was asked to visit the baby in hospital where he was in an intensive care unit. Fears for his survival led to consideration of his baptism in hospital. In the event it was decided to wait in hope and happily Alexander lived to be baptised at Barnwell and to become an extremely energetic and active child. During this anxious period both Launcelot and Jane became very much attached to the young couple. Jane was able to be of great help to the Duchess. It is usually something of an ordeal for any girl to be introduced to her fiancé's family. When your future in-laws are members of the Royal Family and when you yourself are not of royal blood and a foreigner the ordeal must be infinitely greater. Needless to say her in-laws welcomed her warmly and she has undertaken her new role with a natural charm and very successfully. However she has found Jane, an older and understanding person, one in whom she can confide, and it is not surprising that Launcelot has now, with Jane, travelled to Barnwell to baptise all three of her children.

Although Prince Charles was less at Windsor in Launcelot's years as Dean than in Bishop Woods' day, Launcelot came to know him well and was invited by him to be a Trustee of the Prince's Trust. The Queen Mother he had known at Sandringham and he has preached frequently in the Chapel of Royal Lodge, Windsor Park, which she attends. She has let it be known that she has always found him to be an immensely valued friend and adviser. At Christmas and Easter he inevitably came into close contact with the whole family. It was a life which could have gone to the heads of lesser mortals. Launcelot emerged from these years unaltered, but grateful and glad that his affection and admiration for a remarkable family was reciprocated. In his years of retirement they have not forgotten him.

In addition to the official duties at Windsor there were many opportunities to undertake work outside the Castle walls. Launcelot became one of the elected Deans who were members of the Synod but he took little part in the debates. He was no great lover of synodical government, finding the meetings wearisome and believing that the existence of the Synod unnecessarily tied a Bishop's hands when dealing with his diocese. He found that he was *ex officio* a member of the Oxford diocesan Synod but in this he took no part at all. Since St. George's Chapel was not in the Oxford diocese it seemed both wrong and pointless to attend its meetings.

Far more to his taste was his work as a member of the Royal Commission on Environmental Pollution under the Chairmanship of Lord Ashby. This subject mattered to him more than ever. Speaking in Liverpool Cathedral in April 1972 he said: 'I am staggered to find how widespread is the assumption that Man has an absolute dominion over the world of Nature and can do what he likes with it.' He was distressed that 'we have lost the Christian doctrine of Nature

. . . It is significant that this is the only major doctrine of the Church that is not celebrated by a great festival.' The result of this is 'the tragic fallacy that the natural and the supernatural, the human and the divine, are to be thought of as two quite separate things. This is contrary to the teaching of Jesus. The great dividing line which he makes is not between the natural and supernatural but between good and evil.' Since the saving of the world from destruction by pollution often calls for international action he was glad to be Chairman of the Associates of the Inter-Parliamentary Group for World Government.

He continued to show an active interest in the doings of the Schools Hebridean Society and in the Young Explorers Trust. His contacts with schools, notably Bryanston, Wellington, Rugby and Tonbridge remained close, while Magdalene College at Cambridge saw nearly as much of him as Trinity Hall.

One activity deserves a more detailed account. In his early years at Norwich Launcelot had become a member of the Sponsoring Committee which set up Atlantic College in September 1962 at St. Donat's Castle, Glamorgan. He had joined this body because of his friendship both with Kurt Hahn and Admiral Hoare, the first headmaster. Atlantic College was founded to enable young men and women from many different countries to spend the last two years of their school life living together. It became part of the United World College movement to promote mutual understanding between the races and to respond to the challenge of the Third World.

South Wales was too far a cry from Norfolk to visit Atlantic College regularly, but at Windsor and in retirement he attended Governors' Meetings and each term at the invitation of the headmaster has spent the inside of a week with the students. The headmaster, David Sutcliffe, has written an interesting account of Launcelot's involvement in the life of the College:

"It was at one of the Board meetings that he made the point, at some length but very sympathetically, that Atlantic College was falling short of its duty to meet the spiritual needs of the students. He saw in their diversity of religious backgrounds not an excuse for neutrality but a challenge for a specially active programme of pastoral care and concern. At that stage, in the mid-1970s, he made a strong case for the appointment of a College Chaplain, much along orthodox public school lines. I believe he saw this person as a tolerant broadminded Anglican, who would have an active personal involvement in College life, but this concept did not carry conviction with the teaching staff here, nor indeed with myself. We felt it to be a grave danger to appoint to the permanent residential staff a person, however tolerant, who was committed to one denomination. Launcelot Fleming came down to the College on a special visit to explore the issue and spent an evening discussing it with the full Common Room. As a result of this meeting he told the Board of Governors that he felt he was on the wrong track for the time being and that it would not make sense to try and impose such a solution on an unwilling staff and headmaster.

"Nonetheless he maintained his basic position and shortly after-wards agreed, to my very great pleasure, to termly visits of his own to the College to act as a spiritual presence here. At the same time we initiated a programme of religious visits of this kind from members of different faiths and denominations and were much helped in this by the local clergy.

"A regular feature of Launcelot's visit down here each term is the Inter-Faith Focus, which he conducts, obviously on a voluntary basis, for the whole College. These occasions are very carefully prepared weeks ahead, in consultation with staff and students. Each Focus has had a theme and past themes have included the following: 'Happiness', 'Suffering', 'Tolerance'."

The purpose behind Atlantic College and the United World Colleges owed much to the vision and drive of Kurt Hahn. Launcelot was attracted to Kurt Hahn's beliefs about the nature of education, and their mutual respect was shown by the invitation to Launcelot to deliver an address at Schloss Salem in December 1974 at Kurt Hahn's funeral service. In words describing Hahn Launcelot expressed his own deep convictions.

'Kurt felt great anxiety about the state of the young. He saw them as exposed to a series of decays – the decay of fitness, the decay of self-discipline, the decay of enterprise and adventure, the decay of skill and care and, most shattering of all, the decay of compassion; and Kurt himself was a man of deep compassion. With all of this he was conscious of the disintegrating power of cynicism. He attributed such decays in no small measure to defective education, which he felt was more concerned with the transmission of knowledge (and he was fully alive to the importance of academic learning) than with the development of character . . . To restore, to defend, to develop human strength in the young – this he saw as the sacred purpose of education.'

On the 23rd of April, St. George's Day, 1975, the celebrations to mark the 500th anniversary of the foundation of St. George's Chapel began. An elaborately mounted exhibition of illuminated books, manuscripts and treasures, ranging from leaden hat badges given to pilgrims visiting the shrine of Henry VI to the Garter Banner of Winston Churchill was open to the public in the Chapter Library from July to September. Music had been an integral part of the worship in St. George's Chapel for more than a century before the present Chapel was begun and has been maintained there ever since, save for one break during the years of the Commonwealth. Thus music rightly played a big part in the celebrations, and in a series of concerts five centuries of English church music were recalled. Planning for an event such as this involved months of hard work, and Launcelot bore part of the brunt of this as chairman of the Advisory Committee.

When it was all over Jane's thoughts, if not Launcelot's, were turning towards retirement. She wanted Launcelot to leave Windsor in good health and not totally exhausted. During the celebrations Launcelot had entered his seventieth year and it was time to begin to think of where to live, though for the moment he was not prepared to face retirement.

It was traditional for the Royal Family to meet together at Windsor for Christmas and to attend the morning Service in St. George's Chapel. It had also become a tradition that every other year the Service should be televised, a task shared alternately by the B.B.C. and I.T.V. As required by statute, Launcelot preached.

Because what proved to be his final Christmas sermon at Windsor expresses so fully Launcelot's deepest beliefs, it deserves to be quoted at some length.

'There is so much in our life and world today to make us worried and anxious and, if we are not careful, it can all too easily make us bitter and cynical . . . Does the wish of "a happy Christmas" sound rather hollow? . . . The wish of a happy Christmas can be an anaesthetic wish, or just a cliché. But that is not what it really means.

'Christmas brings us back to what life is all about. It declares what a human being most truly and fully is. It tells us that God has been born into the world. He is within us, now and always – here and everywhere . . . There is one central fact which in particular I wish to underline – a fact which you and I and our society need above all to recognise and uphold – namely "the sanctity of human life". The sanctity of each and every individual human being, each of supreme value, each a child of God, made in the image of God with possibilities of truly priceless worth.

'For let us be clear about this. When we celebrate the Holy Child born in a manger at Bethlehem, we are not isolating him in the sense of extracting him from the rest of humanity. We are not treating him as a superman who came to do what ordinary mortals cannot do, nor suggesting that he was a God who grew up disguised as a carpenter. What we are celebrating is a man – bone of our bone and flesh of our flesh – a man who shows us what our human nature is made of and what we have it in us to become . . .

'The sanctity of life is threatened where in any institution, be it Government, Church, School or Business, there is perpetual dominance of the System over the Person, for then the individual's sense of responsibility tends to be crushed and his freedom smothered. And when this happens people's confidence is sapped and that leads to sheer indifference. How often you see this. Someone is in desperate need and the cry goes up "Leave it to the social worker" or "The Head Teacher will take care of that." And that is just not good enough. We do less than justice to the principle of the sanctity of life if we treat everyone in precisely the same way.

We are all different. People are always particular people with their own particular qualities, their own distinctive make-up. This is the great thing about humanity. There is no one in the wide world, and never has been, who is quite like you . . . So we must learn to be sensitive to each person's particularity. It is always in the particular that we find God's presence and activity and it is an essential part of the Law of Love to recognise this . . .

'So in our imagination we follow the shepherds and the wise men to that simple manger, there to offer our adoration to that tiny child: the baby who can inspire us to recognise the sanctity of every individual – his own and other people's – the sacredness of all life.'

The last six months at Windsor were difficult and Jane longed to get away to a more private life. She was far more aware than Launcelot of problems within the Chapter which, with his characteristic belief in the goodness of all those with whom he worked, he found difficult to credit. The continuing kindness of the Royal Family, however, did much to compensate for the unhappiness which at times she felt. Far more worrying was her anxiety about Launcelot, who was more tired than he cared to admit.

His increasing tiredness had earlier struck a young doctor friend. "We went swimming in the Queen's swimming pool. I remember Launcelot's delight at showing me some, to me quite extraordinary, equipment which the Royal Family used for practising polo indoors . . . I remember that afternoon particularly because Launcelot almost completely exhausted himself in the swimming pool and was obviously finding it extremely difficult. It was a long and difficult walk back to the Deanery where we had tea and sat for a long time having a conversation about his present predicament and reflecting on its effect on his life. It was one of the few times that I can remember when he spoke at length about his problems."

Like many men who have led a full and absorbing life, Launcelot was finding it difficult to face retirement. He had come to the conclusion that at the age of seventy he ought to leave Windsor but beyond that he had no clear idea of where to go or what to do. Jane found it almost impossible to make him – never good at reaching a decision on matters affecting his own life and comfort – agree to anything. Scotland was too far away for a permanent home. Cambridge was an obvious place to which to return and he had been sounded by the Master of Trinity Hall on the possibility of once again becoming Dean of the College. It was tempting but he was sure that it would be wrong. Jane had no wish herself to live in Cambridge where even Launcelot admitted that the climate was unpleasant and the surrounding countryside unattractive. Friends would have welcomed him back but some were fearful that he would find the University too much changed to ensure his happiness. The modern undergraduate was a different person from the men whose company he had once so greatly enjoyed, and his beloved Trinity Hall had decided to admit women students, a decision to which he has only slowly become reconciled. Wisely, both Launcelot and Jane saw the danger of looking back too much to the "good old days" or being thought by others that one was doing so. Quite quickly they both realised that Cambridge was not the answer.

Time was getting on and Jane was becoming desperate in her efforts to find a new home which they both would enjoy. In the end she took matters into her own hands and a letter written by Launcelot to Owen Chadwick in June 1976 tells of her success:

"Yes – we are leaving Windsor. We move on August 9th and my resignation takes effect on 1st September. We thought of living at Rannoch but soon decided that this would be too cut off and eventually settled on Dorset. Jane has with great imagination and with the aid of a delightful young architect, converted an early 17th century barn in the village of Poyntington, 2½ miles from Sherborne, into a "dwelling" – and very nice it is too. It is built of Ham Stone and there are lots of walls and outhouses for growing things up. The village – it's really a hamlet – has no shop and no pub but boasts a charming small church. And we like all the people."

On the last Easter Sunday that Launcelot and Jane were at Windsor a rather charming incident had occurred. Jane's eldest grandchild, Pippa Morgan, was staying in the Deanery and had been told that she could come into the drawing-room after the Service when a very large number of the Royal Family would be present, and that she was now old enough to curtsey to the Queen. Jane, very busy with her guests, had only time to notice Pippa standing in the doorway and then running away. Attributing this to the child's shyness Jane was disappointed but thought no more about it. A few minutes later she saw her granddaughter standing in front of the Queen, curtseying and presenting a bouquet, consisting of two narcissi taken from a vase in the hall and wrapped in tissue paper. The Queen was charming to her and clung to her "bouquet" taking it back with her in the car.

Before Launcelot finally left Windsor his work was recognised in two ways. The Birthday Honours in June 1976 carried the announcement that the Queen had created him a Knight Commander of the Royal Victorian Order. As is customary when members of the Household are honoured the actual conferring of the honour took place at a private audience and not at an Investiture. 'As is the case of any other clerics I did not kneel and be touched with the sword on my shoulder. She handed me the Star and medal and in doing so said some very nice things. And then we talked.'

A man in Holy Orders who is made K.C.V.O. does not take the title "Sir" nor is his wife addressed as "Lady". This convention stems from the origins of knighthood when the presumption was that a Knight would protect the Sovereign if need be with his sword and the clergy by virtue of their office could not do this. The continuance of this practice has become somewhat anomalous in an age when the receiving of the accolade is no longer associated with fighting.

Jane had not witnessed the ceremony but shortly before they left Windsor she and Launcelot were honoured by the Queen and Prince Philip who dined with them and Jane's family in the Deanery. For Jane it was a lovely ending to all her hard work. Next day the Queen wrote a charming letter of thanks not only for the dinner party but for all that Launcelot had done as Dean. It had been an exacting and at times difficult five years, but in retrospect both Launcelot and Jane had no doubt that the happiness which they had experienced far outweighed the times when it had seemed impossible that anything could be achieved.

"RETIREMENT"

The break between full time work and retirement can be difficult. In Launcelot's case it soon became apparent that the word "retirement" was not part of his vocabulary. Although the pressures were now less and he could more easily pick and choose his engagements, a good train service from Sherborne to London and his enjoyment of driving a car meant that his diary was often almost as crowded as it had been at Windsor.

Requests for sermons and talks came from many parts of the country. He confessed that it now took him longer to write a sermon than it had done in the past. This was less due to any slowing up with advancing years than with having more time to re-examine basic propositions and to be more self-critical. As his beliefs were often re-interpreted in the light of growing insight, so an old sermon no longer sufficed and a new one had to be prepared. Letters continued to pour in on him and to the delight of his friends were answered in good measure. Most men accustomed to secretarial help find that the lack of a secretary is often the worst loss in retirement. Launcelot was spending so many hours in his study that Jane at last succeeded in persuading him not to work after dinner in the evenings.

Retirement made it possible for him to increase considerably his ties with Atlantic College and Bryanston School, of which he had long been a governor. Since 1976 he has spent the greater part of a week in each of the two terms in the year at Atlantic College. At the invitation of the headmaster of Bryanston he visits the school for forty-eight hours three times a term. As the headmaster wrote: "I never feel that he needs to be chaperoned or given special V.I.P.

treatment. He wanders into the school and moves from houseroom
to houseroom and study to study meeting junior and senior boys and
girls in a very relaxed way . . . On these visits he makes a special
point of meeting staff and members of the community with special
jobs . . . However, he does not limit his talks to pupils and staff; he
also wanders around the kitchens to meet those responsible for
catering and into the rest room to have coffee with those who have
the thankless task of sweeping the corridors and keeping the school
tidy. What is remarkable is to see him at his present age, with his
physical infirmity, going down to the river and taking his place with
the First Eight." What Launcelot regards as remarkable is the
kindness of an ordained headmaster and the School Chaplain in not
regarding a 'superannuated Bishop' as an interfering interloper.

The kind of talk which Launcelot had given at Atlantic College
proved very suited to schools. As he himself said, 'There is one
general activity which has taken up a good deal of time and which I
have felt to be worthwhile – namely the talks which I have given on
subjects which are not themselves theological, but issues of common
experience to man and which seem to me an appropriate way into
the framework of Christian belief. Subjects such as happiness,
suffering, peace and violence, loyalty, personal relationships,
tolerance, time, the generation gap, failure and creativity, have been
discussed. There is nothing in the least original about this method
but it has the merit that it does not involve assuming theological
presuppositions on the part of those to whom one is speaking. And
it is particularly important, I think, when talking to young people.'
Certainly they were successful at Bryanston, Tonbridge and
Gordonstoun.

In addition to sermons and talks there was now time to make sure
that he attended the meetings in London of the various bodies of
which he was a member. A mere recital of these gives an idea of his
interests: the Royal Geographical Society, the Young Explorers
Club, Endeavour Training, the Brathay Hall Management
Committee, the Schools Hebridean Society, the British National
Scientific Committee on Antarctic Research, the Trident Trust, the
Prince's Trust and the Queen's Silver Jubilee Appeal Committee.

The Scott Polar Research Institute provided a good reason to visit Cambridge for the annual meeting of its Committee of Friends.

Rather less than a year after leaving Windsor Launcelot showed that he was very far from being a spent force. From late June until the end of July 1977 he lived on board the Guided Missile Destroyer H.M.S. *Kent* as Chaplain. Captain Jock Slater, who was in command and from whom the invitation had come, was the great-nephew of Admiral Cunningham under whom Launcelot had served in H.M.S. *Queen Elizabeth* thirty-five years earlier. The ship took part in the Silver Jubilee Review by the Queen and Captain Slater invited Jane to come on board that day. After the Review H.M.S. *Kent* moved up Channel for exercises in the southern North Sea. Later Launcelot found himself once again at Scapa Flow and thence in the Rockall and St. Kilda areas of the eastern Atlantic on a NATO exercise. On 20 July he disembarked at Fishguard in order to go to a Silver Jubilee Reception at Buckingham Palace. He returned to the ship, sailed round to Plymouth and on to Portsmouth where he finally left her. As no Admiral was on board Captain Slater moved into the Admiral's quarters leaving his own quarters free for Launcelot, who thus never actually lived with the Captain and so could go about the mess decks freely as he had done years before in the *Queen Elizabeth*, and the sailors quickly accepted him.

Like many another man who has led a busy and rewarding life Launcelot has found it difficult to break a lifetime's habit of intense activity. Domestic chores, when paid help is either very costly or unobtainable, are less attractive than continuing to follow one's accustomed pattern. However his wish to be fully occupied springs from a deeper impulse. He believes that the service to which he had committed himself at his Ordination over forty years ago is a service from which, while health and strength remain, there is no discharge.

> "This sanctuary of my soul
>   Unwitting I keep white and whole,
> Unlatched and lit, if Thou should'st care
>   To enter or to tarry there.

>   With parted lips and outstretched hands
>   And listening ears Thy servant stands,
>   Call Thou early, call Thou late,
>   To Thy great service dedicate."

C. H. Sorley's poem expresses Launcelot's belief in the sustained demands of his calling.

There have been some who have regretted that the Church did not make greater and recognised use of Launcelot's gifts in the years immediately after leaving Windsor. He himself had pondered much about where he could best be of use. He declined an invitation from the Bishop of Salisbury to become an Assistant Bishop in the diocese, feeling that there were already enough retired Bishops in the area. To be an active parson in the group of parishes around Poyntington would have been impossible without giving up all his other interests in order to find time for visiting and doing all that a parish priest should do. Some hoped that with his vision of what the Church should become his work might have lain with Ordinands. This could only have been effective had there been a Theological College close at hand. In his work for Atlantic College and Bryanston he was not appointed to fill an existing post but with the goodwill of both headmasters he was able to perform the kind of pastoral work for which he was so well fitted. In an age of earlier maturity he found the intelligent sixth-former, the type with whom he was most readily at ease, very reminiscent of the undergraduates of Trinity Hall days.

In a sense the whole of Launcelot's life has been a struggle to discover the right thing to do – in his own personal life, for other people, for a parish, for a school or for anything with which he has been called upon to deal. Hence his constant agonising about the right course of action, the right advice to give, the right words to use. 'More than any man I know,' said a very close Cambridge friend, 'Launcelot always seems to be living in the presence of the burning bush.' For such a man time was God given and must never be wasted. This made a deep impression upon a young undergraduate: "I visited him many times when I subsequently became an undergraduate at Cambridge and again this concept of the way in which he organised his life made a strong impression on me. He would write and say that it would be delightful for me to go and visit him between 2.30 and 4 o'clock on a particular afternoon months ahead. When one arrived one would realise that the time scale had to be exact but he would suddenly appear and be able to relax completely and transform the mental pressures of the rest of his working day genuinely to enjoy the company of other people as an active way of coping with his own very hectic life but also, of course, to contribute to the lives of those around him."

Thus everything, however enjoyable it might be, has always been done with a purpose. Physical fitness being, in his view, essential to mental and spiritual health, it was right to set aside in his diary times for taking exercise and to continue playing games for as long as possible. A walk was seldom taken for its own sake or on his own, but as a chance to talk to an Ordination candidate or to someone needing his help. So while in retirement the pressures inevitably lessened there could be no relaxation of his sense of dedication. To Launcelot seems to have been granted in generous measure something of that ultimate vision which the Shepherds of the Delectable Mountain gave to the Pilgrim from the Hill called Clear. Since all are on pilgrimage that vision must be shared with any who are ready to receive it.

One example will suffice. This particular friend's experience of Launcelot's organised life is something which many others who have sought Launcelot's help will endorse. "When faced with a major career decision that I could not resolve . . . I 'phoned Launcelot in Sherborne. I had not in fact contacted him for several months and I remember asking Jane whether it was practicable to speak to Launcelot for a lengthy chat. He came to the 'phone and I briefly outlined that I needed to discuss something of considerable importance to me. He then paused to get pencil and paper, and we spent nearly an hour and a half on the 'phone, when once again this remarkable ability to put something else first and to counsel me as a true friend was very humbling. There are many people who enjoy giving advice and it is always flattering to be asked to do so, but Launcelot has this extraordinary quality of communicating with people to allow them to see the rights and wrongs of situations for themselves in the way in which he can lead a conversation without being directive."

In a Whit Sunday sermon preached in Norwich Cathedral in 1966 Launcelot quoted some words of Edward Wilson, who had died with Scott in the Antarctic. 'The secret of life is this – to get to know and love Christ through love for all his brothers and sisters. In every person we meet in whom we see something to love we are seeing something of Christ. For what we recognise as Christlike in them is the Holy Spirit in them – and the power to recognise it is the Holy Spirit in ourselves.'

A man who was reputed to have received some 3,000 cards one Christmas at Norwich was clearly a man who loved his fellow men. Every friend of Launcelot knows that Launcelot thinks more highly of him than he deserves but this only makes the friend try to live up to what Launcelot believes him to be. In recent years Launcelot has been much struck by a saying of Cardinal Basil Hume which seemed to him to epitomise his own conviction: 'There is no one you can meet who is not superior to you in some respect.' So in his dealings with people of all ages his outstanding quality and his greatest asset is his humility. As a Bryanston master wrote: "Confident in his own value (in God's eyes) as a human being, he has no need to erect barriers to cover any inadequacies and so there is no distancing between him and those with whom he comes into contact. Youngsters feel this instinctively."

Launcelot's humility is totally unselfconscious and genuine. He cannot but be aware that he has been greatly blessed and "endued with singular gifts". His attitude is best shown in a letter written to a young doctor friend who had expressed his admiration at Launcelot's courage in facing serious disability at a moment when the final and more encouraging diagnosis of his illness had yet to be made. "I can only think that if what you say is true, and I'm sure you were sincere in saying it, it only goes to prove that God moves in a mysterious way." It was right for everyone "to have that kind of self-respect which I believe comes from realising that life is something to be lived as God's gift and therefore to be developed in soul and mind and body with the discipline this requires and the freedom this gives to the best of one's ability – and then used."

'The power of the Holy Spirit,' Launcelot had said in the same Whitsun sermon, 'is to reconcile, because when the Holy Spirit is allowed to influence a man's personality He creates in him those gifts which come from Him and are not man-created – the gifts of love, joy, peace, long-suffering, goodness, faith, meekness, temperance. How can we receive this Spirit? . . . The answer is that God asks for nothing but our attention. The way to receive His power and influence in ourselves is sensitively and prayerfully to wait upon the Spirit.' In his love for his fellow men, in his respect for the sanctity of all created things, in his reverence for life is expressed in action Launcelot's central belief, transcending the theological barriers which divide Christians, the invincible power of Love.

To lesser mortals the "unco' guid" can be tedious. Excessive virtue usually repels rather than attracts. The mildly wicked are often far better company than the godly. Launcelot may have his shortcomings like every human being but dullness is not one of them. To be with him is to be with a man whose bubbling sense of humour and sheer joy of living are infectious. The almost childlike openness and innocence are, on first meeting, a surprise and then a delight. There is nobody quite like him.

In the last resort Launcelot's elusive personality defies capture. As one of his oldest friends has written, his virtues of "friendship, love, generosity, humour, modesty are really secret virtues" and cannot be confined within the covers of a book. What Launcelot has meant to his friends often cannot be told, at least not in his life time. For it is the personal and private expressions of his love for them that they treasure and secrets are for keeping. Jane once said to a friend whom she known long before her marriage to Launcelot, 'You don't know how wonderful it is to be married to a truly good man.' That is the kind of remark which no husband should hear. Rather let the last words be the simplest and words which every one of Launcelot's countless friends would echo. They are the final words of Thomas Hardy's novel *The Woodlanders* in which the humble Marty South recalls the man whom she loved so dearly. "No, . . . I'll never forget 'ee. For you was a good man and did good things."

Tithe Barn, Poyntington

Launcelot and Jane at Tithe Barn